THE
JAZZ
Experience

CHARLES T. BROWN

Saginaw Valley State College

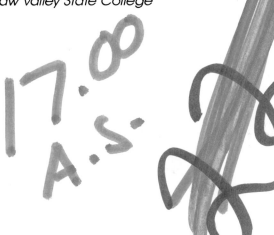

wcb
Wm. C. Brown Publishers
Dubuque, Iowa

Consulting Editor   Frederick Westphal

Cover design by Kay Dolby Fulton. Cover photo by Bob Coyle.
Saxophone courtesy of Faber Music Co., Dubuque, IA.

Library of Congress Catalog Card Number: 88–70408

ISBN 0–697–03057–1

Printed in the United States of America by Wm. C. Brown Publishers
2460 Kerper Boulevard, Dubuque, IA 52001

10 9 8 7 6 5 4 3 2 1

Dedication

*This manuscript is dedicated to Jeff Hall,
colleague and friend.*

Contents

List of Analysis Pieces

The following list indicates pieces that are analyzed in the textbook. In each chapter, the first piece listed is discussed in that chapter. Other pieces associated with that chapter can be found in Appendix B. If the piece is from the revised edition of the "Smithsonian Collection of Classic Jazz" (SCCJ), a record letter and band number are given under SCCJ (for instance, C-4 means cut 4 on record C). If the piece is not from SCCJ, you can find the record in the Discography.

Chapter	Name of Piece	SCCJ
3	"Dippermouth Blues"	A-5
4	"Struttin' with Some Barbecue"	B-2
5	"Weather Bird"	B-5
6	"Maple Leaf Rag"	A-2
7	"Sweethearts on Parade"	B-6
8	"Stampede"	B-11
9	"Ko Ko"	D-13
10	"All Alone"	F-11
11	"I Can't Believe That You're in Love With Me"	D-2
12	"Night in Tunisia"	F-5
13	"Body and Soul"	F-10
14	"Watermelon Man"	
15	"Alabama"	I-3
16	"Watermelon Man"	
17	"Koto Song"	
18	"Blues for Poland"	
19	"Original Rays"	

Preface

Having taught jazz history and appreciation for fifteen years, I have always struggled with the disparity between my students and me. As a person skilled in the technical language of music and as a practicing jazz musician, I have consistently walked a tightrope between being too complicated and not saying enough. However, I have always felt that my role in life is to communicate with the broadest possible audience, thereby educating more people regarding what is, to me, the most important communication medium—music.

This book is designed to provide a method by which nonskilled students of music might come to greater appreciation and facility with jazz and that the readers of this book might do so without having to take music theory classes in preparation for the course. I contend that it is important to find methods by which we can remove the necessity for technical language, because the usage of technical terms and language cuts out a large population of students and readers who could be reached if other means were used. Since it is my stated purpose in life to communicate with the largest possible audience, I feel that a non-technical approach is essential.

Therefore, this book will not contain musical examples other than the analyses, nor will it discuss extensively harmonic chord changes. I contend that nonmajors taking a course in jazz appreciation to fulfill their humanities requirement or simply because they are interested in the subject should not be deluged with material that means nothing to them. This limitation will require us to find new approaches to the discussion of jazz, but the obvious reward will be a group of new appreciators, at whatever level their technical expertise allows them to understand.

The actual text will refer to representative musicians and groups of musicians instead of offering the traditional encyclopedia approach. Starting with chapter 3, there will be one representative analysis example; more analyses can be found in an appendix. The point of this book is to provide analyses that will generate continued work on the types of music discussed in each chapter.

It is my intention to provide usable models for those reading the book, and therefore all readers are encouraged to take those analyses seriously. Many will want to go beyond the information in this book, and for them there are the Bibliography and Discography. Obviously, no book on jazz can be complete, and this book does not attempt to be definitive, only representative, for the particular audience for which the book is designed. Few of us will completely agree with any one approach to teaching jazz or even defining it.

My thanks go to the publisher, to my wife and children, for letting me take time away from them to write the book, and to my students in jazz appreciation over the last fifteen years. After all, it was those students who told me in no uncertain terms when a particular way of explaining something worked and when it failed. This book is a result of that fifteen-year experiment.

Charles T. Brown
Saginaw Valley State University
University Center, Michigan

Part I
Introduction and Origins

Chapter 1
Introduction

BASIC PREMISES

Before students begin the study of jazz, it is always wise for them to learn certain basic facts about this musical art form; these facts become the building blocks for their learning experience. The following basic premises, designed to serve as those building blocks, may require leaps of faith on the part of the reader, because they cannot be proven until one has heard much of the music discussed in this book. However, they are, in fact, true.

1. For a student just beginning the study of music, jazz is just as valid a form for serious consideration as is European classical music. Jazz has not always been accepted as a valuable communication medium, however. In fact, at certain points in its history, jazz has been associated with decadence. However, jazz is now recognized throughout the world and is generally considered one of our most cherished exports. Few things are as truly American as jazz.

Despite its American-ness, however, jazz does possess many of the traditional elements of European classical music, and it exhibits a great deal of technical complexity in its various performing styles.

2. Jazz reflects the culture that produced it. It is imperative to understand jazz within the context of the society that gave rise to it. Out of the early twentieth-century New Orleans culture came Dixieland jazz; in the 1940s, Harlem produced bebop. Each of these two jazz forms was aided in its development by specific cultural influences. To ignore this influence is to miss the point of jazz: It intends to communicate something to a particular group of people. This kind of thinking is usually described as the "sociology of music."

3. We must become familiar with some characteristics of all music so that we can do comparative analysis. Since we are not going to use complete musical notation, we must find some means by which to describe the things that happen in a jazz composition. We will do this in nontechnical terms and in a personal way that works for each individual reader.

4. We will establish a personalized analysis system with which each student can describe and compare many pieces of jazz music. If we do not do analysis, we will not learn as much from this study. The point of this book is to propel us through the fascinating history of jazz and to listen to representative examples of jazz music. As we listen, we will take notes on the pieces we hear. Our analyses or notes about music will then provide the basis for our comprehensive understanding and for continuing study after this course ends.

HOW TO USE THIS BOOK

Many of my students, especially those who are not music majors, ask me how to use music books. If you have taken a previous course in music and you already know how to read music books, you may simply skip this section. If you have no musical knowledge, however, please read on.

Common sense tells us that we ought to read an assigned chapter before the teacher lectures on that subject; this is particularly advisable in music classes. Music is like a foreign language or a type of nonverbal communication; it will take you some time to be comfortable with it. Many beginning jazz students discover that they like the music but have not the foggiest idea what to say about it. Reading these chapters in advance of the lectures about them, and thinking about what you have read helps a lot, especially at the beginning.

Like intelligent listening, intelligent reading requires a strategy. I suggest the following:

1. Read groups of chapters in one sitting. The book is so short that you can easily read whole sections at one sitting. After you do so, go back through the text and underline or put check marks by those parts which stand out as the main points.
2. Listen to the recordings that are analyzed in each chapter, and compare the analyses with what you hear. Listen a sufficient number of times so that the analysis makes sense to you.
3. Last, do some analyses of your own and compare your results with the analyses presented in the chapters.

The Analyses

For many people, the analyses will be the most challenging part of the book, and that is certainly my intention. It is my belief that any book that discusses music must do analyses in one form or another. The main focus of this text is music analysis, and much of the chapter material reinforces that activity. In that sense, you cannot and should not skip over the analysis pieces.

The first thing you must do is to gain access to the recordings, either by borrowing them from the library or by purchasing them yourself. Careful reading of the first two chapters will prepare you for the analyses, the first of which appears in chapter 3. Basically, the following components comprise the analyses in this book:

1. Introductory material, including the name of the piece, musicians, source, often the Smithsonian Collection of Classic Jazz (SCCJ), meter signature (usually in four-beat measures), tonic key, beats per minute, and instrumentation
2. Phrase units divided into measures
3. Descriptive remarks about what is happening in each phrase
4. Chord changes above measure numbers

Each of these components is introduced in the first three chapters.

It is not imperative that you understand everything in the analysis charts, but you should strive to understand more and more as you gain practice in hearing pieces and in making charts from those pieces. For instance, chord changes have been placed in the analysis charts, even though many people will not be able to hear the differences between all chords. However, your goal as a student is simply to recognize a chord change, not necessarily the character of each chord.

If you play the guitar or the piano, you could play along with the pieces by reading the chords. However, one can tell quite a bit about changes in musical sections simply by seeing the different chord structures in written form. If you see that the chord changes are essentially the same throughout a piece, you should verify that the basic sound of the background instruments remains the same. If you see one section that is radically different in its chord changes, you should verify that in your listening. In a sense, it is not imperative to know which chord is which, but rather to know that the chord changes at a particular point in the musical phrase. Once you begin counting beats, that concept should become obvious.

The analysis charts, or models, have been simplified so that they present phrase lengths, measure numbers, and basic chord changes. These technical elements of music are explained in the first chapters so that all students reading this book will find the analysis charts useful. For those students who want more information, particularly about chord changes and their more complex alterations, more complete chord changes can be found in the Teacher's Manual. Therefore, if you desire more information on chord changes, please ask your teacher to share that information with you.

A few analyses are not divided into phrases of measures, but rather are charted on the basis of certain things happening during a timed reading. When this technique is used, the reason for doing so will be fairly obvious, but suffice it to say that some jazz pieces are so free in structure that the types of charts normally used throughout this text simply will not work for them. This is a good example of how analysis can be personalized, not only according to the individual but also according to the characteristics of the music.

Boxed Biographies

Two brief biographies of prominent jazz musicians will be included in each chapter, beginning with chapter 3. The purpose of the biographies is to give additional information about selected representatives of the style discussed in each chapter. Although there are sometimes fifty or so worthy representatives from each period, only two could be chosen for the book. It is my hope that readers will be sufficiently inspired by the biographies to search out the bibliography for more information on other musicians.

The Smithsonian Collection of Classic Jazz

Most of the recorded examples referred to in the text are from the "Smithsonian Collection of Classic Jazz," revised edition, although in the last few chapters some other recordings are cited. This collection is available through the Smithsonian Institution, and most libraries own a copy of it. A great deal of information is available in the booklet accompanying this collection, written by jazz authority Martin Williams.

DEFINITION OF JAZZ

Jazz is a form of music that originated in the United States around the turn of the century among various ethnic groups, primarily black musicians in the South. It is primarily a performer's art form in that a musical composition is not always as important as the improvised performance of it. True jazz involves relative degrees of spontaneity. As a popular—and continuously evolving—art form, it stresses contemporary communication.

This definition is a distillation of many sources on jazz and of my own thinking about jazz over the past fifteen years. It is impossible, however, to describe jazz definitively.

The musical elements of jazz are really the standard elements found in all music. Jazz has many variants, all having a unique combination of the following musical characteristics.

Musical Elements

Rhythm defines the time organization of music. In pop music, this is usually associated with drums. Rhythm is closely associated with life and the harmony of nature: Our bodies are rhythmic devices and depend on their own regular rhythms to function.

In fact, the heartbeat was the organizing unit of music through the Renaissance. Most music before the seventeenth century organized its basic pulsation and the speed of that pulsation according to the heartbeat of the human being; in a sense, music was tied to bodily rhythms. *Tempo* is the speed of music; it also describes the number of beats per minute. One can describe the tempo of one piece of music as being slower than, the same as, or faster than the tempo of another piece of music.

Beat is usually a regular pulsation that repeats continuously, like a heartbeat. There is a fundamental difference between beat and rhythm. *Rhythm* defines the irregular accents, rests, and time changes within the basic beat. If you listen to the basic beat of a simple composition, you can pick out the drumbeats and then listen for the tempo or beat, implied by the melodic instruments.

Listen, too, for changing accents or rhythmic patterns. We must gain experience in listening to rhythmic patterns within the overall musical texture.

Syncopation is a specific kind of rhythmic pattern in which the accent is placed in an unusual or unexpected place. Although syncopation is a normal element of several kinds of music, it is of great importance in jazz, in which it is the rule instead of the exception. Perhaps the easiest way to illustrate syncopation is to provide the following time chart:

```
Regular beat          X   O   X   O   X   X     O
Syncopation             O X    O O X    O O   X    O O X  O
```

In this chart, "x" stands for an accented beat, and "o" stands for a weak or unaccented beat.

Melody is an organized set of notes consisting of different pitches (high or low sounds). It is organized horizontally in the sense that the pitches occur one after another, rather than being sounded together (which would be vertical organization). It is probably easiest to start out listening for the different pitches associated with a song or piece with lyrics. Listen to the way the pitch goes up or down with the lyrics. Once you understand what a melody is by hearing one connected with a set of words, turn to music that has no words. The main, or lead, melody is the horizontal set of pitches that make up a song or composition. Untrained musicians may need to alternate several times between compositions with lyrics and those without lyrics to find the lead melody. But once you have learned to identify it, finding other types of melodies is easy.

Other kinds of melodies include bass, background, and countermelodies. Bass melodies are low-pitched patterns that provide a basis or foundation for an entire composition. Background melodies fill out the texture formed by the lead and bass melodies. Countermelodies are pitch combinations that accompany the lead.

Form is the overall structure of a piece of music, which is usually explained in units of time. Many jazz pieces are variations on one particular unit or melody, so the overall form is often described as "theme and variation." However, often the melody itself has a formal logic to it, such as a two-part form (AB) or a three-part form (AAB or ABA). Many ballads have more complex structures to the thematic or melodic content, such as AABA or ABAB.

Listening for form is hard at first, but it gets progressively easier as your knowledge grows. For the first few times you listen to a piece, simply compare the sound to what you are told the form is. Then you can simply generalize that knowledge to other pieces of your own choosing.

Improvisation, another word for spontaneity, is usually considered by music writers to be the most important characteristic of jazz. Improvisation is the act of spontaneously making up new music and exists in greater and lesser degrees in all the various forms of jazz.

Improvisation always follows some logic, although in each new style it will take you some time to figure out the logic. Clearly, the spontaneous improvisation and communication among jazz musicians during a jam session is one of the most exciting qualities of jazz.

The easiest way to listen for improvisation is to listen to a theme-and-variations piece in which the original melody is played at the beginning, and various musicians then make up music based on that melody. For instance, many of the early Dixieland tunes in chapters 4 and 5 feature the entire group of musicians playing the melody at the beginning of the piece, and then each musician plays an improvised spontaneous solo that uses some qualities of the original melody. The character of jazz improvisation has changed from one period in history to the next. The style of improvisation depends on the way that the rhythm section plays, the types of pieces upon which spontaneous improvisation is based, and a variety of other factors which will be discussed in this book.

LISTENING TECHNIQUES

Most of us can listen to various sounds around us with little concentration and effort. We can listen to two or more conversations at the same time, to the sounds of things happening outdoors, and to the radio or television, all at once. As we do this, we are not hearing every sound that is being made by any of these sources. Yet, even when we do manage to focus on a single source of sound, we may not be listening effectively, simply because we have never been trained in the art of effective listening.

Any successful communication requires both a good speaker and a perceptive listener. It always fascinates me that many college courses in communication attempt to describe communication methods without giving any attention to the receiver. Communication, even when presented in a sophisticated and clever fashion, is wasted unless someone else perceives the message. Good listening skills can often make the difference between a solid relationship and a failed one, such as a marriage or a business partnership. Good listening can help us to pick up hints about correct behavior in a variety of intimate and business settings. Although we will soon be talking about music listening, one should keep in mind that the listening skills we will be developing in this course have applications outside music appreciation.

As a general rule, most of us like to listen to music as background noise for some other activity, such as dancing or studying. Music can be used as background sound in supermarkets to actually cause people to buy more. It can be used as a psychological painkiller in the dentist's office. And of course music is nice to have when you want to dance. However, this function of music is as background, or secondary, communication.

One of our first tasks is to raise the importance of music so that it becomes the primary source, and then the only source, to which we give our attention. To make it easier for you to concentrate as you listen to music, I suggest that you create the right atmosphere by following these steps:

1. Go to a quiet room—one to which you can close the door, thereby blocking outside noises.
2. Turn off all sound-producing devices in the room, especially the telephone.
3. Sit in a chair in a position that is not *too* comfortable (you don't want to fall asleep!).

It is very difficult to concentrate on a single sound source, if we have not had practice in doing this. We are trained by our society and environment to respond to many aural and visual stimuli at once. Therefore, we need to purposefully set up our environment so that we can block out other distractions. A sound-proof room is the best place to do this, although you can achieve somewhat the same effect by using a cassette player with headphones.

TECHNICAL SKILLS

Basic Terminology

While this book is intended to be nontechnical, there are a few simple technical skills we simply must master before we can make much progress. Two of these skills are counting beats and recognizing the sounds produced by different instruments.

A beat in music is the regular pulsation that defines the tempo. Interestingly, the basic beat of music is based on the many beat patterns found in life, including the heartbeat. Our first task is to understand and experience beat, so that we can clap, stamp our feet, or move our bodies in time to the beat of music.

We can begin to do this by having an instructor play a piece of music—either a recorded piece or a piece on the piano—while counting out the beats for us. Then we can count and clap along with the teacher. Eventually, we should be able to count and clap or stamp without the instructor's assistance.

A measure in music is an arbitrary grouping of beats into a slightly longer unit. Much of Western music is grouped into measures of two, three, and four beats, called, respectively, 2/4 meter, 3/4 meter, and 4/4 meter. The top number in each meter signature indicates the number of beats in each measure, and the bottom number indicates that a quarter (or 1/4) note gets one beat. You will need to have an understanding of meter signature when you start to do the analyses in later chapters, but for now it is important only to determine what the basic beat is and then count beats in measure units. If you can do that, then you can do the following:

1. Count beats in phrase units that are longer than one measure.
2. Count beats through an entire piece of music.
3. Follow my analyses.

One Musical Element at a Time

I believe that, in order for us to use the maximum amount of brain power available to us, we can pay attention to only one thing at a time, and in a specific way. I recommend concentrating on one musical element at a time to effectively hear the music's meaning. Especially in the beginning stages of learning how to listen to music, this is difficult; to do so requires that we dissect what we hear. Music is obviously intended to be heard as a whole, but it is often easier to make sense of its complexities by breaking it down into elements.

As one begins to listen, one should listen to the lyrics. Most of us have had extensive experience listening to words as a part of everyday life. And most of us have had the opportunity to analyze lyrics in high school English classes. Therefore, in music, as in English, we begin by analyzing words and repetition schemes.

Musical sounds are organized into units, like sentences; in jazz pieces that have lyrics, one can break the lyrics into sentences and phrases and compare the organization of the lyrics to the organization of the musical sounds. We can count the beats, measures, and longer phrases so that we can experience, physically, the time quality of music. Since jazz is not all vocal music, our recommendation is to use a two-pronged attack that will (1) allow us to concentrate on lyrics when they exist, and (2) help us to become equally skilled in counting beats and phrase units.

It will then be our purpose to learn the skill of relating other qualities of jazz and music in general to the structural framework of counting beats and phrase units. In a sense, we are trying in this study to follow a time line or beat and phrase units and compare all other qualities and elements of music to that basic structure.

The point of all this is that analysis should become a personalized activity, and any analysis chart should be modified by the individual to meet his or her expectations and skills. Some of us will be drawn to instrumental textures, and some to drumming patterns, keyboard textures, or some other quality. However, we must develop together the skill of counting beats, eventually perceiving longer units of measures and phrases, and then share in a lively discussion of why each of us hears different things.

Sounds of Different Instruments

There are a number of schools of thought on how to teach the sounds of different musical instruments to beginning listeners, but they all boil down to effective listening. As with learning to count beats, if you can make yourself do one thing at a time, you can learn, for instance, the difference between a piano and a trumpet. It is simply a matter of experience.

The first time you listen to a piece, make sure you can clap with the beat. Then count measures and phrases. Then listen to the piece again, picking out one instrument at a time. The most obvious ones are usually the solo instruments and the drums.

When you first begin defining for yourself the difference between a trumpet and a saxophone, you may be in for some rough going. Some discriminations are easier to make than others. The difference between a soprano saxophone and a trumpet in certain styles is slight, and it takes considerable experience before one can make that discrimination. Consult the analyses in this book for the entrances of specific instruments. Then simply follow the chart until the particular instrument is introduced and you recognize its sound. Next, try to identify it without watching the chart. Anyone can learn to identify the different instruments simply by listening carefully.

MODEL FOR LISTENING

Creating a structural chart for pieces analyzed in this book and for other pieces you hear is of paramount importance. As you begin to collect a number of structural charts of your own, you will have a library of material that you can analyze for general trends. Once you have analyzed ten or fifteen bebop tunes, you can make some valid generalizations about that style. Although your teacher can make those generalizations for you, you will understand these concepts more fully if you do it yourself.

Questions for Discussion

Choose a music selection, and answer the following questions.

1. Analyze the lyrics. Identify any repetition schemes.
2. Discuss how the lyrics explain or reflect the cultural attitudes of the time in which the piece was written and performed.
3. Describe the musical instruments used in the piece, and draw a textural chart. A textural chart is one that shows the presence or absence of particular instruments through the entire piece; this presence or absence is known as textural density. For example:

Saxophone   _____   _____

Guitar _____   _____

Drums _____

Bass _____   _____

Flute
Measures   1   2   3   4   5   6   7   etc.

4. Are there any instrumental solos in the piece?
5. Is the accompaniment by the background instruments continuous?
6. What is the meter signature; how many beats are in a measure?
7. What is the metronome marking; how many beats are there per minute? (Use your watch.) Is the song slow, medium, or fast?
8. How many counts are in each major section of the piece?
9. Within each measure, which beats are strongly accented?

Other Activities

Use the same piece of music to complete the following activities.

1. Describe melodies, harmonies, important rhythms, and the lyric content.
2. Describe the performing environment, and research the lives of the musicians.
3. Describe the musical style.
4. Compare your results for any of the above with those of other students.

Checking Results

While it may seem redundant to say so, you should check and recheck your results as often as possible. Music is like a good film; the more times you see it, the more you understand from it. You should use as many resources as possible and as many people as well. Do not feel that it is "cheating" to discuss your findings with others. They may clue you in to something that you did not hear, or you may teach them something.

Suggested Listening

1. Scott Joplin, "Maple Leaf Rag"
   For melody, syncopation, rhythm, beat, and tempo.

2. Jelly Roll Morton, "Maple Leaf Rag"
   For improvisation or changing another composition.

3. Bessie Smith, "St. Louis Blues"
   For improvisation, melody, and form. Notice Louis Armstrong's improvisation on cornet on this 1925 recording.

Chapter 2
Origin of Jazz

No other aspect of the study of jazz causes more debate than its origin, precisely because no one really knows exactly when jazz started. No written document exists to prove when and where it began. A frequently contested issue is whether the African influence or the white European influence has been stronger in the development of jazz. It is probably safe to say that both have contributed.

We accept as a basic premise for this discussion that creative art springs from the cultural experiences of its inventors. Prejazz and jazz came from individuals who were expressing their cultural values through music. Therefore, to understand the evolution of American music leading to jazz in the early twentieth century, one must trace the development of black music in the American colonies, beginning in the early seventeenth century.

AFRICAN ROOTS

Although clearly slavery is not a civilized aspect of cultural history, it is nevertheless an old practice documented throughout the world, starting as far back as the earliest recorded history. Slaves from West Africa were first transported to Europe by the Portuguese more than 500 years ago, and by the time Africans were brought to the American colonies, slavery was a common practice. Although there is a moral dilemma regarding its existence, we must accept its influence on the development of black culture and eventually culture in general in the United States.

To understand the impact of slavery, we must view its business practices to assess the acculturation that occurred as a result of migratory patterns. The first black slaves were brought to Jamestown, Virginia, by a Dutch ship in 1619; twenty slaves were purchased. The first slave ship to arrive in upper New England was in Boston in 1638.

In 1641, slavery was officially recognized as a legitimate act by laws in the colony of Massachusetts. Interestingly, the first slave baptized as a Christian occurred in that same year in Dorchester, Massachusetts.

Slavery as a business actually created what were called "slave factories," a practice through which slaves were procured in West Africa for shipment to other countries. The term describes a castle or compound which was used as a holding cell for slaves collected from the African interior (these castles were on the coast). Tribal chieftains and black government bureaucracies in Africa often helped with the trading.

The slave district covered the western coast of Africa from Senegal down to the Congo but actually developed around tribes such as Fon, Yoruba, Ibo, Ashanti, Jolof (Wolof), Fanti, Baoule, and Mandingo. Africans from these tribes were taken as slaves to the New World, but from different locations depending on the European slavers' relationship to specific tribal organizations. Generally speaking, slaves who were brought to Latin America and the Caribbean were treated differently than those brought to the Colonies and Canada. The primary difference in their treatment was usually a result of philosophical or religious attitudes toward Africans.

The American colonies were populated with slaves brought primarily by the English and Dutch, who brought slaves from the Gold Coast and the Slave Coast. There were three major areas of slave production: the Ivory Coast, the Gold Coast (Ghana), and the Slave Coast (Dahomey and Togo). In particular, the Ashanti of the Gold Coast and the Ivory Coast, as well as the Baoule, were taken for the Colonies. For the Louisiana Territory, controlled by the French, the Fon, Yoruba, Ibo, and Fulami were taken from Dahomey and Nigeria.

The use of slave routes (see Bibliography for additional sources) resulted in certain tribes making up the bulk of slave populations in certain areas of the American colonies. Obviously, the music and culture of those tribes had an important impact on the culture of the black Americans living in those areas.

The cultural traditions of the Colonies in terms of black slaves were radically different from the experiences of the Louisiana area, which did not become a part of the United States until 1803. For the most part, slaves in the original thirteen colonies were acculturated in an English Protestant society; slaves in Louisiana were influenced by French Catholics.

Slaves in the New World did not recognize themselves as Americans, but rather as Africans. They were not brought here to be a part of this new land, but rather to be labor animals. At least in the Colonies, Africans were generally not thought to be human beings, or at least they were not considered to be significant enough to join in Protestant religious thought, which influenced Colonial life.

Colonial Protestant thinking in New England was based upon a rather severe form of Protestantism called puritanism. Believing strongly that the New World represented a place where they could practice their religious beliefs without persecution, our puritan forefathers had strong beliefs, founded on the principle that people must observe specific religious practices to gain a position in heaven. Some of these beliefs taught that many activities could potentially lead people to the devil. Unfortunately, the Black African fell under this area of influence. It was felt that the African was a heathen and barbaric, and that proper Christians would be better off leaving them alone.

There are some rather fundamental reasons why tribal tradition is inconsistent with Protestant Christianity. African tribal tradition in general was a polytheistic system, in which there were many gods, each representing a certain natural force or being, such as animals. There is also a tendency for African tradition to be integrated; religious activity was not separated from everyday life. For instance, music as both a life activity and a religious experience is a constant in most African philosophies. And both music and dance (most often combined) are exuberant and emotional experiences—a radical departure from the beliefs of staid Christianity in the early history of the United States.

While there are noticeable differences between tribal traditions which led black Africans in certain areas to produce different evolutionary results than they would in other areas, the greatest difference in U.S. black music is between those areas that were primarily influenced by English Protestantism and those influenced by French Catholicism. Louisiana has tended to produce very different results from much of the rest of the black communities in the United States.

Slave Music

The most striking characteristic of African tribal music in general is its rhythmic character. African music is not at all "barbaric" or "primitive." The polyrhythmic (two or more different rhythm patterns going on at the same time) character of much tribal music is one of the most complicated rhythmic configurations in world music.

The instrumental accompaniment of African tribal music is primarily rhythmic, although melodic instruments are used as well. As early as the late eighteenth century, the "banjar" was mentioned in the writings of Thomas Jefferson; the "banyo" is a four-stringed African instrument that was brought to the New World by slaves. It eventually became the American banjo, which has five strings.

Generally speaking, the texture of polyrhythmic music relies on drums or other instruments used rhythmically to play different patterns to produce a complex composite texture. The following chart illustrates this type of texture (using x for beat and o for no beat):

```
Instrument 1   x x o o x o o x o o x x x o x x o o x o o x o o x
Instrument 2   x o x o x o x o x o x o x o x o x o x o x o x o x
Instrument 3   o x o x o x o x o x o x o x o x o x o x o x o x o
Instrument 4 etc.
```

The composite, or total sound, is far more complex than any individual part.

From a melodic point of view, tribal tradition varies greatly from the relatively sophisticated society of the Fon of Dahomey to the Mandingos of Guinea. Generally speaking, vocal music is always joined with instrumental performance. Vocal music ultimately had its first impact in the Colonies because white people could not stop black people from singing in the fields. Much of the vocal music is antiphonal, or call-and-response. Call-and-response, in which the leader sings a phrase and then the group responds, is a retentive trait of African music in all American popular music.

The actual vocal melodies are quite diverse, depending on the meaning of the words. A pentatonic (five-note) scale is used quite often, and there are a variety of scooped notes, grace notes, or embellishments and changes in accent and volume. Tribal music in general is quite sophisticated, even when it is radically different from the European mind-set of what "proper" music should be. Many of the melodic patterns present in tribal tradition from which slaves came are present in early slave music and in later stages of evolution.

The most common instruments used in African music are rattles, bells, scrapers, xylophones, thumb pianos, and drums of various constructions. However, African instruments also include various types of flutes, single- and double-reed instruments, trumpets and horns, musical bows (one-stringed violins), zithers, lutes, harps, and lyres. Although the double-reed instruments tend to be found only in those areas with a Middle Eastern influence, virtually every other type of instrument is used throughout tribal tradition, depending only on the degree of migration of the tribe.

The only common Western musical element that is relatively rare in African tradition is harmony, although many Western-influenced forms practice traditional harmonic singing and playing. It is probably best to assume that tribal tradition is polymelodic rather than harmonic ("harmony" being a word deriving from a theory of music that evolved in western Europe). There are examples of singing styles that use more than one melody at a time, but more common is the use of melodically tuned percussion instruments, such as xylophones and thumb pianos, used for playing different melodies at the same time.

Many of these practices were continued in the Colonies by African slaves, although their frequency was severely limited. For instance, slaves were not allowed to construct or play native instruments in many parts of the Colonies. As such, the vocal tradition continued even when the instrumental tradition could not.

Slaves continued to sing in African dialects throughout the nineteenth century, and they developed some specific forms of music that were used in the New World—the cry, the field holler, and other work songs. The field holler is the most obvious of African songs because it is based on the traditional practice of communicating over long distances with music—in Africa with the "talking drums." The field holler is simply a two-note descending phrase (a minor third) which communicates over a distance. The particular interval became the basic interval of the blues some two hundred years later. The cry is more associated with work songs and, although more complicated, it also features that same descending pattern. In lullabies and other work songs can be found both African qualities and incipient blues style.

Secular Acculturation

At some point in America's history, black Africans in America began to think of themselves as black Americans, or Afro-Americans. Although there is no precise point at which that time can be fixed, it probably occurred about the time that cultural habits began to shift in the mid- to late eighteenth century. It is possible that secular acculturation occurred the minute that a black African sang a song in English or adapted an African text to an English folk song. It was at this point that we can truly begin the development of musical forms leading to jazz.

SACRED MUSIC

For reasons given earlier, blacks were not brought into the mainstream of the Colonies because they were thought to be outside God's domain. However, by the end of the eighteenth century, this attitude had begun to change. With it came the conversion of many blacks to Christianity. By 1780, Christianity was strong in the black community. Black Protestantism adopted most aspects of traditional Christian religious practices, although the new converts altered slightly the style of music.

      Religious music among whites in the New England colonies was simple in character; religious philosophy suggested that music should be single-melody hymns without ornamentation. Most white secular music was solely of European origin as well. Throughout the nineteenth century, most religious and secular music in the United States continued to be imported from Europe.

The first significant change in music in the Colonies occurred in black sacred tradition, although black fiddlers received attention as early as the 1730s. Hymns became imbued with a new emotionalism at about this time, which marked the beginning of the Great Awakening, a series of religious revivals that swept through the American Colonies. By 1780, tunes called spirituals had replaced many hymns, especially in black churches. These spirituals were deeply emotional folk songs or popular songs of the day, often with a biblical text. They were performed in a lively fashion, often involving hand-clapping and vocal utterances not present in the original compositions. Thus began improvisation in American music.

IMPROVISATION

Improvisation is the act of making up music on the spot, sometimes in a very spontaneous way and sometimes in a controlled way. One example of improvisation is *embellishment,* taking a basic melody and simply adding some notes to it to make it more complicated. Much of the improvisation in spirituals was in fact just embellishment using words, notes, or both, or changing slightly the spirit of the hymn to make it more emotional and spirited.

African elements of the spiritual are call-and-response (minister and congregation responding to each other) and changing rhythmic patterns. The spiritual did not become polyrhythmic, but the melodies were changed so that accents did not fall on the main beats. This is a direct outgrowth of tribal practices and ultimately is defined in Western music as *syncopation.* Syncopation (music that contains offbeat accents) probably was introduced in the spiritual. Both improvisation and syncopation are found in most styles of jazz, and the existence of these practices in spirituals argues strongly for black religious music as a major precursor to jazz.

BLACK MINSTRELS

In the mid-nineteenth century, white vaudeville began in America. The most significant form of this entertainment was black minstrelsy, which had actually given rise to vaudeville. Minstrel shows were stage entertainment by white performers made up in blackface. Black minstrels were influenced by two earlier practices—camp meeting revival songs and spirituals.

Some elements of African music were present in the songs sung at camp meetings. These gatherings were religious extravaganzas at which thousands of people got together for two or three days of religious experiences; they were usually held outdoors. The first such camp meeting was held in Kentucky in 1800. Interestingly, most camp meetings were interracial.

One highlight of these camp meetings was singing by the entire congregation, during which black members sang with great jubilance, often stamping their feet or slapping their thighs. By the 1820s, *shouts* were performed at camp meetings. A shout is a secular African song sung while the group forms a circle or ring. Shouts were reminiscent of African tribal songs; these ultimately led to the ring shout, which was a popular tradition of the mid-nineteenth century. Of interest was a particular form of shuffle-step dancing that signaled the ends of the meetings.

Spirituals, which were being performed in England by the mid-eighteenth century, were parlor songs based on the lives of black people; they usually depicted blacks as either comical or sad. Interest in these songs continued even through the early twentieth century in both England and America.

Blackface, or "Ethiopian," minstrelsy arose from both of these earlier traditions and gave rise to the following: (1) blackface theatrical performances, starting in the 1820s; (2) touring groups, such as Daniel Emmett and his Virginia Minstrels in New York, in 1843; and (3) the hayday of touring, from 1850–1870.

Touring black minstrel shows developed in the late nineteenth century; the circuit was called "black vaudeville." There were, by this time, two distinct circuits touring the country—one black and one white. It is possible that from these shows came the constituent parts of jazz, or at least syncopated singing, polyrhythmic instrumental texture, and a continued representation of black attitudes in the United States.

Ultimately, black attitudes would be expressed through dance forms, both African-influenced folk dancing in European white tradition, and in the continuation of African tribal dances. Although the influence of African culture was retained in many locations in the United States, probably the strongest influence was found in New Orleans.

One of the most popular places for African practices was the Congo Square, or Place Congo. Of the many dance forms performed there, the Juba, the Bamboula, the Counjaille, the Babouille, the Cata (or Chacta), the Voodoo, the Congo, and the Calinda were particularly popular (Courlander 1963).

One of the most delightful examples of early Afro-American dance style is the *cakewalk*. The cakewalk, most popular in the 1870s and 1880s, was originally a parody in which black dancers imitated the way in which upper-class whites appeared as they danced European dances. The cakewalk, however, was essentially a square dance. The most glaring caricature was at the corners of the square, where blacks would spin around, making elaborate dips and bends. At some point, some white people observed black people dancing this strange new dance and were amused—not understanding that it was they themselves who were the butt of the joke. In a perverse turnabout, cakewalk soon became a parody performed by whites to poke fun at black dancing.

The standard argument that jazz was created out of a careful blending of European and African styles is probably overstated. More precisely, it was a black development that was influenced by the acculturation process forced upon African slaves by white society. Quite often, black music and dance forms were parodies of European forms or were African-based with some European influence.

Suggested Listening

1. "Anthology of Music of Black Africa" (Evergerest 3254)
2. "Afro American Spirituals, Work Songs and Ballads" (Lib. of Congress AAFS-L3)
3. "Negro Church Music" (Atlantic 1351)
4. "Ballads of the Civil War" (Folkways, FH 5004)
5. "Fisk Jubilee Singers" (Folkways FA 2372)

Chapter 3
The Blues

The last subject with which we need to deal before we get to a discussion of musical forms that are clearly recognized as jazz is the blues. Pervasive in American music in the twentieth century, the blues was pivotal in the beginning of jazz and has been influential throughout its history. As well, the blues has had strong impact on country music and is the basis for rock-and-roll.

The blues can be defined in a variety of ways, including the following: (1) a feeling of sad or strong emotions that pervades a person's life; (2) a temporary feeling of melancholy; (3) any song that contains the word "blues" in either the lyrics or the title; and (4) a particular musical structure. It is the last definition which we will use for this discussion.

BLUES ROOTS AND THE BASIC FORM

Although it is speculation to suggest that the blues was sung or played before 1900, the style must certainly have developed from prior practice that had many of the musical characteristics of the blues style. One bluesman, Bunk Johnson, suggested that blues had been both sung and played as early as the 1880s. Two of the earliest musicians associated with the blues, Ma Rainey and W. C. Handy, reported that they first heard songs that were clearly blues in 1902 and 1903, respectively. The first published blues composition, "Memphis Blues," was composed by W. C. Handy, first written down in 1909, and printed in 1912. Although one could argue that the blues is a twentieth-century invention, the most likely reality is that the style was performed before 1900, although perhaps the term was first used and associated with that style after 1900.

The roots of the blues are undoubtedly rural and black, even though eventually white singers and players got in on the act. Early blues was often called primitive or rural. For a variety of reasons, I prefer "rural" because it suggests its cultural origin rather than making

a value judgement about its quality. As a rural form, the blues was not formalized when it was first sung but was rather crafted according to the length of the lyrics. The blues communicated certain feelings of black people living in rural America. Although certain parts of the South would become the center for blues production, especially as it developed into jazz forms, it is also clear that blues singing and playing probably existed wherever there were pockets of blacks.

We cannot generalize about the number of lines that existed in early blues forms, since this is undocumented. However, we do know that early blues music was irregular in form, totally dependent upon the number of syllables in each line. Sometime prior to the codification of the blues in the 1910s, the structure of the lyrics settled into a three-line or three-part form, with the first two parts or lines being essentially the same and a third line that contrasted and finished the thought. The blues should be thought of as a poetic form that evolved the way most poetry has—from an oral form to a written form.

Early blues were sung to the accompaniment of a guitar, usually played by the singer. This relationship of instrument to voice being controlled by one musician did not require exact forms; it was only when more than one musician performed that consistency of musical accompaniment developed.

HARMONY AND CHORD PATTERNS

Harmony is the simultaneous sounding of more than one pitch at a time, in blocks of sound that are dependent upon one another. It is possible to have two or more melodies happening at the same time, and this occurs in jazz. However, two or more independent melodies occurring simultaneously is called counterpoint. Harmony is a different concept; it defines blocks of sound that often serve as the building block of musical textures, and for that matter the foundation of the rhythm section in a jazz group.

Harmony, then, defines two or more notes sounding at the same time so that the listener and player perceive them as belonging to one group or chord. Individual chords have character and textural sound that can be analyzed, but the most interesting quality of harmonic chords is in a progression of chords, or a collection of chords moving from one to another so that they make up a distinctive sound and foundation.

The blues progression is commonly a twelve-measure phrase of four-beat measures, making forty-eight beats in the entire progression or unit. As you begin to listen to songs that are based upon blues progression, you should proceed as follows: (1) Simply count the beats in units of forty-eight beats, starting at the beginning, or after the introduction, if there is one; (2) count the beats in twelve four-beat units, such as 1234 2234 3234 4234, and so on; and (3) count the beats in your mind while saying aloud the scale degrees that define the sound quality of the blues. To learn this material, it is absolutely imperative that you go through all of these steps. The blues progression must become second nature for you, so that you can generalize this knowledge and apply it to other analyses.

The blues progression is both a unit that is forty-eight beats long and a progression of chords that are based upon a musical scale. A musical scale is a collection of notes going up and down in a stepwise motion. It is like a melody, but it defines the notes that are used in music rather than a specific tune or song. In that sense, Western music is in one of two types of scales, from which many melodies exist. An example of a typical scale is as follows:

C D E F G A B C B A G F E D C

These notes are simply the notes on a piano, starting at C, going up one white key at a time to the next-highest C, and then back down again. To avoid reading the actual letters, the scale can also be expressed in numbers, as follows:

1 2 3 4 5 6 7 8 7 6 5 4 3 2 1

In the analyses, which begin in this chapter, we will use actual letter names for chords. In this discussion, we will use numbers and letters interchangeably to illustrate the blues progression. However, it is the *relationship* between notes of a scale, and not just the letter names, that determines the basic structure of the sound of the blues. Chord progressions other than the blues can be understood either relatively by numbers or exactly by letter names, although most musicians tend to use letter names in popular practice.

In the scale above, what is important for the blues is the 1, 4, and 5 chords, that is, the chords or clusters of sound based upon the sound of the first, fourth, and fifth degrees of the scale. (Given in letters, those important notes would be C, F, and G.) Although it would be a luxury to spend time learning about the exact nature of chords and how they function, for our purposes it is important only to learn how to hear chord changes. This works in time as follows:

Letters   C///C///C///C///F///F///C///C///G///G///C///C///
Numbers 1///1///1///1///4///4///1///1///5///5///1///1///

Notice that there are actually forty-eight beats represented by both the letter chart and the number chart. To use this, go through the exercise listed earlier while listening to a blues progression in a song. It is actually easiest to hear the chord changes when a teacher plays an example for you, with one chord on each beat. Count, first, one through forty-eight through as many progressions or units as the instructor plays. Then count 1234 2234 3234 4234 5234, up to twelve measures. This activity should neither be skipped nor shortened, because if you drum it into your head, it will pay enormous dividends in time. Besides being able to count the phrases and keep up with the progression, you should also concentrate on what it sounds like when you move from the 1 chord to the 4 chord and other changes. In a sense, one does not need to know what a 4 chord or a 5 chord sounds like, only that a change has occurred. If you can hear and count changes in the blues progression, you will be able to hear changes in other, more complicated chord progressions. This is the essential purpose of this entire process.

BLUES FORMS

Classic Blues

The written history of the blues begins in the 1910s. By 1920, many orchestrations of blues tunes had been written. The blues came to be recognized as folk music—the music of the people—and was probably the first form of popular music that was totally American. Although black string bands and other, smaller ensembles performed the blues before it existed in the form of sheet music, how far back they began is anyone's guess.

Classic blues is the structured form of the blues that followed rural blues. The distinction between classic and rural is primarily a cultural one. Rural blues is associated with rural environments and with singers who create musical performances primarily for themselves, usually accompanying the song on a guitar or piano. In that sense, rural blues is quite often a solo phenomenon. It is also quite flexible in its musical structure, basically a lyric that is accompanied by strummed chords that simply last long enough for someone to sing all the words. The actual structure, therefore, can be everything from seven to thirty-five or thirty-six measures of music. While rural blues often had blueslike structures, in which the 1 chord eventually went to the 4 chord, back to the 1, up to 5, and back to 1, there was no set pattern. Often, parts of that general progression were not even present.

The beginning of the twentieth century saw major migrations of population into cities, primarily because of industrialization. Many ethnic groups, including Afro-Americans, moved to cities, and their culture changed accordingly. Blues music began to reflect the different attitudes found in the city. Cities reflect themselves in ordered constructs because of the interaction of groups of people. It is rational that a blues form would develop out of the organization of a city, as manifest in its emotional and physical aspects.

Besides the obvious cultural differences that developed as a result of migration, there were also entertainment opportunities that developed as a result of major growth of city populations. Towns like New Orleans had a long history of sophisticated city life and offered entertainment opportunities for a number of musicians. The history

King Oliver's Creole Jazz
Band with Louis
Armstrong

of cultural activity in New Orleans and the rather unusual and unique racial mix that existed there probably were the catalyst for the development of Dixieland jazz, but these also were significant in the development of classic blues (which was often performed in Dixieland style).

Blues began to develop around the turn of the century in many growing cities, such as St. Louis, Kansas City, Memphis, Detroit, Chicago, and Philadelphia. The development of musical entertainment (which included the blues) occurred in Detroit in the early 1920s primarily because of the development of the auto industry. In some senses, the best way to understand the development of classic blues is to define the difference between rural expression and city expression.

Classic blues is a continuation of rural musical practices (i.e., the emotional content, musical scales, types of chords, and singing technique). But it adopted a consistent structure. The twelve-measure progression discussed above evolved as the most popular blues form, although eight-measure country blues and twenty-four-measure form progressions were also used. The irregular structures of thirteen measures, seventeen measures, and other asymmetrical structures lost favor, with musicians clearly identifying those irregular forms as rural blues.

Lyrics were more codified in classic blues as well, although they continued to express emotion as well as communicate historical and philosophic ideas. The ideas themselves changed to reflect the values of the city, but the emotional content still retained older traditions that developed from African music of the seventeenth and eighteenth centuries. There still existed call-and-response, blue notes (flatted or lowered), minor feeling, and often an earthy quality. The structure of lyrics codified into a three-line (or three-section) stanza, in which the first two lines or sections were equal in length and often in meaning, and the third line was different and summed up the entire unit.

Blues, which was one of the early forms of Dixieland, shared the same functional quality. It was used in the context of classic blues primarily as an entertainment medium, and most musicians supported themselves by entertaining. Rural blues were often done simply for the sake of singing the blues; classic blues were usually performed for financial remuneration. Rent parties (groups of people gathered for the primary purpose of getting contributions toward paying the rent), camp dances (such as those around New Orleans), black church socials, funerals, and dances were usually the places where professional musicians performed.

Although black musicians originally copied their white counterparts by performing society music (which, in the early twentieth century meant European dances, light classical music, and nostalgic American music such as that written by Stephen Foster), these same black musicians eventually discovered that there was a real market for blues, or "folk music," as it was often called. Although these musicians began playing the blues informally at first, they quickly realized that the blues was a viable medium, first for black audiences, but also for white audiences.

Boogie-Woogie

In the mid-1920s the boogie-woogie craze hit American cities and towns. Primarily a piano style, although later translated into big-band music, boogie-woogie is pure, classic blues in that it follows the chord progression exactly. The piano player plays a left-hand broken chord that uses the same pattern over and over and follows the twelve-measure progression given as the blues model. The right hand plays rhythmic and melodic variations that change for each progression. Often the relationship between the left hand (which has a short-long rhythm) contrasts with the right hand, producing a poly- or multiple-rhythmic effect. Listen carefully to the analysis piece of boogie-woogie to hear the three-against-two rhythm set up in several of the variations.

The history of boogie-woogie is rather interesting because, like the development of the blues, it had a specific function. It usually was played by piano players who traveled constantly, looking for work; often these itinerant musicians played for rent parties, where they were usually rewarded for their labors with a nominal payment: simple food and drink.

Since many traveling musicians hitched rides on the under-carriage of freight trains, they were well accustomed to the sound of the train on the tracks. It was this sound, some say, that gave rise to the long-short quality of boogie-woogie. The term itself comes from "bogey," meaning "spirit," and "woogie," the term used to describe railroad ties.

Urban Blues

Urban blues is really no different in structure from classic blues, but it is perhaps different in emotional content. Generally a term used to describe blues after about 1930, urban blues reflects city life in an urban environment. While that may seem a subtle distinction, urban attitudes spring from the development of racial and ethnic pockets of civilization within a large city. Urban blues is often associated with big band music and with entertainment locations that cater to a very specific and local clientele, such as the neighborhood bar. On the black circuit, there was a form of music called urban blues that responded directly to the needs of big-city blacks. The character of this music was earthy and strong. The music of Duke Ellington and Count Basie may be seen as an extension of this cultural phenomenon.

Jump Blues and Rhythm-and-Blues

Jump blues developed in the 1940s. Although much of the history of the blues is relatively black oriented, jump blues is almost completely so. The primary artist of this style was Louis Jordan, who had a five- or six-piece small ensemble from 1938 to 1951. His music was straight classic blues in structure and featured an ensemble that played music punctuated with shouted lyrics. Undoubtedly the most important single influence on the development of rock-and-roll, jump blues was intended almost solely for black audiences, who wanted to dance and who were also very interested in watching the musicians move onstage. Jordan's band was very physical in its presentation, moving onstage in ways that would later become the stock-in-trade of rhythm-and-blues, soul, and later funk. Rhythm-and-blues describes a phenomenon of black "popular" music that emerged as a commercial phenomenon in the 1950s. Along with rock-and-roll, blues influence has continued in forms of music besides jazz.

In conclusion, the blues—from W. C. Handy and Count Basie to the contemporary Herbie Hancock—has been a constant in jazz. However, the most significant structural development of the blues was the codification of the twelve-measure unit. There have been important variations on the basic scheme, but, like jazz improvisation in general, each innovation is a variation on a basic theme.

"Dippermouth Blues"
King Oliver's Creole Jazz Band (SCCJ A-5)

MUSICAL ANALYSIS

The instrumentation of King Oliver's Creole Jazz Band is two cornets (played by King Oliver and Louis Armstrong), clarinet, trombone, piano, banjo, and drums; the ensemble recorded "Dippermouth Blues" in 1923. The meter signature is 4/4, which means that there are four quarter notes (beats) per measure; the tempo or speed is 192 beats per minute. It is in the key of C-major, although the actual key of the recording is halfway between B and C. Other than the introduction, the piece is a fairly standard blues progression.

In the first complete twelve-measure unit, the chord changes are C,F,C,C7,F,F,C,C,d7,G7,CF,C. Translated into numbers, this yields 1,4,1,1,4,4,1,1,2,5,1 4,1, with the standard progression being 1,1,1,1,4,4,1,1,5,5,1,1. By comparing those two, you can see that the form is fairly close to the standard progression. The main point is to count the beats and measures so that you can hear the return to the beginning of the next twelve-measure unit; then you can try to differentiate between chords within the progression. Be sure to listen to this piece enough times so that you can make those discriminations.

Louis Armstrong, ca. 1936

This particular piece is fairly easy to follow. Listen carefully to the way in which the group collectively improvises their first time through the progression. Then the clarinet takes over, with continuous group activity for one chorus (twelve-measure unit), then as a solo for two choruses, with background figures from the other instruments. The group returns to set up the trumpet solo and concludes with group improvisation.

For those of you who are reading chords, "7" following the chord means a seventh chord, a capital letter means a major chord, a lowercase letter a minor chord, and "o" means "diminished." In this piece, C is 1, F is 4, and G is 5.

Intro

Co	Ao	F#o	G7F#7		G7
1	2		3		4

Group

C	F	C	C7	F	F	C	C	d7	G7	C		F	C
1	2	3	4	5	6	7	8	9	10	11			12

Group (High Clarinet at Beginning)

C	F	C	C7	F	F	C	C	d7	G7	C		F	C
1	2	3	4	5	6	7	8	9	10	11			12

Clarinet with Stop Time

C	Co	C	C7	F	F#o	C	A7	d7	G7	C	F	C
1	2	3	4	5	6	7	8	9	10	11		12

Clarinet

C	Co	C	C7	F	F#o	C	A7	d7	G7	C	F	C
1	2	3	4	5	6	7	8	9	10	11		12

Group

C	F	C	C7	F	F	C	C	d7	G7	C	F	C
1	2	3	4	5	6	7	8	9	10	11		12

Trumpet (Light Clarinet Obligatto)

C	F	C	C7	F	F	C	C	d7	G7	C	F	C
1	2	3	4	5	6	7	8	9	10	11		12

Trumpet (Skipping Melody)

C	F	C	C7	F	F	C	C	d7	G7	C	F	C
1	2	3	4	5	6	7	8	9	10	11		12

Trumpet (Higher and Fancier)　　　　　　　Vocal Break

C	F	C	C7	F	F	C	C	d7	G7	C	F	C
1	2	3	4	5	6	7	8	9	10	11		12

Group

C	F	C	C7	F	F	C	C	d7	G7	C	F	C
1	2	3	4	5	6	7	8	9	10	11		12

Extension

C	C/Off on beat 3.
1	2

T-Bone Walker　　　　　　　　　　　　　*SIDE-NOTES*

Aaron Thibeaux Walker was born on May 22, 1909, in Linden, Texas; he died in Los Angeles on March 16, 1975. As the first country bluesman to make use of an electric guitar, he influenced both rock and jazz guitarists.

"T-Bone" (derived from the pronunciation of his middle name) was born to a musical family, which moved to Dallas when Walker was 2 years old. His stepfather, Marco Washington, was a street singer. By the age of 10, Walker was regularly accompanying his stepfather out on the streets. From 1920 to 1923, he was the lead boy for Blind Lemon Jefferson, one of the most popular and influential blues singers of the 1920s.

By 1923, Walker had learned to play the guitar and was entertaining at private parties. He went on the road for the first time at the age of 13 with Dr. Breeding's Big B Tonic Medicine Show. From 1923 to 1934, he toured with several different groups, one of which included Ma Rainey. He also played with several big bands, including Les Hite and Fletcher Anderson. In 1934, he moved to the West Coast and married the next year. His wife inspired the tune "Viola Lee Blues," which was eventually played by other musicians, including the Grateful Dead.

Walker began using an early electric guitar in 1935. In 1942 he recorded as T-Bone Walker for the first time. In 1942 he had his biggest hit, "Call It Stormy Monday," which was covered (played by other musicians) many times. He toured both the United States and Europe throughout the 1950s and 1960s and won a Grammy Award in 1970 for "Good Feelin'." He died in 1975 at the age of 64.

Big Bill Broonzy

William "Big Bill" Broonzy was born in Scott, Mississippi on June 26, 1898 and died in Chicago on August 14, 1958. Broonzy was considered one of the most influential of the Delta blues singers. His style was a transition between the old style of Robert Johnson and the electronic blues style of Muddy Waters. His influence was strong in blues, country music, and rockabilly.

One of seventeen children, Broonzy grew up working the crops on the family farm. At the age of 10, he started learning to play a homemade fiddle and then the guitar. By age 12, he was playing for picnics, as an informal entertainer, for what were called two-stage picnics: whites on one side and blacks on the other.

After serving in the army from 1917 to 1919, Broonzy moved to Chicago, where he worked first with Papa Charlie Jackson, and then others, including Blind Lemon Jefferson. In 1923, he cut records of two of his songs: "Big Bill Blues" and "House Rent Stomp." He continued to make recordings for various companies throughout the late 1920s and the 1930s, especially for Champion Records.

He continued to perform successfully throughout the 1940s but supported himself with other work. In 1950 he joined a Chicago folk group called I Come for to Sing, which gave concerts across the United States, primarily on college campuses. He toured Europe in 1951 and returned to the United States to critical and financial success. By 1953, he was working as a full-time musician.

Broonzy died of cancer in 1958. His influence has been important in blues, country music, and rockabilly.

Suggested Listening

1. "Boogie-Woogie Rarities" (1927–1943) Mile. 2009
2. "Gut Bucket Blues and Stomps" Her. 112
3. "Atlantic Rhythm and Blues," Vols. 1–7 Atlantic 7–81293–9
4. "Good Morning Blues" (Lead Belly) Biograph 12013

Part II
Dixieland and Classic Jazz

Chapter 4
Dixieland

Dixieland jazz, sometimes called "classic" jazz, was developed more or less during the years 1900–1925. Despite the many styles of jazz that have evolved since Dixieland began, one can always find examples of its continued influence in contemporary music.

The term "Dixieland" comes from the term used to describe the southern United States—while Dixieland is said to have developed in New Orleans, it is reasonably certain that a similar type of music was being developed in other cities at the same time. In Chicago, for instance, a different style of Dixieland was being developed, primarily as a result of prime New Orleans players such as Sidney Bechet and Louis Armstrong moving there both to play and to make recordings.

The most important quality of both early Dixieland and New Orleans style is collective improvisation, a concept that will continue to be important for us through free jazz into the 1980s. Improvisation is the act of making up new music by varying some aspects of the original composition. Quite often in jazz, only one player—a soloist—improvises. However, the basis of New Orleans Dixieland is that all the players of melody instruments improvise at the same time; at certain times, one player takes a more dominant solo role while the other musicians play simple background figures or countermelodies.

DEVELOPMENT IN NEW ORLEANS

Racial and Social Milieu

At the turn of the century, New Orleans was a relatively large and sophisticated city, with a varied racial and ethnic population. Its large black population had retained many African cultural traits. The probable reason for that retention was the relatively relaxed attitude that

Sidney Bechet, late 1950's

Louisiana French Catholics had toward other religious and philosophical traits. There was also a great deal of intermarriage between blacks and whites, which formed the population body called Creoles, a group unique to the United States.

New Orleans was—and still is—a party town, with many opportunities for entertainment; parties were thrown for all the usual festive occasions, as well as to celebrate during Catholic feast days, African feast days, religious camp meetings, secular camp parties, society balls, and riverboat activities. New Orleans supported a vast entertainment industry; there were a great number of orchestras and bands, which led to musical competition and high standards.

Street Bands

One of the most important jazz phenomena in New Orleans was the development of street bands. These organizations, which predated jazz, included traditional brass bands playing marches, and string bands playing European dance forms. Because of its temperate climate, New Orleans maintained several bands that played music outdoors year round.

Street bands were also associated with black and Creole tradition, a distinction that remains important in the history of early jazz. Creoles at one time were allowed certain freedoms that blacks did not have, which created a dual class system, both within society and in music. However, both racial groups had musical practices that were clearly retentive of African influence, such as the playing of music at funerals. Among blacks, this practice continued at least through the eighteenth century; by the early twentieth century, New Orleans street bands were the medium for that continuing practice.

At the end of the nineteenth century, funeral music was limited to brass bands; but soon ragtime, blues, and eventually Dixieland began to be used. The street band usually would consist of brass instruments, metal clarinets, tuba (for bass), and drums. The early form of Dixieland, however, was already in place before 1910 in street bands.

A similar development of more traditional European-based music occurred in society orchestras such as the W. C. Handy Orchestra. Before 1900, Handy was the leader of a society orchestra that played transcriptions of European light classical music, Viennese waltzes, and other European-influenced music. In the early 1900s, he heard a black string band of guitars and country fiddlers playing blues-type music; he was soon inspired to write formal arrangements for his orchestra. Handy was only one of several bandleaders who recognized the commercial value of the blues.

Street bands frequently performed at camp parties. Often these were held on the waterfront of Lake Pontchartrain. During the 1910s and the 1920s, as many as sixty bands would perform at the same time at different parties. Although there were black parties and white parties, some parties were often racially mixed; when both blacks and whites were in attendance, a rope or ribbon frequently divided the audience into halves—one black, one white.

Collective improvisation and experimentation probably came from bucking contests, a method that was used to entice people to attend the parties. In bucking contests (also called "cutting"), two or more players or bands compete musically. This attracts a crowd, and the winner gains recognition. In New Orleans, people would follow the winners to wherever they were playing next. Ragtime competitions were legendary; boogie-woogie musicians continued the practice in the 1920s.

Musicians of the time—Buddy Petit, Chris Kelly, Sam Morgan, Kid Rena, Punch Miller, and many others—were paid to parade up and down the streets of New Orleans on furniture trucks, with signs and posters on the sides of the truck, advertising the dance that would be the following day, usually a Monday. Therefore, on a Sunday, as many as five or six trucks would cruise the streets, playing music. Quite often, the truck musicians would meet at a corner, where an informal bucking contest would occur. The young Louis Armstrong watched these contests as he was maturing as a player; he termed the best players "head choppers."

Street musicians had to come up with unique musical concepts to beat the competition and win work. Quite often, some little device that the other musicians could not pick up (or "cover") determined who would win. But more often than not, it was simply the players' abilities that allowed them to win. The best buckers were simply the best musicians. The best band was the group that made the most harmonious and exciting group improvisations.

Some of the most significant early New Orleans musicians, including Kid Ory and eventually Louis Armstrong, played in very mundane situations as they learned their trade. Out of the competition came not only the willingness to try new things, but also the necessity.

CLASSIC DIXIELAND

Classic New Orleans–style Dixieland came from the brass band and evolved into a relatively set instrumentation. The pre–Dixieland brass band was made up of players who provided the melody of a composition, and a rhythm section (drums) that provided the beat. Bass instruments (tubas), played the lowest notes of the melodic and harmonic texture but also tended to play on all four beats of a measure, so that they had rhythmic function as well. Harmony defined the whole texture (minus drums) working together.

Many street bands were small, much smaller than the complete marching brass bands of the 1970s and 1980s. Often, they were made up of eight to ten players, with each instrument having a clear function; that is, the drum kept the beat, the trumpet played the melody, the clarinet played high notes, and so on. The overall texture was fairly thin.

The tuba and the drums began to be thought of as one unit, a kind of rhythm section. Sometimes a banjo was used as part of that unit. Metal clarinets began to be used because of their inexpensiveness and availability; these and other melodic instruments were treated as another unit, primarily responsible for playing melodies in harmony. When these bands started playing blues-type music—probably in the early 1900s—the function of the two units (melody instruments and rhythm section) separated so that they were more distinct.

The basic texture of the Dixieland band is rhythm section (tuba, banjo, and street drums) and melody instruments (metal clarinet, cornet, and trombone). In the late 1910s, the instrumentation changed somewhat. Tuba eventually was replaced by string bass. Piano was introduced when Dixieland began to be played indoors, and street drums were replaced by a complete drum set. Although the metal clarinet was eventually replaced by the more sophisticated wood clarinet, many New Orleans clarinetists continued using metal clarinets into the 1940s.

Instrumentation

The function of the rhythm section in New Orleans Dixieland is simply to play chords or beats on every beat of each measure. New Orleans Dixieland generally uses fairly static rhythm, although when the tuba is replaced by string bass, the texture quickly gets much lighter. One of the most obvious differences in later Dixieland styles (such as the Chicago style) was the occasional use of rests in the rhythm section; that is, every once in a while the rhythm section did not play the notes on the score.

Zutty Singleton

The function of melody instruments as a group is to provide the melodic texture. Both units together provide the harmonies, because banjo or piano play full chords, and the tuba or string bass play the bottom note of the chord. The melody instruments also play background for each other during the collective improvisation.

The actual structure of New Orleans–style Dixieland can best be understood from the analyses for this chapter. Only the Red Onion Jazz Babies selection represents classic style, in that there are no solos; improvisation is always collective. Note that the later Armstrong recording does have noticeable solos. The Jelly Roll Morton piece is halfway between, in that the important sections are really the group sections; this is an informal arrangement because it was not written down.

The primary model of New Orleans style is essentially a group of variations on a particular melody, with the melody instruments playing the melody the first time through, then collectively improvising through several variations, and then concluding with a less varied repeat of the original melody. Some people call this "group grope," but the technique is really very precise.

The function of the clarinet is to play a high obligatto (countermelody), which often doubles the speed at which the cornet or trumpet is playing; the clarinet also tries to fill in the spaces that the trumpet leaves. The trombone plays a low countermelody that is essentially a duet with the trumpet, although the trombone also fills in the spaces left by the other two players.

Warren "Baby" Dodds

It is important to note that all future developments of Dix-ieland were based on this model. Sidney Bechet's development of the soprano saxophone was essentially a combination of clarinet- and cornet-style playing. Louis Armstrong took the basic function, as learned from King Oliver, and expanded it to create pure solo func-tion, without the group. But his technique is based on how he played with a group.

Some of the important players from New Orleans were as fol-lows: Louis Armstrong, Buddy Bolden, Joe "King" Oliver (trumpet and cornet); Sidney Bechet, Johnny Dodds, Jimmie Noone (clarinet); Kid Ory (trombone); Lil Hardin Armstrong, Jelly Roll Morton (piano); Pops Foster (bass); Lonnie Johnson (guitar); Johnny St. Cyr (guitar and banjo); and Baby Dodds and Zutty Singleton (drums). Although some of these players achieved worldwide fame playing Dixieland into the big band era and beyond, New Orleans musicians of the 1910s and 1920s were the ones who created the essence of jazz.

"Struttin' with Some Barbecue" Louis Armstrong and His Hot Five (SCCJ B-2)

MUSICAL ANALYSIS

The piece was recorded in 1927. The instrumentation is cornet, trombone, clarinet, piano, and banjo. The meter is 4/4, and the tempo is 192. The key of the piece is Ab. This piece is clearly a Dixieland piece probably derived from ragtime. The piece starts with a twelve-measure introduction and then is based upon sixteen-measure phrases. Note the extensions and the fact that the rhythm section normally plays on beats 2 and 4 only.

You will notice a number of different chord changes in this piece, so even if you do not use the chords extensively, you should look at those changes and try to perceive that there are different things going on, depending on the instrument that is playing. There are two distinct, alternating, harmonic units. The solos are excellent examples of New Orleans musicians who were in the process of building a new style. In this piece, Armstrong clearly develops melodically in ways that New Orleans style generally avoided.

Intro

Ab	Eb	Ab	Eb	Ab		bbm	Eb	Ab	Eb	Bb7	Eb7
1	2	3	4	5	6	7	8	9	10	11	12

Trumpet

Ab					F7		bbm	Eb	f	Bb7		Eb7		
1	2	3	4	5	6	7	8	9	10	11 12	13	14 15		16

Trumpet

													Banjo	
Ab		Ab7		Db		Db	dbm	Ab	F7	bbm	Eb7	Ab		
1	2 3	4	5	6	7	8	9	10	11	12 13	14	15	16	

Clarinet

													Break	
Ab					F7		bbm7	Eb7	fm	Bb7		Eb7		
1	2 3	4	5	6 7	8	9		10	11 12	13	14	15	16	

Trombone

													Break	
Ab		Ab7		Db		dbm	Ab	F7	bbm	Eb7	Ab			
1	2 3	4	5	6	7 8	9	10	11	12	13	14	15	16	

39

Trumpet

																Break
Ab						F7		bbm	Eb7	f		Bb7		Eb7		
1	2	3	4	5	6	7	8	9	10	11	12	13	14	15	16	

Trumpet

															Group
Ab			Ab7		Db			dbm	Ab	F7	bbm	Eb7	Ab	Eb7	
1	2	3	4	5	6	7	8	9	10	11	12	13	14	15	16

Group Extension

Ab	Eb7
17	18

Group

																Banjo
Ab						F7		bbm	Eb7	f		Bb7		Eb7		
1	2	3	4	5	6	7	8	9	10	11	12	13	14	15	16	

Group

							Stop time								
Ab			Ab7		Db			db	Ab			Bb7	Eb7	Ab	
1	2	3	4	5	6	7	8	9	10	11	12	13	14	15	16

Extension to Hold

Ab
1   2

SIDE-NOTES

Louis Armstrong

Daniel Louis ("Satchmo") Armstrong was born in New Orleans on July 4, 1900 and died on July 6, 1971. His parents separated when Armstrong was 5. He started singing on the streets for pennies when he was 7. In 1913, Armstrong celebrated New Year's Eve by firing a gun in the street, for which he was arrested and sent to the Waifs' Home in New Orleans. It was there that he learned to play the cornet.

After he was released from the home, Armstrong began playing with variety bands in New Orleans. King Oliver, undoubtedly the most important trumpet player of that time, heard Armstrong and encouraged him in his playing. When Oliver moved to Chicago in 1918, Armstrong took over his spot in the Kid Ory Band, working the riverboats, camp parties, and street parades. In 1922, Armstrong joined Oliver in Chicago to play in his band; he also married the piano player, Lil

Hardin, in 1924. That same year, he left Oliver to join the Fletcher Henderson band in New York, then in 1925 Lil's Dreamland Syncopators in Chicago. On November 12, 1925, Armstrong made the first "Hot 5" recordings which continued through 1928. Many of the recordings featured pianist Earl Hines. Back in New York City in 1929, Armstrong began playing with big bands.

He toured the United States and then traveled throughout the world, becoming America's greatest jazz ambassador. He appeared in numerous films—"Ex-Flame" (1931), "Pennies from Heaven," with Bing Crosby (1936), and "Hello Dolly" (1969).

Sidney Bechet

Sidney Bechet was born in New Orleans on May 14, 1897 and died in Paris, France, on May 14, 1959. Trained classically on the clarinet from the age of 8, he had played with Buddy Petit, Jack Carey, and the Eagle Band by the age of 17. In 1914 Bechet toured the South, and in 1916 he joined King Oliver's Olympia Band in New Orleans. Bechet moved to New York in 1919, where he joined Will Marion Cook's Southern Syncopated Orchestra. In 1919, the group traveled to Europe as the first concert jazz band. It was on this trip that Ernest Ansermet was so impressed with Bechet's playing that he published the first piece of jazz criticism.

Bechet remained in Paris until 1921 and then returned to New York, where he started to develop his soprano sax playing. He made the first records with Clarence Williams' Blue Five and worked with a variety of blues musicians while in New York. In 1925, he worked briefly with Duke Ellington and then returned to Europe. Bechet split the rest of his musical career between Paris and New York; when in New York, he usually made important recordings. Bechet's influence in the development of saxophone playing was major. His influence on the use of soprano sax has been most keenly felt and is apparent in the works of John Coltrane and others.

Suggested Listening

1.	"Armstrong and Hines, 1928"	Smithsonian 2002
2.	"Louis Armstrong and King Oliver"	Milestone M47017
3.	"Armstrong and Bechet in New York"	Smithsonian 2026
4.	"Louis Armstrong Story," Vols. 1–4	Columbia CL 851–4
5.	"King Oliver's Jazz Band, 1923"	Smithsonian 2001

Chapter 5
The Growth of Dixieland

The greatest legacy that any style of music can have is lasting influence. The greatest legacy of New Orleans Dixieland is the countless musicians who took that basic style and expanded it. The purpose of this chapter is to discuss some of the styles of Dixieland that evolved. Chicago-style Dixieland is discussed at length because it is a definitive style, but it should be understood that Dixieland of different types developed in many other cities across the United States.

The expansion of Dixieland style can be explained in several ways. Traditionally, most of the Dixieland styles in most towns were thought to have been started by New Orleans musicians who migrated there. Clearly, in the case of Chicago style and to a certain extent, Kansas City style, that is true. New York Dixieland was developed primarily as a result of musicians going to New York to record and to make money.

However, one could also argue that other Dixieland styles developed naturally in towns other than New Orleans; that city—while having a unique blend of cultural traits—was not the only place in the United States that could support artistic development.

A generic influence on the development of early jazz styles was the ragtime pianists, many of whom traveled a regular circuit from New Orleans, up the Mississippi River. For instance, the early history of Kansas City jazz was heavily influenced by piano players who had been pupils of Scott Joplin.

Brass bands like those popular in New Orleans existed in other towns as well. And of course, some African activities existed in black populations in other cities, although again perhaps without the sense of acceptance that the unique New Orleans attitude allowed. But by far the most significant support mechanism for the development of jazz as an entertainment vehicle was the existence of high-society behavior such as that associated with the Roaring Twenties.

DEVELOPMENT IN CHICAGO AND KANSAS CITY

Some people have said that the entire history of jazz can be explained by illegal or immoral behavior. While I think that this is stretching the truth, in the case of Chicago jazz there is at least a little truth to it. There can also be no question that piano players have long been associated with bars, nightclubs, and even bordellos (particularly in the red-light district of New Orleans).

Chicago

Music tends to develop in areas where there is support for musicians to make money performing for the public. Part of the reason musicians went to Chicago was to record, as is certainly the case for musicians in New York as well. However, the most compelling reason that black musicians, in particular, went to Chicago as a musical center of the 1920s was that there was opportunity there. Musicians could rather easily find employment in nightclubs, speakeasies, gambling joints, and brothels. Organized crime supported activities that welcomed entertainment and dance music. In fact, much of the jazz of alternative Dixieland styles functioned as dance music. Louis Armstrong came to Chicago because King Oliver wanted him there; Sidney Bechet and many other New Orleans musicians went to Chicago because work was available there for them.

A variety of musicians—primarily white—from the upper midwest were attracted to Chicago and developed an alternate jazz style of their own. Interestingly enough, this was the first time that white musicians developed a style of jazz; the spiritual leader probably was Bix Beiderbecke, although there were older musicians who wielded more power.

Chicago of the 1920s was a large, industrialized town. During this time of Prohibition, it earned itself a reputation in gang warfare. Chicago is also quite mixed ethnically, with large pockets of ethnic groups represented, especially on the city's west and south sides.

Kansas City

Kansas City, a southern city, differs from Chicago ethnically, but, like Chicago, it has a strong political identity. Musical activity was prevalent from the 1890s on. Having a fairly large black population, Kansas City became a center for the vaudeville circuit and for the boogie-woogie players of the 1920s. Probably the most significant musical director to emerge from Kansas City was Count Basie. In some senses, the ultimate success of Count Basie and many other Kansas City musicians hinged on the activities of Bennie Moten (see Biography).

Wolverines, Des Moines, Iowa, 1925 or 1926. From left to right: Frank Teschemacher (Sax, Clarinet), Jim Lannigan, String Band, Bud Freeman (Sax, Clarinet), Jimmy McPartland (Cornet), Dave Tough (Drums), Floyd O'Brien (Trombone), Dave North (Piano), and Dick McPartland (Banjo, Guitar)

CHICAGO-STYLE INSTRUMENTATION

Although specific instrumentations were created in towns other than Chicago, the style of music that evolved in Chicago is highly representative of alternative Dixieland styles in general. The influence of Chicago-style Dixieland is perhaps more pervasive than other styles.

Of course, the migration of New Orleans musicians to Chicago was the first step in the evolution of Chicago's jazz style; many musicians began to develop their own personal styles after their arrival in Chicago. The continuing influence of Sidney Bechet and especially Louis Armstrong is important in Chicago style.

Chicago-style Dixieland is essentially like New Orleans style, but it is based on solo activity rather than on collective improvisation. The instrumentation is basically the same, although saxophone was added and the use of string bass became common. However, the general structure is different. The melody instruments play the melody first (similar to New Orleans style), but then each melody instrument plays an individual solo, rather than collective improvisation, as in the New Orleans style. They conclude by playing the melody again.

What is important about Chicago-style Dixieland is its concentration on individual improvisation. In Chicago-style jazz, musicians had to develop their own improvisational style, without support during the solo from other melody instrumentalists, who would play in New Orleans style. Collective improvisation creates a texture in which one player does not do everything. Individual improvisation is both freer and more demanding.

Louis Armstrong was terribly important in the development of the New Orleans style, but his influence was perhaps more important on the Chicago style. He moved clearly from the group player to

Jimmy McPartland

an individual improviser. His solos became studies in contrast, using the entire range of the instrument, changing speed and quality of style, going from melodic playing to leaping sounds.

At the same time that Armstrong and other New Orleans musicians were creating new ideas in Chicago and other towns, other musicians were generating new ideas as well. For instance Frank Teschemacher, a white clarinetist from Chicago, had excellent technique; his style was more fluid than that of other clarinet players from New Orleans. Also, young Benny Goodman started playing Chicago-style Dixieland.

The so-called Austin High group—all from Austin High School—was significant in the 1920s. This group developed a solo concept that was ultimately identified as the Austin High style. They began in 1922 while the players were still in school. Jimmy Mc-Partland and Frank Teschemacher were members, as well as Bud Freeman. Gene Krupa (discussed later) was from Chicago. Although Earl Hines was originally from Pittsburgh, he moved to Chicago when he was 21; ultimately he influenced Nat "King" Cole, Art Tatum, Teddy Wilson, and others.

One of the big jazz players of that era was Bix Beiderbecke, who was part of the Chicago scene, although only peripherally. He did not remain in Chicago, but his solo technique was radically different from Armstrong's and was also influential. Beiderbecke was a consummate soloist.

Generally speaking, the most significant difference between New Orleans–style music and the Dixieland styles of other places is the relative amount of collective versus solo improvisation. New Orleans style tends to be dominated by collective improvisation, with very few solos. Traditional Dixieland played in New Orleans today is still much that way.

Chicago Dixieland tends to be very solo oriented, with very little countermelody from the other players. Kansas City Dixieland tends to use background activity but of a melodic or rhythmic riff type (one short phrase played over and over in the right chord).

Chicago-style Dixieland tends to use a full rhythm section, employing string bass, piano, guitar or banjo, and drums. They also tend to play a two-beat style (on beats 1 and 3) rather than on all four. As they moved into big-band style, they allowed rhythm players to play complementary parts rather than doing the same thing all the time.

Early Chicago and Kansas City styles blended into the growing tendency toward big-band textures. Chicago Dixieland also tended to be more elaborate in structure, employing introductions, interludes, and codas or finishing sections. Big bands at first were essentially Dixieland bands with several saxophone players and perhaps two trumpets. The bands played in whatever Dixieland style was current. As the arrangements became more elaborate, the traits of individual Dixieland styles began to fade. But collective improvisation of New Orleans traditional style did not remain a major influence on big-band arrangers. It was Chicago style, along with influences from Kansas City and New York City, which would shape the next stage of evolution.

MUSICAL ANALYSIS

"Weather Bird"
Louis Armstrong and Earl Hines (SCCJ B-5)

The instrumentation of this piece, recorded in 1928, is Louis Armstrong on trumpet and Earl Hines on piano. The meter signature is 4/4, and the tempo is 195. The key is Ab. Although again the chord progression is quite difficult to follow, the piece does divide neatly into eight-measure phrases. Notice that the trumpet introductory statement is A (sixteen measures) and B (sixteen measures). The following piano statement is exactly the opposite structurally.

Probably the most intriguing aspect of this tune is that it illustrates improvisation by just two players, without the support of an entire rhythm section. However, it is important to note that only a very good player can sustain this type of activity. Make sure that you listen carefully for interaction between the two players. Slashes have been placed under some chords to clarify the number of beats.

Intro

Dbdb		c	F7	Bb	Eb	Ab
////		/	///	//	//	////
1		2		3		4

Trumpet Melody-A

Ab	Db	Ab		g	f	G7	c	Eb7	Ab	Db	Ab	F7		DbD	Ab	F7	Bb	EbAb
1	2	3		4	5	6	7	8		1	2	3	4	5	6		7	8

B

Eb		Ab		bb	Eb7	Ab		bb	Eb7Ab			Dbdb	c	F7	bb	EbAb
1	2	3	4	5	6	7	8	1	2	3	4	5	6		7	8

Piano-B

Eb		Ab		bb	Eb7	Ab		bb	Eb7Ab			Dbdb	c	F7	bbEb	Ab
1	2	3	4	5	6	7	8	1	2	3	4	5	6		7	8

A

Ab	Db	Ab		g	f	G7	c	Eb7	Ab	Db	Ab	F7		DbD	Ab	F7	Bb	EbAb
1	2	3		4	5	6	7	8		1	2	3	4	5	6		7	8

Trumpet

Ab	Ab	Ab	Eb7
1	2	3	4

Piano

Ab		Eb7	Ab			Ab	Dbdb	c	F	Bb	Eb	Ab
1	2	3	4	5	6	7	8	1	2	3	4	5	6	7	8

Trumpet Break

1	2

Trumpet **Breaks. . . .**

Ab	A	Eb	Eb	Ab		AoDbdb	c	f	Bb	Eb	Abbb	Eb7
1	2	3	4	5 6 7 8	1	2	3	4	5	6	7	8

Ab **Eb7** **Ab** **Piano Break.Ab DbD AbF BbEb Ab**

1	2	3	4	5	6	7	8		1	2	3	4	5	6	7	8

				Free Hold
Do		**DbDoAb**		**Ab**

1	2	3	4	5	6	7	8	1	2	3	4	5	6	7	8

Bix Beiderbecke

Leon Bismarck ("Bix") Beiderbecke was born in Davenport, Iowa, on March 10, 1903 and died in New York on August 7, 1931. He was one of the earliest white musicians to influence black players. Having one of the shortest careers in the history of jazz, Bix Beiderbecke was not really appreciated by many during his lifetime, but many have since come to relish his trumpet solos and his compositional genius. Beiderbecke's life was probably the inspiration for the 1950 film "Young Man with the Horn." The film, which starred Kirk Douglas, Doris Day and Lauren Bacall, was directed by Michael Curtiz for Warner Brothers.

Self-taught on the cornet and the piano, Beiderbecke became the star of the Wolverines, a group from Chicago, in 1923. He went to New York in 1925 to play at the Roseland. He returned to Chicago later to sit in with King Oliver, Louis Armstrong, and Jimmie Noone. In 1926, he went to St. Louis to work with Frankie Trumbauer at the Arcadia Ballroom. After that, it was off to Detroit with Jean Goldkette and then Paul Whiteman, from 1928 through 1930. He worked last with Glen Gray and the Casa Loma Orchestra.

Although he did not play with bands that were known for their technical ability, he was a trumpet virtuoso and played in a style considered unusual for the time. Perhaps rivaling Louis Armstrong in inventiveness, Beiderbecke played long melodic improvisations that were much more fluid in execution than were those of musicians from New Orleans. Clearly, Beiderbecke would have achieved even greater fame had he lived longer, but he did leave a lasting influence through his approach to improvisation.

Bennie Moten

Bennie Moten was born in Kansas City on November 13, 1894 and died there on April 2, 1935 from a mishap during surgery. Although he was a piano player, he was best known for his leadership of early big bands and as a Kansas City political leader. Moten directed bands from 1922 until his death in 1935; his big band became the Count Basie Big Band in 1935.

Moten began his career as a baritone horn player in a brass band while a teen-ager and then shifted to ragtime piano. He took lessons from Charlie Watts and Scrap Harris, two leading piano players who were pupils of Scott Joplin. In 1918, Moten put together his first group, a trio. In 1921, he had a six-piece band that played at the Panama Club; this band played ragtime and blues. In 1923, Moten's group was recorded by Ralph Peer of Okeh Records—six tunes with blues singers, and two instrumentals.

By 1926, Moten's band had expanded into a prototypical big band. In 1927, the Victor Talking Machine Company (now RCA Victor) moved into on-site recording and hired Ralph Peer away from Okeh. They signed several artists of note, but Jelly Roll Morton and Bennie Moten were the major successes. By this time, the Moten band had ten players, and over the next ten years the band would grow to a full big band. Perhaps two of the most important additions were Walter

Page (bass) in 1931 and Count Basie in 1929; Eddie Durham (trombone) and Ben Webster were significant as well. In any event, the Moten band eventually became the most important big band in Kansas City, which by this time had become a hot spot of jazz development.

The evolution of Moten's band, from musically mediocre to the springboard for Basie, parallels the development of jazz. Also important was Moten's influence as a politician and musical bookmaker. He literally controlled musical life in Kansas City during the last ten years of his life. And although his name is perhaps not as well known as that of his successor and others, Moten continued to influence others through his techniques and charismatic control.

Suggested Listening

1. "The Bix Beiderbecke Story," Vol. 2   Columbia CL 845
2. "Count Basie in KC, Bennie Moten's Great Band of 1930–32"   RCA LPV–514
3. "Kansas City Jazz"   Decca 8044
4. "Warm Moods (Ben Webster)"   Reprise 92001
5. "The Chicagoans "The Austin High Gang" 1928–1930"   MCA–1350

Chapter 6
Ragtime and Other Piano Styles

The purpose of this chapter is to place into historical context the significance of the piano and styles of piano playing in the development of jazz. In some senses, the piano was on the periphery of the development of jazz, although some of the playing styles were highly important to its early development.

Probably the most significant reason that the piano was not used more in early collective New Orleans Dixieland was the location in which jazz bands played (usually in streets, where instruments were carried by horse-drawn wagons and later trucks), and the tendency for musicians to think of the piano strictly as a solo instrument. This is not to suggest that pianos were hard to come by; they were the second most abundant instrument in the United States, after the guitar. But their sheer size and weight made them difficult to transport.

In New Orleans, at least, the piano was associated with ragtime and stomps and was always played by a flashy solo performer. (A stomp is a piano style that is highly percussive; stomps could be in ragtime style, blues, or gospel playing.) Jelly Roll Morton was one of the few solo piano players to play the piano in a group, which is probably his major contribution to the development of jazz.

The most interesting kinds of piano music in the early twentieth century included ragtime, stomps, and eventually stride. *Boogie-woogie* was a specialized piano style that developed from stomps; it was very popular in the 1920s and into the big-band era. Many modern piano players who were pivotal in jazz (Count Basie for instance) recognize their roots as going back to earlier players who all played ragtime, boogie-woogie, stomps, and stride.

DEFINITION

Ragtime is a formalized piece that contains elements of classical structure and American folk music; although it was developed primarily between 1895 and 1915, its roots went back before 1895, and it continues to be popular. There is no question that ragtime was the first black musical form to attain great popularity and to be widely published.

In the late nineteenth century, a common form of entertainment was vaudeville, which was performed in a slightly different way than what we know today. Vaudeville in the nineteenth-century American tradition was a traveling show that consisted of everything from boxing matches to acts from Shakespearean plays. By the 1870s, there was clearly a black vaudeville circuit and a white vaudeville circuit; that is, there were traveling troupes that entertained white audiences and traveling troupes that entertained black audiences. They played in different locations and developed slightly different shows. They were sometimes called "medicine shows" because potions touted as cure-alls were sold as money-making schemes.

An important part of vaudeville was always musicians and singers. Although most traveling vaudeville shows did not carry a piano with them, a piano was used whenever it was available. However, vaudeville troupes and early Dixieland players did sometimes carry a portable pump organ.

Ragtime was the result of a conscious attempt by piano players to create music that had both white and black elements to it. As such, it was structured the way that parlor piano was composed—in even phrases and fairly consistent chord progressions. But it also had syncopation (off-beat accents) and break sections that contrasted with the smoothness of some melodies. In short, it was European music that had been "jazzed up." Critics constantly debate whether or not ragtime should be classified as jazz, but most concede that it had a strong influence on early jazz styles.

Ragtime piano is formally an AB structure with rather marked differences between the two sections (although each section is usually broken up into two smaller parts). Typically, ragtime has a strong rhythmic pulse with an emphatic left hand. The right hand normally plays chords and running passages. There are consistent chord progressions, strong movements toward cadences (or endings), and specific breaks in the movement to provide interest and transition.

Ragtime has the feel of improvisation, even though many ragtime pieces are written compositions. Most early ragtime composers tried out their bits first and then wrote them down when they found a publisher who would buy the piece. Some ragtime composers leaned toward a classical approach and some toward a jazz-improvisation approach. Although this is not to suggest that one is better than the other, there is little doubt that the jazz approach had the more lasting influence.

Scott Joplin

RAGTIME STYLES OF JELLY ROLL MORTON AND SCOTT JOPLIN

Jelly Roll Morton and Scott Joplin are generally recognized as the two kings of ragtime. Although Morton earned a significant reputation for his small ragtime orchestras, Joplin also orchestrated some of his ragtime in a set of pieces called the "Red Back Book" (a recording is available by the New England Conservatory of Music Ragtime Ensemble; see Discography). The two ragtime artists can be characterized as follows:

Scott Joplin, Composer and Player

> Clean classical style, very formal
>
> Even phrases and repetitions
>
> Well-established drive to cadences and strong endings
>
> Fairly simple melodies
>
> Little dynamic variation

Jelly Roll Morton, Player and Composer-Arranger

> Raucous, nonformal style of playing
>
> Open-ended, long, nonsymmetrical phrases
>
> Melody that is difficult to describe; mixed texture
>
> Left hand and right hand blended together
>
> Loud, pounding rhythm
>
> Makeshift cadences

STRIDE AND BOOGIE-WOOGIE

Stride piano is a style of playing rather than a musical structure, but it is perhaps even more important than other piano styles discussed in this chapter. Stride developed directly from ragtime, stomps, and, to a certain extent, boogie-woogie, but actually took these playing techniques one step further.

Jelly Roll Morton

Stride style is simply playing bass or low notes on the piano in octaves with the left hand on beats 1 and 3 of each measure, and chords in the mid-range of the piano on beats 2 and 4. This is combined with a melodically active right hand. Of course, that is a basic definition of ragtime style as well, but it is somewhat less formalized. As well, there is a great deal more improvisation in the stride style, and generally the tempo is faster than in ragtime.

Stride playing tends to be rather intense and rhythmically active. The standard way of playing the piano in a jazz band at one time was to simply play chords with two hands on all four beats. Therefore, stride piano was exciting when it began to be used in Dixieland, blues, and larger ensembles.

Boogie-woogie has already been discussed, but it is significant in any discussion of stride playing, as well. A style that was incredibly popular from the mid-1920s on, boogie-woogie follows the blues chord progression exactly. Like ragtime, it uses a consistent left hand with melodic and rhythmic variations on the right hand. Although boogie-woogie is not hard to play, it is incredibly difficult to play it well, as some of the masters did.

As a solo style—first associated with rent parties and black entertainment and then with larger ensembles—it was technically more demanding than ragtime. To be a successful boogie-woogie player, one had to make up new ideas and develop tricks; boogie players suffered the trials and tribulations of "cutting" contests on a regular basis. Boogie-woogie was popularized further during the big band era by bands such as Count Basie's, Woody Herman's ("Woodchopper's Ball"), and Tommy Dorsey's ("Original Boogie-Woogie"). Boogie-woogie also had a rather marked influence on early rock-and-roll; tunes like "Rock Around the Clock" are essentially boogie-woogie.

RAGTIME MUSICIANS

New Orleans had piano players, many of whom were associated with brothels and the 1920s Dixieland bands. However, in general, the collective improvisational style of New Orleans Dixieland did not emphasize the role of the piano player, with the exception of Jelly Roll Morton. Therefore, while there were certainly important piano players from New Orleans, not many of them had a major impact on other players because of the way the instrument was used in classic Dixieland. Lil Hardin (Armstrong) was an excellent Dixieland piano player in the New Orleans style.

However, in Chicago a number of fine piano players prospered, both in boogie-woogie style and within the context of instrumental groups. As previously discussed, the general style of Chicago music was oriented toward solo improvisation. As such, piano players began to develop more freedom, and that experimentation led to greater visibility of the piano player. As well, both the general public and the recording and publishing industry supported boogie-woogie players from Chicago.

For instance, Albert Ammons, Cow Cow Davenport (Cleveland based), Meade Lux Lewis, "Pine-Top" Smith (famous for his "Pine-Top Boogie"), and Jimmy Yancey were all popular boogie-woogie players who were either based in Chicago or associated with it. Earl Hines was certainly one of the very significant players of early jazz. As a stride player, he had a profound effect on many musicians, including Count Basie.

Important boogie-woogie musicians in New York and on the East Coast included the following: Fletcher Henderson (arranger, pianist, and director of Ethel Waters' band in 1921–1922, and significant early big band leader); James P. Johnson (Pittsburgh-born stride player and one of the first jazz composers he composed his best-known composition, "Charleston," in 1913); Willie "The Lion" Smith (New York stride player and a favorite of Duke Ellington); Fats Waller (New York stride player); and Clarence Williams (composer, arranger, and Dixieland piano player).

This list illustrates that piano stylists were indeed important, even if that impact came rather late to the development of jazz. Ultimately, what piano players did affected jazz directly. For instance, Earl Hines ultimately influenced Count Basie, Teddy Wilson, Nat King Cole, and Art Tatum, among others.

MUSICAL ANALYSIS	## "Maple Leaf Rag" ## Jelly Roll Morton (SCCJ A-2)

This version of *Maple Leaf Rag* was recorded by Jelly Roll Morton on piano in 1938. While it is essentially the same piece as the original by Scott Joplin, Morton plays the piece a bit faster (170 instead of 160) and in the key of G, which is easier than Ab. The basic melodies and chord changes are very similar, but the technique is quite different.

Fats Waller

The Jelly Roll Morton version has quite a bit of swing; the Joplin version has very even subdivisions of the beat. The melodies and chord changes are not so clean on beats 1 through 4, but rather fluctuate and shift. Also, the melodies are not repeated each time, as in the Scott Joplin version. (See Appendix for analysis of the Scott Joplin version.)

Intro

Dbo	GEbo	GDbo	G	Dbo	G	Dbo	G
1	2	3	4	5	6	7	8

A Melody

G D7	G D7	EbG	EbG	Dbo		Dbo	G	Dbo	D	GDbo	G A	D	G
1 2	3 4	5	6	7		8 1		2 3		4 5	6 7		8

B Melody

D7	G	D7	G	D7	G	GF#FE a	A	D	G
1	2	3	4	5	6	7	8 1	2 3 4	5 6 7 8

A Melody

G	D7	G	D7	EbG	EbG	Go		Dbo	G	A7	D	G	Dbo	G	A	D	G
1	2	3	4	5	6	7	8	1		2	3	4	5		6	7	8

C Melody

‖: G7		C		G7		C		A7		d	Ad	FF#C	A	D	G	C :‖
1	2	3	4	5	6	7	8	1	2	3	4	5	6		7	8

D Melody

C	G		D7		G		C	C#	G		E7	a	D		G
1	2	3	4	5	6	7	8	1	2	3	4	5	6	7	8

D Melody

C	G		D7		G		C		G		E7	a	D	GD	G
1	2	3	4	5	6	7	8	1	2	3	4	5	6	7	8

SIDE-NOTES

Scott Joplin

Scott Joplin was born in Texarkana, Texas, on November 24, 1868 and died in New York on April 1, 1917. A prolific composer of ragtime and other compositions, Joplin was popular during his own lifetime but not to the full extent which history has accorded him. He wrote one full-length opera, "*Treemonisha*," the whole of which was never performed during his life; however, Joplin did produce a scaled-down version of it in Harlem in 1911. He is perhaps best known for his "Maple Leaf Rag," published in 1899.

Joplin traveled extensively during his lifetime and was best known as a solo piano player in St. Louis and Chicago during the 1890s. He played at rent parties and various other types of engagements. He was a well-known musician and widely published composer during his lifetime and was a featured performer at the Chicago World's Fair in 1893.

SIDE-NOTES

Jelly Roll Morton

Ferdinand Joseph La Menthe (Jelly Roll Morton) was born in New Orleans, on October 20, 1890, and died in Los Angeles on July 10, 1941. He began playing the guitar at age 7 and the piano at age 10. From 1902 he was an entertainer in the red-light district of New Orleans, playing ragtime. He was also a pool hustler and engaged in other methods of earning money. Before 1917 he had traveled to Memphis, St. Louis, and Kansas City, and in 1917 he moved to California. In 1923, he moved to Richmond, Indiana. From 1926 through 1930 he recorded piano solos in Chicago for Victor with Morton's Red Hot Peppers; these were probably his most significant recordings. His career took an unexpected nosedive in the 1930s, and although he later managed to make a series of recordings in New York in 1939–1940, he passed away in 1941 without retaining the glory he had known in the late 1920s.

A flamboyant personality and piano player, Jelly Roll Morton attained cult status to many musicians, although he also was criticized for his ego and bragging. There is no question that Jelly Roll Morton was influential in establishing ragtime as an instrumental and improvisational style. He also helped to expand the style of New Orleans Dixieland in Kansas City and Chicago.

Suggested Listening

1. "Boogie-Woogie, Jump and Kansas City, Jazz"   Vol. 10
   Folkways 2810
2. "King of New Orleans Jazz" (Morton)   Victor LPM 1649
3. "Piano Roll Ragtime"   Sounds 1201
4. "Texas Barrelhouse Piano"   Arhoolie 1010
5. "Earl "Fatha" Hines"   Everest FS246
6. "Cuttin' the Boogie"   New World 250
7. "Piano in Style"   MCA–1332

Chapter 7
Jazz Singing

The subject of vocal jazz is usually given little attention in books about jazz for two reasons. First, most jazz writers tend to be either instrumentalists themselves, or critics of instrumental jazz. And second, much of the interest in jazz has to do with instrumental interplay and the development of major instrumental soloists. However, it is imperative to understand that vocalists have had a profound effect on many forms of jazz and have also increased the popularity of jazz to a wider audience.

Jazz was a popular form of music until the bebop era of the mid-1940s, after which it became primarily an intellectualized form that appealed to only a small minority of listeners. Popular music can be defined in many ways, but the simplest definition is that it is music that people like. Early jazz singers were charismatic and very visible. They used their voices as jazz instruments, singing the melody and then improvising with vocal embellishments and changes. In this chapter, we will briefly discuss different styles of jazz singing and some of the people involved in jazz singing through 1930.

THE BLUES

The first significant jazz singers were blues musicians. They included Ma Rainey, Bessie Smith, Mamie Smith, and Ethel Waters. One could argue that it was blues recordings which popularized jazz. The first blues record was "Crazy Blues," which was done by Mamie Smith in 1920. This recording was incredibly popular and ushered in the production of numerous blues recordings (primarily by Okeh Records). The fact that these records sold all over the United States certainly contributed to the growing popularity of jazz. While blues records were initially sold as "race" records (a term that was used until the late 1940s to describe recordings made by black performers) they were also sold to white fans.

Most of the major blues vocalists were women, although male blues vocalists such as Blind Lemon Jefferson, T-Bone Walker, Robert Johnson, and later Muddy Waters were also popular. The first recordings by Mamie Smith were done by Okeh Records, which was a subsidiary of the General Phonograph Company. Although the popular career of the blues singers started in 1920, most of the early recording artists had performed these tunes on the road for years before they were recorded.

In 1921, Harry Pace formed his own company, Black Swan Records, and started releasing blues recordings. He hired Fletcher Henderson to be musical director and began doing what he considered to be high-quality recordings of the best singers available. He recorded Ethel Waters for the first time in 1921, along with Alberta Hunger, Katie Crippen, and Elizabeth Taylor Greenfield (who was known as the "Black Swan").

Bessie Smith started recording for Columbia in 1923, and Clara Smith immediately followed. The vocal quality of Bessie Smith— "Empress of the Blues"—was full-voiced and Deep South. Clara Smith had a thinner voice, but it had a delicate style which was appealing to white audiences. The other company to join this growing market was Paramount, which recorded Albert Hunter and eventually Ma Rainey, whom they billed as the greatest blues singer ever.

Interestingly, Okeh Records also sent a young recording manager, Ralph Peer, to the South to record country blues, which eventually led to his recording fiddle musicians such as Fiddlin' John

Carson and later Jimmie Rodgers and the Carter Family. So in some senses, the popularity of black female blues singers led peripherally to the development of a market for country music as well.

Ethel Waters and Bessie Smith created—or had created for them—a rivalry similar to the bucking contests of New Orleans. The big-chested Smith could belt out the blues like no one else, but Waters could sing technical circles around her.

At the same time that blues singing (primarily by females on record) was gaining popularity, singers associated with Dixieland bands were also gaining recognition. Interestingly enough, Louis Armstrong was one of the first vocalists to gain recognition as a Dixieland singer, although he also did blues tunes. Armstrong began singing backup vocals for other musicians, including Bessie Smith, but soon became popular as a singer himself. Armstrong sang first within the context of his nightclub act but then made recordings because he was so successful in live performances. In fact, many people may remember Satchmo better as a singer than as a horn player.

Most Dixieland tunes are based upon songs with words and as such, singing a chorus makes perfect sense. In fact, a chorus provides one more element of contrast to a jazz performance. Louis Armstrong and other early singers used the Dixieland jazz bands as an accompaniment to both singing the song in its original form and in creating melodic improvisation based on the original song. Listen carefully to Armstrong's rendition of "Sweethearts on Parade," in which he clearly changes the original melody.

Vocalization was also present in band vocals, which is also given scant attention by most writers. Band vocals are sung phrases or whole sections of lyrics by two or more members of the band. Eventually this concept led to vocal groups as a part of the big band, like the Mills Brothers or the Andrews Sisters, but they started within the context of the Dixieland-style band. Often these were novelty effects and were sung in neither a highly imaginative style nor a vocally pleasing one; they were used as an attention-getting device or as an element of contrast. The example of the duo singing in "4 or 5 Times" is representative.

Later in the big band era, band vocals would become very important, such as Glenn Miller's "Pennsylvania 6-5000," in which the band simply sings those words at the end of the three phrases. The effect is novel and maybe it is not even jazz, but as a popular device it was certainly functional. Many bands, in fact, used group vocals as a kind of signature for their band.

In conclusion, the artistry of the female blues singers, as well as the continued tradition of blues singing by both males and females in Chicago, Kansas City, New Orleans, Memphis, New York, and other cities, successfully popularized blues jazz styling with the voice. The improvisational ability of many of the earlier singers had a massive impact on the playing techniques of instrumentalists and a continued influence on piano styles. Louis Armstrong, like other musicians, transferred many techniques he had created for the cornet to the voice. Vocal embellishment and nuance created new emotional expressions through slightly changed melodies. Some musicians created complete improvisations that were very far from the original melody. Scat songs—vocal solos based on nonsense syllables and imitating an instrument—were created during this era and were further developed by singers in the big band era and beyond. In short, singing laid the foundation for other forms of jazz and continues to influence the shape of jazz solos, regardless of whether they are played on an instrument or produced by the human voice.

*MUSICAL
ANALYSIS*

"Sweethearts on Parade" Louis Armstrong and His Orchestra (SCCJ B-6)

The instrumentation of this piece is two trumpets, one trombone, three saxes, piano, banjo/guitar, bass, and drums. Recorded in 1930 by a small big band, the song's texture is big band rather than Dixieland. The meter signature is 4/4, the tempo is 126, and the key is F.

The song is a popular song from the big band era and is not at all bluesy. The piece breaks into thirty-two-measure units, the total length of the song, with the melodies being A A B A (each eight measures). The chord progression is easy to follow as soon as you get to the vocals: F is 1, Bb is 4, and C7 is 5. The only really difficult part of the piece is the beginning trumpet solo. Armstrong both introduces the melody and improvises at the same time. And the thirty-six measures that he takes can confuse the listener. My advice is to listen to his marvelous improvisation and then listen to him sing the melody in order to understand the structure. His trumpet solo, after he sings, is thirty-two measures in length and follows the same chord progression that the vocal uses. Note the brief introduction of the "Reveille" melody at the end.

Trumpet Exploration
A Melody   **A Melody**

F						C7		F	C7C	F			C7		
1	2	3	4	5	6	7	8	1	2	3	4 5	6	7	8

Transition

FF7	Bbbb	F	F7
1	2	3	4

B Melody   **A Melody**   **Saxes**

Bb		C7F	D7	g	D7	G7	C7	F		C7		F7	Bbbb F		g C7
1	2	3	4	5	6	7	8	1	2	3	4	5	6	7	8

Vocal
A Melody   **A Melody**

F		C7		F	C7	F	C7	F		C7		F	Bbbb F		F7
1	2	3	4	5	6	7	8	1	2	3	4	5	6	7	8

Vocal

B Melody								A Melody					Saxes		
Bb	F	D7	g	D7	G7	C	F		C7		F7	Bbbb	N.C.		
1	2	3	4	5	6	7	8	1	2	3	4	5	6	7	8

Saxes (Extension)

NC	
1	2

Trumpet Solo

A Melody								Trumpet Break A Melody					Trumpet Break		
F		C7		F	C7	F		F		C7		F	F7Bbbb	F	
1	2	3	4	5	6	7	8	1	2	3	4	5	6	7	8

Trumpet

B Melody								Break A Melody					"Reveille"		
Bb		C7F	D7	g	D7	G7		F		C7		F	Bbbb	F	
1	2	3	4	5	6	7	8	1	2	3	4	5	6	7	8

Trumpet Extension

1	2

SIDE-NOTES

Ethel Waters

Ethel Waters was born in Chester, Pennsylvania, on October 31, 1896, and died in Los Angeles on September 1, 1977. She performed for the first time in church as "Baby Star" in 1905. As a teen-ager in Philadelphia and Baltimore, she was billed as "Sweet Mama Stringbean." In 1917, she went to New York to work at the Lincoln Theatre. Throughout the 1920s, she sang with many bands, including Fletcher Henderson, and recorded for a number of record labels. In the 1930s she moved to stage presentations, first in nightclub revues and then in dramatic parts. She introduced several important songs, including "Dinah" in 1924 and "Stormy Weather" in 1933. She appeared in the motion pictures, *Mamba's Daugher* and *Member of the Wedding,* and was in the starring role in "Beulah," a television series in the late 1950s. She has generally been known as an actress rather than as a singer.

However, as a blues singer she was quite significant. She sang with a full-bodied voice and projected it well on-stage. Although she was not quite as flamboyant as others, her overall career was probably more successful.

Bessie Smith

Classic blues singer Bessie Smith was born in Chattanooga, Tennessee, on April 15, 1898, and died in Clarksdale, Mississippi, on September 26, 1937. Her family was extremely poor, and it was only because of a fortuitous visit by Ma Rainey's Rabbit Foot Minstrels that she was able to escape lifelong poverty; Ma Rainey took the young Smith out on the road, and for a while she worked tent shows, carnivals, honky-tonks, and private parties. While she was performing in Selma, Alabama, a Columbia record man heard her. Ultimately, Clarence Williams (pianist and promoter) was sent to bring Bessie Smith to New York.

Smith made her first recording in 1923, and her records were very well received. Between 1923 and 1930, Clarence Williams accompanied most of her blues recordings, some of which he also wrote. Smith was very popular in the 1920s and performed with many other musicians of note, including Louis Armstrong, Don Redman, and Fletcher Henderson. A large, robust woman, she was known for her physical presentation and for the sensuality she gave to her performances.

In the 1930s, Smith began battling alcoholism, and had little commercial success in the ensuing years. In September, 1937, she was injured in a car accident and bled to death between hospitals because the first hospital to which she was taken refused to operate on a black person.

Suggested Listening

1. "The Bessie Smith Story," Vols. 1–4   COL. CL855–8
2. "Oh Daddy (Ethel Waters)"   Biograph BLP12022
3. "Ethel Waters' Greatest Years"   COL. KG 31571
4. "The Louis Armstrong Story," Vols. 1–4   COL CL851–4

Part III
Big Band Era

Chapter 8
Golden Age of Big Bands: The Swing Era

In this introductory chapter on big band music, we will learn generalizations about the big band, almost as if it were a static musical organization. It is not, of course, for the big band was an evolutionary stage in the history of jazz, and that is what makes its story most interesting.

The golden age of the big band is traditionally thought to have run from 1925 through 1945. The classic big bands did not reach full strength until the 1930s. Since big band music is still played, this arbitrary ending of the big band era is questionable, although there are clear differences between big band music of the 1930s and 1940s and the big band sound of the 1970s and 1980s.

We speak of the golden age of jazz as the time when the style of music was homogeneous. But the big band era of the 1930s and 1940s was a kind of golden age in American society at large, the time when the country pulled together to defeat the Great Depression and win a world war.

Some writers do not believe that big band music can be considered jazz, because at times big band music is not spontaneous at all, but is rather read completely from individual written parts. However, I believe that big band music *is* jazz, even when it is completely prepared in advance. The arranger creates music which, when recreated, yields spontaneity in the manner in which sections and soloists play together.

There are certain stylistic characteristics that exist for every improviser in specific styles of jazz. The quintessential difference between free improvisation and the controlled improvisation of big band music is that the stylistic spontaneity is done by the arranger, within the style of jazz as it had evolved by the big band era.

The rest of this introductory chapter on big band music will present various aspects of the big band style. The main task for the reader is to establish a technique of listening to big band music so that the individual character of big band music (as it represented its era in American history) is understood and comprehended through individual examination of specific representative pieces.

CULTURAL SETTING

We have already discovered that Dixieland was the product of a few places, New Orleans in particular. While the roots of Dixieland jazz are found in rural America, the roots of big band music are primarily urban, specifically the towns where Dixieland development was concentrated in the 1920s.

The United States in the mid-1920s was very optimistic and booming, both psychologically and economically. The Roaring Twenties, often associated solely with Dixieland, supported the beginnings of the big band movement because of its urban-centered activity. Many U.S. citizens were migrating to large cities because of industrialization, and this created a market for mass-recreational activities; one could assert that this was the biggest cauldron in which big bands boiled.

Although the Great Depression of 1929 would create different attitudes on the part of Americans, the late 1920s were to many Americans joyous years. Many Americans enjoyed great success during the first three decades of the twentieth century (see Bibliography). It is certainly a factor in the development of big band music out of Dixieland bands that times were good.

Big band music represented an exciting experiment with music and one that received rave reviews. The very idea of putting more musicians on stage and having them play in harmonies was very exciting, and it fit the times, too; many people congregated for socializing and dancing.

The basis for big-band music was firmly established by the 1930s. One might be tempted to suggest that the depression should have killed the big bands. One might wonder, Who could afford to go dancing when people were losing their shirts? Interestingly enough, entertainment does well regardless of the situation in society. When people are doing very well, they want to celebrate; and when they are doing poorly, they want to party to forget how badly society is treating them. Even though America experienced the worst economic times in its history during the early 1930s, big bands continued to entertain, although on a reduced scale. Some have even suggested that big bands provided necessary and substantial relief to a downtrodden society.

The depression ended in the mid-1930s. The election of Franklin Delano Roosevelt in 1932 signaled an economic recovery, at least to the Democrats. With the exception of the 1960s, the 1930s was the decade responsible for more social legislation than any other period in American history. Government acts set up mechanisms that

Original members of Jimmy Lunceford's "Harlem Express." Photo taken 1945–1946. From left to right: Earl Carruthers (Baritone Sax), Russell Bowles (Trombone), Edwin Wilcox (Piano), Jimmie Lunceford, Joe Thomas (Tenor Sax), and Al Norris (Guitar)

would prevent another total collapse of the stock market, which had led to the Depression. As a result, by the end of the 1930s America's economy was prospering again. And with this revitalization of America came continued success for the development of big bands.

The late 1930s and early 1940s were consumed by World War II, and much of the American economy and spirit were put into defeating Hitler and the Axis powers. Although wartime is certainly not a desirable time, America prospered during World War II if for no other reason than that Americans were united by a common cause. Again, big-band music moved with the times, providing social release as well as many songs associated with the patriotic feelings of the time, such as "American Patrol."

Societal attitudes that could be attributed to this time are patriotism, optimism, comradery, growth, invincibility, financial security, and belief in the American way. Americans simply felt very good about themselves and what they were doing in the world. These attitudes were reflected in the arts of that time, particularly big band music.

FUNCTION OF THE BIG BANDS

Big bands played for large gatherings and for people who wanted to dance to a particular style of music. They played for specific clienteles, such as white or black audiences, urban or rural audiences, or specific ethnic groups. At the beginning of the era, big bands were primarily associated with big towns and rather limited audiences. By 1940, however, big-band music could be found all over the United States and for a variety of types of audiences.

The social function of the big band was to provide background music for ballroom dancing. Such an event also provided an opportunity for socializing, generally a formal experience. The big band functioned as a symbol for that particular group of people, and many of the specialty tunes they played and the stage tricks they used were designed to appeal to that special clientele. Big-band music was especially filled with communication tricks. The very essence of a particular big band was found in the unique communication packages presented as its individual signature.

The growth in number and strength of radio stations during the late 1930s and the 1940s had a great deal to do with the rising popularity of big-band music. The radio had become in this period the center of family communication. In some senses, the popularity of big bands was tied to their radio performances, which allowed them to play their theme songs to a much larger audience than they could have done live. Of course, generally speaking, radio has always been the medium for the presentation of popular music, which big-band music certainly was.

Every big band had a charisma all its own, and the social identification which people had with bands—such as the Glenn Miller or Duke Ellington bands—was as important to their listeners as the identification which people in the 1960s had for the Beatles. Therefore, the big band was an important symbol for the society of its time.

INSTRUMENTATION AND TEXTURE

The most important stylistic characteristic of a big band is its precise instrumentation, and it is in that instrumentation that the quality of sound of a big band resides. While other musical elements may be important in other forms of jazz, it is the way in which instrumental groups fit together that makes big band music interesting. Therefore, while this particular topic may be inconsequential in other styles of jazz, it is of paramount importance to big band music.

As was said earlier in this chapter, we will consider a standard model for the instrumentation of big bands rather than exhaustingly describe the growth of bands from the small big bands of the 1920s to the full-blown ensembles of the 1940s. However, it should be understood that big bands did not suddenly appear; rather, they evolved over time.

The standard instrumentation of a big band is as follows: four trumpets, four trombones, five saxophones, piano, bass, guitar, and drums. Early ensembles had three saxes and three brass instruments, and then gradually increased in size through the 1930s and 1940s until the standard ensemble of five saxophones and eight brass instruments was reached in the mid- to late 1940s. Four sections provide musical texture: trumpets, trombones, saxophones, and rhythm. Sometimes the trumpets and trombones are treated as one section, simply called "brass." Each of these sections has specific responsibilities within the context of a piece, and it is the interaction of the sections which provides the interest in big band music. And it is the instrumental textures which provide the individual signatures of specific big bands and arrangers.

There are differences among big bands with regard to instrumentation; for example, the Glenn Miller band used a clarinet in lieu of one of the saxophones. However, the model just described provides the standard big band sound and therefore serves as a good starting point for our discussion. Of course, the significance of the instrumentation is *how* the instrument families are used.

The rhythm section is the most important unit in the big band because it provides the continuous framework for the musical texture; it serves as the organizational unit for everything else. The rhythm section gives the big band sound its jazz flavor; it is the one common element in all jazz. Its function is fairly consistent throughout the history of jazz, even though the specific instruments used in the section have changed over time. One change, for instance, from Dixieland to big band music, has been the substitution of the string bass for the tuba, and the guitar for the banjo. However, the rhythm section that we will consider for the standard model is made up of piano, bass, guitar, and drums. The specific function of the different instruments is as follows:

> Piano plays chords on all four beats of each measure, providing both tempo function and harmonic function. There are basically two different styles of playing—straight chords with both hands, and a ragtime style as defined earlier.
>
> Bass plays either a walking bass (a bass line which melodically implies the basic chord), or the first and fifth note of each chord providing a tempo and harmonic bass line.
>
> Guitar plays chords on each beat in a continuous style.
>
> Drums play continuously and on every beat.

Big band rhythm style is basically continuous music with little rhythmic variation and with a great deal of overlap in function among the four instruments. Occasionally, the rhythm section will do different things, such as play brief solos or accent specific whole band passages, but the basic style is continuous rhythm without much variation.

The saxophone section is the most interesting, melodically, in the big band style. The section itself consists of two alto saxophones, two tenor saxophones, and one baritone saxophone; the different ranges of these instruments provide the widest pitch texture of any section in the standard big band. At the beginning of big band arrangements, the saxophones play the melody of the song, usually in harmony. Traditionally, the saxophone section will play the complete melody right from the beginning of the song (or after a brief introduction), and if the melody is repeated then the brass will take over the melody. When the brass instruments are playing the melody or when there are solos, the saxophone section will usually play background melodies or *riffs* (a riff is a short melodic phrase with a memorable rhythmic quality).

The trumpet and trombone sections are normally treated as one unit, although occasionally they will play separate roles. In big band style (1925–1945) the trumpet had a relatively limited range and therefore tended to be somewhat limited in its arrangements. The harmonizations tended to be close-position chords (all of the notes

Dorsey Brothers, 1935

were relatively close to each other). The trumpet section was the leader in brass section melody playing or background melodies, with the trombones playing the lower harmonies.

The trombone section was not developed to the extent that the other sections were in big band style. The instrument has a relatively large range, but the range was seldom used in big band style (except in compositions like Tommy Dorsey's "Song of India"). The traditional approach to writing for trombone was in close-position chords such as those for the trumpet section; this style of writing led to a muddy sound when it was used by itself because of the low pitch of the trombone notes. Quite often, the most effective trombone writing was in thirds (doubling two instruments) or in unison (all the trombones playing the same notes).

The trumpet and trombone sections were used together and separately as solo instruments and for novelty effects. With a variety of mutes and special playing effects, the brass instruments could be used for emotional effects, such as "growling" or for humor. The brass instruments were also used purely for loud accenting or for major excitement at the end of a composition.

All the melody instruments could be used at once for a big textural sound, usually at the end of a composition. Many big band standard arrangements (called standards because many people played them using the same arrangement) featured one rather short melodic and harmonic unit that was played ten or fifteen times to make up one piece. Often the last three or four sections would build in volume to a fever pitch at the end, with all the instruments playing. This shout chorus (or last chorus) usually brought people to their feet applauding and generally ended the composition with great excitement; it was called a shout chorus because the volume usually was quite loud at this point, and quite often the crowd shouted with excitement. These different textural combinations were often coupled with various sections standing or sitting down when they came in (and moving their instruments back and forth in unison). The shout chorus usually used all the players, all of whom were standing. This stage technique was very successful; in fact, it still is.

ANALYSIS OF FORM AND TEXTURE

In defining form for big band music, one must use texture as one of the identifying characteristics. Traditionally form is defined in terms of the melodic or harmonic unit that is repeated. Although one could do that with a big band unit, more satisfying results are obtained when the melodic and harmonic units are combined with textural units in big band style.

We will consider two different styles of big band form, with the understanding that there are other types of forms. However, the two types (two melodies in a ballad form or one melody in a theme and variation form) are the most common and prevalent. Therefore, we will consider only those two types in this introductory chapter.

The first type (represented by "In the Mood") has two different melodies in the composition. The first melody is the one associated with the song and is readily identifiable. These melodies will quite often have lyrics to them, but our consideration is with the instrumental style and the standard way of doing the composition. The second melody will be a contrasting melody quite different from the first melody, providing both relief and variety. If the first melody were described as A, and the second as B, the following combinations in standards, as well as others, would be possible:

AAB, AABA, AABB

The saxophone section usually plays the melody first, and then the brass section plays it the second time or at a later time in the composition. Traditionally, both the saxophone section and the brass section will play the basic melodies before there are solos or unique characteristics. Traditionally, all of the instruments will play at the end. Transition figures usually occur at the ends of melodies, moving the music smoothly to another variation.

In the type of form that repeats one melody over and over in variations, it is harder to generalize about the kind of instrumental textures that are used. Often the saxophone section plays the basic melody continuously, with occasional brass work or solos.

Often the two-melody type is in slower songs. If there are two melodies, two very different types of sounds are being played by the same instrumental unit. It is easier to hear the theme-and-variation type, because by the time you have listened to one entire piece it should be obvious that there was only melody and that you heard it many times. As soon as you determine the melody, then you can proceed to listen for specific textures or for which instrumental families are used for the melody at certain points in the composition.

In conclusion, one should analyze big band compositions for melodic repetitions and structures but connect with that analysis information about instrumental textures (see analyses for examples).

BIG BAND IMPROVISATION

There is relatively little free improvisation in big band music, which is one reason it is sometimes not considered to be jazz. However, it is my contention that spontaneity is found within the style and that the arranger is creating spontaneous jazz at the time of composition. Once the arrangement has been created, even the solo passage (improvised sections) will be played the same way in subsequent performances; the solos are often written down.

For instance, the solo passages in Glenn Miller's "In the Mood" and Woody Herman's "Woodchopper's Ball" were written down. They were improvised when the tunes were first performed and then they were written down for a standard arrangement. In riff-oriented bands (see chapter 9) solo sections were not written down—for instance, Charlie Barnett's "Cherokee," Jimmy Dorsey's "Johnson Rag," and Count Basie's "One O'Clock Jump." However, the opportunities for free improvisation were limited for the following reasons: (1) audiences wanted recognizable music, (2) the recording industry required that compositions take about three minutes to play, and (3) the interest was in instrumental textures rather than in individual solo efforts. When a solo was especially important to a particular song, it was simply written down so that it would be recognizable.

Big band improvisational style was based on Dixieland at first and then became consistent with the different types of compositions big bands did. While Dixie musicians played solos based on chordal passages, big band improvisation became increasingly melodic in character; in this sense, big band jazz helped make the transition to later styles (for instance, the 1939 rendition of "Body and Soul" as played by Coleman Hawkins—see chapter 12).

The main improvisational impetus in the big band era was provided by the arranger of the standard and specialty songs for big bands. Typically, the arranger would create basic arrangements for the band, leaving spots open for improvised solos. When the soloist created the solo in live performance, the arranger would write down an approximation of that solo.

SWING STYLE

Swing style has to do with a particular rhythmic quality. If you were to take the four quarter notes of one measure of four beats and subdivide those quarter notes into eighth notes, you would have eight

small units in one measure of four beats. Dixieland jazz tended to make those eighth notes fairly even in length, as does rock-and-roll. Boogie-woogie emphasizes a long-short feeling of the eighth notes (the phrase 8 to the bar comes from the subdivision into eight).

Swing divides the eighth notes into something halfway between even eighth notes and the long-short style of boogie-woogie. This gives the music a generally relaxed and "swinging" feel. While you will probably have a difficult time notating the differences, you can hear them quite easily, either in a demonstration on the piano by your instructor or in recordings representing the different styles.

Swing was fairly common in big band music and beyond. Generally speaking, the string bass was used as the bass instrument in the rhythm section and played just on the four beats. However, the piano, guitar, and drums to a certain extent emphasized the swing feel in their playing; the drummer uses the cymbals (particularly the high hat) to emphasize the rhythmic change. The rhythm section tends to be more complementary in that the instruments do not play all four beats all the time, but rather they play different rhythms to create a more complex composite rhythm.

Instrumental ensembles play longer melodies with textures that flow over phrases, emphasizing the swing feel through their playing. The brass instruments, especially, play accented riffs that clearly outline the eighth-note feel appropriate to swing. As well, melodies are written that emphasize a smooth swing style rather than short, choppy phrases.

BIG BAND ARRANGERS

In some senses, the real mover behind popular big bands was the arranger, who created the specialized arrangements that came to define the style of a particular orchestra. For instance, Duke Ellington wrote many of the early arrangements for his band, and was joined by Billy Strayhorn in 1939. It was Ellington and Strayhorn as arrangers who created these distinctly "Ellington" tunes, rather than Ellington as player or leader.

Other significant arrangers of the big band era were Benny Carter, Eddie Durham, Will Hudson, Budd Johnson, Deane Kincaide, Jimmy Mundy, Sy Oliver, Eddie Sauter, and Don Redman. It was largely Redman's experimental success which accounted for the great popularity of the Fletcher Henderson orchestra. In fact, one could argue that a big band would become successful only if it had a talented and skilled arranger.

The bands of Fletcher Henderson, Jimmie Lunceford, and Benny Goodman developed intriguing textural sounds and also created significant soloists. Other bands, such as those led by Glenn Miller, the Dorsey Brothers, Harry James, Guy Lombardo, Sammy Kaye, Glen Gray, Count Basie, and Duke Ellington, developed distinctive arrangements. Regardless of the level of soloistic excitement, big band music was immensely popular with many people, and the credit for that goes to the arrangers, the musicians and singers, and the stage tricks, in that order.

MUSICAL ANALYSIS

"Stampede"
Fletcher Henderson and His Orchestra
(SCCJ B-11)

The instrumentation is three saxes, two cornets, one trumpet, one trombone, piano, banjo, tuba, and drums. Recorded in 1926 by the Fletcher Henderson Orchestra, "Stampede" is one of the successful arrangements of the young Don Redman. The meter is 4/4, the tempo is 170, and the key is C. The structure is primarily made up of eight-measure phrases which fit into a thirty-two-measure song form (ABAC), as follows: introduction (eight measures), ensemble (thirty-three measures), tenor (thirty-two), trumpet (thirty-three), and concluding solos and ensemble (thirty-two measures).

The most striking quality of this piece is the way in which Redman uses sections for textural reasons. One of the best arrangements by an early big band, the piece has a "defective" rhythm section. The clarinet trio concept is a Redman trademark. Redman used a tuba for the bass instrument, and the plodding style of the rhythm section (which plays on all four beats) is quite static. However, the Coleman Hawkins solo suggests what Redman will do later. The trumpet solo is clearly influenced by Louis Armstrong.

The chord changes are not difficult to follow, but they are subtle. Look carefully at the first eight-measure phrase, and try to memorize the sound of the repeating five-note sequence as you listen to the piece. That is a stock phrase (one that is used quite often) for big band style. Also observe that the actual structure of the thirty-two-(thirty-three-) measure unit is ABAC.

Intro
Brass/WW

G F#	G F#G7	G F#	G F#G7	G F# G	G F#	G G7	
1	2 3	4	5	6	7 8		

A   **B**
Woodwinds Brass Chords   **WW**

D7	G7	C		D7	G7	C		C7		F		D7			G7
1	2	3	4	5	6	7	8	1	2	3	4	5	6	7	8

A   **C**
Tutti

D7	G7	C		g	C7	F		a		D7		G7	D7G7C	D7G7	
1	2	3	4	5	6	7	8	1	2	3	4 5	6	7	8	9

A
Tenor Solo

                                           B

D7	G7	C		D7	G7	C		C7		F		D7		G7	
1	2	3	4	5	6	7	8	1	2	3	4	5	6	7	8

A   **C**
Tenor Solo   **Punch Chords**

D7	G7	C		D7	G7	g	C7F	a			D7		G7	D7G7C	
1	2	3	4 5	6	7		8	1	2	3	4	5	6	7	8

A   **B**
Trumpet Solo   **Ensemble**
                                                                        Interlude   Clarinet

D7	G7	C		D7	G7	C		C7		F		D7		G7	
1	2	3	4 5	6	7	8 1	2	3	4	5	6 7	8			

A   **C**
Trumpet Solo

D7	G7	C		D7	G7	g	C7F	a		D7		G7	D7G7C	D7G7	
1	2	3	4	5	6	7	8	1	2	3	4 5 6	7	8	9	

A Brass/Clarinet Trio								B Clarinet							
D7	G7	C		D7	G7	C		C7		F		D7		G7	
1	2	3	4	5	6	7	8	1	2	3	4	5	6	7	8

A Saxophones								C Ensemble							
D7	G7	C		C7		F		a				D7	G7G		D7G7C
1	2	3	4	5	6	7	8	1	2	3	4	5	6	7	8

SIDE-NOTES

Don Redman

Donald Matthew Redman was born in Piedmont, West Virginia, on July 29, 1900, and died in New York on November 30, 1964. From a musical family, Don was a child prodigy who started playing the trumpet at age of 3. He studied nearly every instrument as a child and completed study at the Boston Conservatory before joining the Fletcher Henderson band in 1924. He worked with McKinney's Cotton Pickers from 1927 to 1931, played with his own band from 1931 to 1940, did free-lance stints in the 1940s, and became music director for Pearl Bailey in 1951. He led a long and productive musical life, influencing many people through his talent as an arranger, although he was also a fine instrumentalist on alto, soprano, and baritone saxophones.

Redman's chief importance was as an arranger, first for Fletcher Henderson. It was in his arrangements for Henderson (see analysis) that he established techniques which would later be used by countless other musicians. He was probably as responsible for the textural conception of big band music as any other arranger. He arranged for Basie, Paul Whitman, and others in the 1940s, but his technique was copied by everyone, from Ellington to Kenton. While not a big name in comparison to others, Don Redman may have been one of the most quietly influential jazz musicians of the twentieth century.

SIDE-NOTES

Benny Goodman

Benjamin David Goodman was born in Chicago on May 30, 1909, and died in New York on June 13, 1986. Like other jazz musicians, he came from a large and poor family; he was trained on clarinet at Hull House. He appeared in public for the first time when he was 12 and made his first recording with the Ben Pollack band in Chicago in 1926. Leaving Pollack in 1929, he moved to New York and became a free-lance musician. He started a big band in 1934 that had a regular radio show. That particular band became very popular, primarily through its recordings and the arrangements of Fletcher Henderson.

The first of Goodman's small ensembles, started in 1935, was the Goodman Trio, with Gene Krupa on drums and Teddy Wilson on piano. The inclusion of Teddy Wilson created the first interracial combo. In 1936, Lionel Hampton was added on vibes; in 1939, Charlie Christian on guitar and Arthur Bernstein on bass were added. The history of growth from trio to sextet is also significant in its impact on the combo era, a phenomenon of the 1940s.

Goodman continued to perform occasionally until his death. There is little question that he was one of the finest clarinet soloists of all times, and he was equally conversant in both classical and jazz repertoires. While Goodman did not have a reputation of having strong personal skills, his musical skills were mammoth, and his impact on the growth of both swing and contemporary combo style was significant. Toward the end of his life, he held out strongly against certain modernist tendencies in jazz, but in actuality he was during his time of major importance, both modern and traditional at the same time.

Suggested Listening

1.	"Complete Benny Goodman," Vol. 1	RCA AXM2–5505
2.	"Carnegie Hall Jazz Concert"	COL. OSL 160
3.	"Big Band Jazz"	Smithsonian RC030

Chapter 9
Riff Bands

The solo tradition of big bands continued in the 1930s with the evolution of the riff band. The style derived primarily from black musical style, although white musicians felt its influence, and many white big bands imitated the style. Most big bands that structured their music around riffs—or solo improvisations—were also swing bands.

Riff bands played pieces that were structured around short riffs, or brief rhythmic melodies, as the primary musical material, . . . as opposed to many repetitions of a long melody. To illustrate the difference, listen to "In the Mood" and then "One O'Clock Jump." "In the Mood" is based on very recognizable melodies, which are repeated in their entirety in different sections. The same could be said about most big band ballads.

"One O'Clock Jump" is based upon a melody, but in the background is a short melodic phrase whose whole character is based upon a rhythmic idea. Rhythmic fragments drawn from the blues tradition are used to back up the melody as it is played at the beginning, and they also function as the background figure for solos.

Riff bands tend to be solo bands in which various players create improvised solos with only the rhythm section for background, although occasionally other sections will provide background riffs for accompaniment as well. Some of the greatest riff bands have been made up of players who all could solo, whereas many of the swing bands had very few high-caliber soloists. The actual solos were similar to Chicago style Dixieland during the early part of the big band era, although they evolved to a smoother and more melodic style later in the era. Actually the improvisational influence of big band style was primarily accomplished by riff-type players who developed unique styles, such as the growling style of Ellington's trumpet and trombone soloists. The background riffs done by instrumental sections behind a soloist were quite often based upon some idea in the melody of the piece; better riff bands tended to improvise them on the spot.

I remember vividly an experience with trumpeter Clark Terry, an alumnus of the Ellington organization, when my college band did a concert with him in the mid-1970s. We wrote a simple arrangement of the "Flintstones" theme song, with the melody first, followed by the solo section. The solo section had three different backgrounds, which were basically short riffs in harmony for the saxophones, trumpets, and trombones. These backgrounds could be played at the director's discretion—one group at a time or in any combination.

When we rehearsed the song with Terry, he said, "That's the way we used to do it in the Ellington band. Some guy would make up a short riff and the other guys would follow it, filling in the right harmonies." Quite often, riffs are used in blues tunes, and the players simply follow the changes, especially to back up solos. In that sense, the riff becomes an improvisational unit, similar to what boogie-woogie musicians did. The rhythm section just keeps "filling in the right harmonies" and time, while the horns fill in the background.

Improvised at first, these riffs were finally written down into arrangements. The solos were written down, as well, so that others could reproduce the sound. Players would also copy these ideas and use them to create different solos of their own.

This evolution eventually led to the creation of "head charts." In this type of arrangement, all one needed to do was to write down a version of the melody for big band, write some transitions and riff backgrounds for soloists, and then write a concluding chorus. Although one might be tempted to conclude that this is simplified big band arranging, what it actually led to was freedom from the melody.

One model of big band writing (that was primarily the province of commercial white bands) was continuous recreation of the melody. The smooth sounds of Glen Gray, Guy Lombardo, and Freddy Martin, for example, recreated total melody within differing textures. However, the actual diversity of textural possibilities was not that great. With riff bands, the freedom from repetition ultimately allowed arrangers to freely experiment with unusual textures. Certainly the Duke Ellington band is a good example of that, beginning as a riff band but ultimately becoming a symphonic unit using all sorts of unusual instrumental combinations to create very different sounds and effects.

Many of the more traditional society orchestras of the time created music that was functional and limited in special effects, so as not to irritate audiences. Although riff bands also were in the business of pleasing audiences, they tended to be more experimental with the rhythm section, with solos, with the use of unusual mute effects, and with instrumental tone. As such, they also tended to become technically more proficient and in the long run had more influence.

The rhythm section of riff bands evolved subtly toward more efficient use of the four instrumentalists. Players either stopped playing on all four beats, or at least played off the beat every once in a while. For instance, the piano style of both Basie and Ellington became very spartan; they played very few notes. While Basie in particular was capable of very technical stride piano, when he played in his rhythm section he was known as almost a "one-finger" or one-chord player; he would just hit a short chord every once in a while. The effective use of silence and complementary playing actually did more to make those rhythm sections swing than anything else. Ultimately the general style of jazz rhythm playing was altered immeasurably as a result.

One can trace very easily the development of big band music through riff-oriented groups, perhaps even more easily than through the more commercial-oriented white bands. Many of the white organizations built up the size of their musical forces for visual, as well as musical, effect. Many of the popular big bands of the late 1930s and 1940s used a full complement of players, whereas big bands overall evolved into bands of twenty players and more.

The Fletcher Henderson band of 1926, for which Don Redman wrote "Stampede," was made up of three saxophones (who doubled on clarinet), two cornets, one trumpet, one trombone, piano, banjo, tuba, and drums. As previously noted, the rhythm section was the weakest part of the ensemble; piano, banjo, tuba and drums simply played one note or chord on each beat of every measure. However, the early big band sound is adequately communicated with the seven-instrument group. This band was clearly riff oriented in style, although the use of different textural groups is evident.

The work of arrangers Will Hudson, Sy Oliver, Eddie Wilcox, and Gerald Wilson for the Jimmie Lunceford Orchestra in the 1930s was highly significant in the development of riff style. Although Lunceford's orchestra contained few major soloists, the sound emphasized high-register trumpet playing and very exciting shout choruses. In actuality, Lunceford's horn section played in swing style, and

Duke Ellington, 1945

the rhythm section played in an older style. Benny Goodman's big band—and especially his smaller ensembles—played an approximation of riff style, as evident in "Sing, Sing, Sing." But the best-known riff band was the Count Basie Orchestra, which developed from the defunct Bennie Moten Orchestra in 1935. From Moten, Basie inherited many of the best jazz soloists available; but even if this had not been the case, Basie's piano style and directing still attracted musicians who could solo expertly and also create interesting backgrounds.

Duke Ellington was also very significant in the development of swing music within a riff tradition, because he, too, had fine soloists. Among these are Johnny Hodges (the first great alto soloist), Harry Carney (baritone sax), Cootie Williams (trumpet), and Juan Tizol (valve trombone). In 1939, he was joined by Billy Strayhorn, who had strong arranging skills. Ellington did not remain solely in the riff tradition, although he always returned to it. He matured in his music beyond pieces based totally on rhythm, to pieces that told bigger stories, with greater and greater flexibility in instrumentation. While Basie's band was certainly the major riff ensemble, Ellington's was musically uplifting. Basie's band was constantly turning over new players (somewhat like Miles Davis in later years); Ellington kept the same players year after year.

Other big bands and smaller groups which played in a riff-oriented way were those of Earl Hines, Chick Webb, Andy Kirk (with Mary Lou Williams), Charlie Barnet, Benny Carter, Erskine Hawkins, Lionel Hampton, Billy Eckstine, and Dizzy Gillespie.

MUSICAL ANALYSIS

"KoKo"
Duke Ellington and His Famous Orchestra (SCCJ D-13)

The instrumentation of this piece is three trumpets (including one cornet), three trombones (Juan Tizol, the soloist, on valve trombone), four saxes (doubling on clarinet), piano, guitar, bass, and drums. The recording was done in 1937. The meter is 4/4, the tempo is 144, and the key is eb-minor. The piece opens and closes with an eight-measure introduction; the body of the piece is seven times through a twelve-measure blues progression. It is in a minor key, but other than that it is fairly standard blues; eb is 1; ab is 4; and Bb7 is 5. The actual progression is 1,1,1,1,4,4,1,1,5,5,1,1, although there is a half-step alteration in measures 9 and 10: B7 to Bb7. Notice that the chart repeats five times with different solos or textures indicated.

The orchestration (use of instruments) is interesting. The baritone sax (Harry Carney) plays an Eb pedal note (long-held note), and the trombones play the rhythmic figure on top of that note. The trombone solos are tastefully woven into the texture of the piece, first valve trombone and then tenor slide trombone. The piano solo is typically Ellington, very subdued. The bass solo actually almost responds to the ensemble.

The most significant thing to listen for in this piece is the way that the sections create unusual textures. This is the trademark of the Ellington band.

Intro

Gb F E eb	Gb F E eb		ab Bb B7	Bb Gb	F		E eb
Eb Pedal by baritone sax							
1	2	3	4	5	6	7	8

—Five Times—
Trombone/Muted Trombone/Muted Trombone/Piano Solo with Ensemble/Reeds + Trumpets/

eb			ab		eb		B Bb	B Bb	eb	
1	2	3	4	5	6	7	8	9	10	11	12

Full Reeds/Bass Solo in Twos

Ebm			Abm	Ebm		B7Bb7B7Bb7Ebm				
1	2	3	4	5	6	7	8	9	10	11	12

Charlie Barnet

Chords and Running Line in Twos

| Ebm | | Abm | Ebm | Bb7#11 | Ebm |
| 1   2 | 3   4 | 5   6 | 7   8 | 9   10 | 11   12 |

Intro   **Extension**
Same as Above Intro   **Ebm**

   1   2   3   4   5   6   7   8   9   10   11   12

Count Basie

William (Count) Basie was born in Red Bank, New Jersey, on August 21, 1904, and died in Hollywood, Florida, on April 26, 1984. He was taught by his mother to play piano. He also picked up ragtime from New York pianists, including Fats Waller. He started performing in public as an accompanist to vaudeville acts and eventually replaced Fats Waller in an act called Katie Crippen and Her Kids.

On the road with a vaudeville show in the late 1920s, Basie wound up in Kansas City, where he played first for silent movies and then joined Walter Page's Blue Devils (1928–1929). He joined Bennie Moten's band in 1929 and remained there until Moten's death in 1935.

SIDE-NOTES

He then started his own band, which contained many of Moten's former players. His band went to New York in 1937 to make its first recordings for Decca Records. From that point on, the Basie band had a huge following and enjoyed tremendous success.

Basie's band, perhaps the most famous of the riff bands, is distinctive because of its rhythm section and because of its swing, but also because of the quality of soloists Basie was able to attract over the years. Although Basie himself was not always considered a great piano player, because his playing had a sparse sound while in the ensemble, he did display virtuosity on occasion. However, in the classic Basie sound, Count Basie did not play very many chords or notes during any one composition. Obviously, Count Basie was very significant for his development of a black big band that set standards for others and had influence far and wide. Many of Basie arrangements, written by a variety of people, have become jazz standards.

SIDE-NOTES

Duke Ellington

Edward Kennedy (Duke) Ellington was born in Washington, D.C., on April 29, 1899, and died in New York City on May 24, 1974. Ellington began studying piano at the age of 7, but in high school he became fascinated with art and later worked briefly as a commercial sign painter. At the same time, he had also started working as a musician and bandleader. He made one, disastrous, trip to New York before moving there, more successfully, in 1923 at the suggestion of Fats Waller. His first band in New York was called Duke and His Washingtonians.

Ellington's band grew substantially between 1923 and 1926. Two musicians who joined during that period were Joe Nanton (trombone) and Harry Carney (saxophone). The rhythm section remained constant through the mid-thirties. On December 4, 1927, the Ellington band began an engagement at the Cotton Club and from then on was regarded as a musical institution. Barney Bigard, Johnny Hodges, and Cootie Williams joined the band during the Cotton Club era.

Ellington was the spiritual leader and the original composer and arranger for the band until 1939, when he was joined by Billy Strayhorn, with whom he continued to turn out creative masterpieces. The Ellington band took on massive artistic proportions, as it played more and more complicated music and extended its technical ability. Whereas the Ellington band may have started as a riff band, it quickly went beyond that to perform pieces that contained unusual voicings and special effects. Starting in 1943, Ellington began presenting annual concerts at Carnegie Hall, which always introduced new experimental compositions. Even after his death in 1974, the Ellington tradition was continued by his son, Mercer.

There is little question that the most significant big band in the history of jazz was Ellington's. The technical proficiency of his players was significant, as was the constancy of their membership in the band. The most important aspect of the band was the fact that arrangements were written for the specific playing abilities of each player. Many have imitated Ellington, but none have duplicated his style.

Suggested Listening

1. "Duke Ellington—1938" Smithsonian 2003
2. "Duke Ellington—1939" Smithsonian 2010
3. "Duke Ellington—1940" Smithsonian 2013
4. "Duke Ellington—1941" Smithsonian 2027
5. "The Best of Count Basie" MCA 2–4050
6. "Big Band Jazz" Smithsonian RC030

Chapter 10
Big Band Vocalists

Vocalists were a very visible—and a very important—part of the big band era, although they were often relegated to reproducing the melody as a soloist or in a group. Occasionally, great jazz singers like Billie Holiday, Ella Fitzgerald, and Louis Armstrong created vocal improvisations that were works of sheer genius, but few others were able to excel in big band style. Excellent bands such as those of Duke Ellington, Count Basie, Stan Kenton, and Benny Goodman, used vocalists, but usually only for commercial reasons. Big bands were, after all, for-profit organizations and there was a tendency among them to use vocalists as a means of making the band visible and commercially salable.

This is not to say that vocalists did not have an important function, because they often did; in big band arrangements, the vocalist would often simply sing along with the melody the first or second time it was presented. Solos and transition sections followed the vocals. In fact, many old "stock" arrangements (original arrangements of the era printed so that others could play them) had instructions for how to change the score if a vocalist was to be used. Invariably, a vocalist was used at the beginning of the composition.

Sometimes group vocals would be sung by the entire band, but these were typically short phrases intended to have a novelty effect. True jazz singing—that is, improvisational—was not often done during the big band era. Exceptions are musicians like Joe Williams with Basie's band, Louis Armstrong, and Ella Fitzgerald.

Some very fine singers, such as Ella Fitzgerald and Billie Holiday, got their start in big bands. Mel Torme's singing is rooted in big band style, as is the singing of Sarah Vaughn. Of course, Louis Armstrong and some of the blues singers continued to sing during the big band era. Bing Crosby is another singer who got his start as a big band singer (originally, he was a drummer). He sang with Bob Wills and

Ella Fitzgerald

Helen Forrest

Billie Holiday, mid-1940's

His Texas Playboys, a pioneer western swing orchestra once reputed to have the finest jazz players in America. June Christy and Anita O'Day got their starts singing with young Stan Kenton's orchestra. Frank Sinatra sang with many big bands, especially the Harry James Orchestra and Tommy Dorsey. And young Dean Martin and Sammy Davis, Jr., started out as big band singers.

The primary female vocalist for Harry James was Helen Forrest. Kay Davis sang for Ellington, as did Ray Nancy, a member of the band. Helen Ward sang for Benny Goodman as a commercial attraction; Ella Fitzgerald also sang for Goodman. Jimmy Dorsey used Helen O'Connell, Bob Eberly and Charlie Teagarden (a trumpet player and Jack's brother). Other top vocal groups were of course the Mills Brothers and the Andrews Sisters.

REPRESENTATIVE VOCALISTS

Big band singers were admired for their charisma and stage presence. Rudy Vallee, the first great American crooner, sang in a smooth style that conveyed to his audience a feeling of security. When Dean Martin sang the words, "powder your face with sunshine," he communicated both the words and the feelings that were associated with them. Although many musicians might argue that those ideas can be conveyed without words, vocalists helped the audience to better understand what the instrumental music was trying to communicate.

Some of course, like Ella Fitzgerald, also did solo work and scat singing (vocal improvisations using nonsense syllables). Billie Holiday, in her 1938 version of "These Foolish Things," with the Teddy Wilson Orchestra, (see "Smithsonian Collection of Classic Jazz, rev. ed.") does some improvisational work, but her 1952 version, with a smaller band, allows her more freedom. The big band style was somewhat limiting for singers, both because of the size of the musical force and because of the perceived function of the lyrics. But some vocalists made some excellent music during that era, and their influence has had a major impact on the development of vocal jazz.

"All Alone"
Sarah Vaughn (SCCJ F-11)

The instrumentation on this piece is four trumpets, two trombones, two saxophones, and piano. It was recorded in 1967. Some of the players involved were Clark Terry, Freddie Hubbard, J. J. Johnson, Kai Winding, Phil Woods, and Benny Golson. The meter signature is 4/4, the tempo is 130, and the key is C. The instrumentation has the essence of a big band, although there is only a piano for rhythm.

The instruments provide only background voicings, with Vaughn carrying everything after the short introduction. But the singing style of this popular standard is beautiful and certainly illustrates the way that a big band sound can be used to back up a vocal. The actual chord progression of this tune is quite a bit more complicated than the version presented here.

Intro

CA7		D7	G7
1	2	3	4

A   **B**
Vocal

C		G7		C	G7	C		b	E7	a	F#B	E		f#		B	e A7 d	G7
1	2	3	4	5	6	7	8	1	2	3	4		5	6		7		8

C   **A**
Vocal

C7		F		a	D	G A	d	G7 C	C7	F		f	e		A d		G Ca d	G7
1	2	3	4	5	6	7		8	1	2	3	4		5 6		7		8

A   **B**
Ensemble Tutti   **Vocal with Band**

C		G7		C	G7	C		b	E7	a		F#B	E	f#B e A7	d	G7 1	2
3 4		5	6	7 8	1 2 3	4		5		6		7		8			

Sarah Vaughan

C Vocal/Band								**A** Vocal							
C7	F	a	D7	G A	d	G C	C7	F f	e	A d	G	CB	E A
1	2	3	4	5	6	7	8	1 2	3	4	5	6 7	8

Extension　　　　**Band Chord**

D7	G7	C		C7
1	2	3	4	5

SIDE-NOTES

Billie Holiday

Eleanor Gough McKay (Billie Holiday) was born in Baltimore on April 7, 1915, and died in New York City on July 17, 1959. One of the most successful and tragic musicians in the history of jazz, "Lady Day" is thought by many to be the quintessential jazz singer. She sang equally successfully with big bands and small combos; she remained a great talent even toward the end of her life, which was overshadowed by drug addiction.

Holiday moved to New York with her mother in 1929 and began singing in Harlem clubs. Her father played banjo and guitar with Fletcher Henderson in the early 1930s. She made her first record with Benny Goodman in 1933 and became famous as a result of the recordings she made with Teddy Wilson from 1935 to 1939. She was also a vocalist with Count Basie and Artie Shaw in the late 1930s, was featured in one film in 1946, and toured Europe twice, in 1954 and 1958. She was addicted to narcotics for much of her later life, which hastened both the end of her career and her death.

Probably the artist with whom she had the most rapport was Lester Young (Prez), the tenor player with the Basie band. Her singing style was very sensitive and sensuous, and her jazz vocalizations made her a true improviser. No other jazz singer, except perhaps Louis Armstrong, has been more imitated.

Ella Fitzgerald

Ella Fitzgerald was born in Newport News, Virginia, on April 25, 1918. While she was singing for an amateur show in New York in 1934, Chick Webb heard of her and asked her to join his band. Her first record was made with the Webb band in 1935. She took control of the band after Webb died in 1939, and she remained in that position until 1941. Probably her biggest hit as a vocalist was "A Tisket a Tasket" in 1938.

In the 1950s, Fitzgerald became a solo singer with small combos, although occasionally she has returned to big band work, as she did for the Duke Ellington Carnegie Hall concert in 1958. She has toured Europe extensively and has remained, until recently, a vibrant performer.

Her low singing voice has a husky quality. However, it is in her free vocal improvisations that Fitzgerald is truly unique. Although her forte is scat singing, she is now known primarily as a combo jazz singer.

Suggested Listening

1. "Big Band Jazz"   Smithsonian RC030
   Bing Crosby, Jimmy Harrison, and Mary Clark are vocalists who appear in this collection.
2. "Billie Holiday's Greatest Hits"   COL. CL 2666
3. "Duke Ellington Song Book"   Decca 4010–4
4. "Greatest Jazz Concert in the World"   Pablo 2625–704

Part IV
Combo-Style Jazz

Chapter 11
Combo Style

INSTRUMENTATION

Dixieland was at the forefront of jazz until the late 1920s, when most musicians were becoming part of the big band craze. Small Dixieland ensembles grew in size until they reached the eighteen to twenty players who typically made up big bands. Then big bands met their demise, primarily for economic reasons: Few people could afford to hire such large ensembles, which were ultimately replaced by smaller combos. The military draft of World War II also accounts for the loss of many musicians and depleted the talent in numerous big bands. Some critics contend that the desire to return to improvisation as the chief activity of jazz led to the demise of the big band and the rise of combo-style jazz.

In our earlier discussions of Dixieland, we talked about smaller ensembles made up of everything from three pieces to eight, made up of a rhythm section of varied instrumentation and one or more melody instruments. Combo-style jazz is made up of just such a combination of instruments, although the combo-style jazz of the 1940s had little in common with Dixieland.

Combo style jazz is a term which describes music of a small instrumental combination (combo), usually consisting of drums, bass, piano, plus one or two melody instruments. Other rhythm instruments are occasionally used, such as guitar and vibraphone; other melody instruments such as clarinet and trombone appear in combos. Although there were instrumental combos throughout the history of jazz, the modern combo (non-Dixieland) period started in the late 1930s. As we shall see in the next few chapters, each of the instruments in a modern-style combo (sometimes referred to as pre-bebop) plays a diversified role. The rhythm section players do not play on every beat as in Dixieland and swing band style; rather they play in

Lionel Hampton, from the movie "The Benny Goodman Story"

such a way that the total texture keeps the beat. All players, including the rhythm section, became soloists. The solos were longer and explored harmonic and melodic areas untouched in previous styles, and the entire combo concept was experimental.

There was always combo jazz throughout the big band era, even when it was simply a part of a big band ensemble. Many big bands, including the Benny Goodman orchestra, carried a small band within the large band, which would play during engagements for contrast. These units were soloist oriented and produced some of the more memorable performances and recordings. For instance, the 1938 combo recordings of Benny Goodman are legendary. Another example is the small ensemble carried within the Bob Wills and His Texas Playboys ensemble. This band played standard big band arrangements similar to other commercial bands, carried a Dixieland band within the organization, and also played Western swing with a progressive string band.

Combo jazz groups shifted slowly from a Dixieland orientation to a more modern style. Some Dixieland-type units still existed, in classic style. But most small organizations moved more toward a contemporary style of playing in which the solos were extended and left the basic chordal framework of the original composition. Perhaps one of the most exciting examples of that slow growth is with the sideman (or band personnel) of the Fletcher Henderson organization. Starting in 1928, sidemen of the Henderson band (known as the

Chocolate Dandies) made records that constantly broke new ground in small-ensemble playing. The first example analyzed in this chapter is a 1940 example featuring Benny Carter on alto, Coleman Hawkins on tenor, and Roy Eldridge on trumpet. Earlier examples illustrate a clear development from East Cost Dixieland to contemporary style.

The standard instruments used in prebop combo style are selected from the following: piano, string bass (eventually electric), electric guitar, drums, alto or tenor sax, trumpet, and trombone. Some of the more historic combo pieces from the late thirties and early forties feature saxophone or trumpet, but many combinations occurred. The rhythm section usually consisted of piano, bass, and drums, although Lionel Hampton played the vibraphone ("vibes") in a combo for Benny Goodman. In that particular group, Hampton used the vibes both as a rhythmic instrument and as a melodic solo instrument.

There is a significant difference between Dixieland-style combo jazz and modern or prebebop combo work. The rhythm section in the modern combo is much more sophisticated, and they do not play four clomping beats per measure. The bass lines are fluid and

actually control the tempo. The drummer plays rhythmic variations around the tempo, providing a different sound for the texture. The piano player quite often plays brief chords designed simply to fill out the harmonies and leave space. The guitar player occasionally solos but typically does what the piano player does, although not at the same time. In short, the rhythm section provides the harmonic and rhythm foundation for the soloists.

It is the soloists who really developed combo jazz to its prebop level. Musicians like Coleman Hawkins, Roy Eldridge, Benny Carter, Johnny Hodges, Lester Young, Dexter Gordon, and even Charlie Parker and Dizzy Gillespie played in big bands and tried to develop advanced improvisational ideas. In certain bands like Basie's and Ellington's, this was certainly possible. In clubs and in session work for recordings, some soloists broke new ground and ultimately influenced the whole style of combo jazz.

One such example is the "Body and Soul" recording of Coleman Hawkins, which is analyzed in the appendix. Hawkins had been an early major power in jazz dating back to the 1920s. He slowly developed a full rich tone, which he used to create emotional nuance

not possible in earlier times. He also created improvisational variations on basic melodies which strayed further and further away from the original melodies. Instead of simply embellishing the original melody, he created new ones and then fragmented those. In his technically important "Body and Soul," he created a new technique on the saxophone.

Johnny Hodges (lead alto for Ellington) did the same thing within the context of the Ellington band and also in combo recordings. Benny Carter was the other ground breaker on the alto sax prior to Charlie Parker. Charlie Christian on guitar created a new musical vocabulary for the electric guitar, and pianists like Nat King Cole, Art Tatum, and later Bud Powell and George Shearing all created prebop piano styles that departed markedly from Dixieland. Benny Goodman's smaller ensembles had great influence as well.

"I Can't Believe That You're in Love With Me" The Chocolate Dandies, Featuring Roy Eldridge and Benny Carter (SCCJ D-2)

The instrumentation of this piece is trumpet (Eldridge), alto sax (Carter), tenor sax (Coleman Hawkins), guitar, bass, and drums. The recording was made in 1940. The meter signature is 4/4, the tempo is 168 beats per minute, and the key is Db. The actual chord changes to this performance are rather complicated, starting on the 4 chord (Gb7), but the structure is fairly easy to hear—thirty-two measures divided into four 8s for AABA.

Fletcher Henderson's sidemen began using the name "Chocolate Dandies" in 1928, when they made recordings separate from the Henderson band. The arrangement and performance have almost a big band sound, with Hawkins and Carter providing background for Eldridge. Both the Eldridge solo and the Carter solo are well worth hearing; they are beautiful renditions.

A   **A**
Trumpet Solo

```
‖: Gb gb Db Eb Ab    Db ab DbGb gb Db Eb Ab      Db
   1  2  3  4  5   6  7  8    9   10 11 12 13 14 15 16
```

B   **A**
Trumpet

```
F7      Bb    Eb    Ab ab Db Gb gb Db Eb Ab    Db Db7:‖
1  2  3   4  5   6  7  8      9 10 11 12 13 14 15 16
```

Alto Solo

```
‖: Gb gb Db Eb Ab    Db ab DbGb gb Db Eb Ab      Db
   1  2  3  4  5   6  7  8    9   10 11 12 13 14 15 16
```

B   **A**
Alto

```
F7      Bb    Eb    Ab ab Db Gb gb Db Eb Ab    Db Db Db7:‖
1  2  3   4  5   6  7  8      9 10 11 12 13 14 15 16
```

A   **A**
Group (Trumpet, Alto, Tenor)

```
Gb gb Db Eb Ab    Db ab DbGb gb Db Eb Ab      Db
1  2  3  4  5   6  7  8    9   10 11 12 13 14 15 16
```

B   **A**

```
F7      Bb    Eb    Ab ab Db Gb gb Db Eb Ab    Db Db
1  2  3   4  5   6  7  8      9 10 11 12 13 14 15 16
```

Coleman Hawkins

Coleman Hawkins was born in St. Joseph, Missouri, on November 21, 1904 and died in New York on May 19, 1969. He studied piano, cello and tenor sax as a youth and attended Washburn College in Topeka, Kansas. He first worked with Mamie Smith's Jazz Hounds in 1922 and came to New York, making his first recording with Fletcher Henderson in 1923. For the rest of the 1920s, he was the principal tenor sax soloist in jazz, although there were others starting in the 1930s. He worked in England and remained in Europe from 1934 to 1939.

In October of 1939 he recorded the important nine-piece rendition of "Body and Soul" (see analysis) and very briefly put together a sixteen-piece band in 1940. He assembled a band for a bop session, which recorded in February of 1944. He continued free-lance work in America and Europe.

Coleman Hawkins played with a very rich tenor tone, especially for his time. As the only significant tenor soloist in the 1920s, he was obviously important and influential. However, there can be little question that his interpretation and solo on "Body and Soul" has had lasting impact. That solo paved the way for the tenor sax to become the most popular jazz instrument of the 1950s and 1960s.

Lionel Hampton

Lionel Hampton was born in Louisville, Kentucky, on April 12, 1913. He grew up in Chicago, and it was there that he began playing drums in a boys' band. His professional career began with another move westward in 1928, this time to California, where he played with Paul Howard, Eddie Barefield, and Les Hite. Louis Armstrong was the major player with the Hite band, and during this time Hampton picked up the vibes. A pioneer on vibes, he made his first recording on the instrument with Armstrong in 1930. He formed his own band to play at the Cotton Club in Los Angeles, where Benny Goodman heard him playing. Joining Goodman in 1936, he quickly became a significant part of the small ensemble. He formed his own big band in 1940, which made its first recordings in 1941. In the late thirties, Hampton made a significant series of Victor recordings with other players.

From the late 1940s on, Hampton has played primarily with small bands and has been continuously active musically. He tours extensively throughout the world. He also occasionally plays a rather unusual two-fingered piano, but he is not highly acclaimed for this. His personal warmth is endearing to audiences everywhere.

Suggested Listening

1. "Steppin' Out"   MCA-1315
2. "Best of Hampton"   MCA2-4075
3. "Prez and Teddy and Oscar"   Verve 2502
4. "Jazz Giant"   Contemporary 7555
5. "Coleman Hawkins and the Trumpet Kings"   Trip 5515
6. "Sweets, Lips and Lots of Jazz"   Xanadu 123

Chapter 12
Bebop

The subject of modern jazz begins with bebop. The term *bebop* may derive from nonsense syllables jazz vocalists used to sing along with this particular type of melody. Or the term may have come from a tune of the same name by Dizzy Gillespie. Generally speaking, bebop is very fast, played by a small combo, and features instrumental soloists who created complex melodies and solos. Bebop musicians used existing compositions, but they altered both the chord structure and the original melodies; they also wrote original compositions. Bebop was agitated, sounded angry, and created tension. By comparison to earlier styles, including the prebop combo jazz described in chapter 11, bebop was exclusive music because it was equally challenging for both player and listener. The bebop players community in the 1940s was mainly based in New York and was primarily black.

The development of bebop marked a turning point in the relationship between the American public and jazz musicians. In one important sense, bebop signaled both the coming of age of jazz as a musical art form and its partial demise as "popular" music. By the 1940s, jazz had lost much of its mainstream audience, many of whom found themselves alienated from it—particularly because of the complexities of free improvisation. The status of jazz remains pretty much the same today, although a few contemporary styles have managed to draw a wider audience.

Regardless of the loss of listeners, bebop clearly raised the level of jazz appreciation on the part of the musical intelligents. Many music critics initially disliked bebop because it was hard to understand, but ultimately jazz followers recognized that this was a startling new style of music that deserved their attention and respect.

Essentially, bebop was established as a technique by a small number of black musicians who gathered in New York City in the mid-1940s. By that time, New York City had become the center of jazz activity and of the music industry as a whole. It remains the place where new things are constantly happening and is also the only viable location for new plays and musicals to run.

As the recording center, New York employed many session musicians (people who worked full time providing music for recording artists), and the resultant competition yielded players of great skill. (The same is true of other towns where there is tremendous activity in one artistic medium, such as the country music recording industry in Nashville, Motown in Detroit in the sixties, and the blues and rockability in Memphis.) Also, New York is filled with clubs where musicians can perform and hear other talented musicians on a consistent basis. The success of the first bebop artists created a snowball effect, and black musicians began arriving in New York in droves to join the emerging new style.

Bebop can also be understood as one of the first black-power movements, in that black musicians created a musical vocabulary that was either indigenously or secretively black. Like earlier musicians from New Orleans, who created tunes that could not be imitated by other bands, and like big band arrangers who created complex textures that could not be easily copied, beboppers established a technique that defied playing by the casual musician. They were purposefully trying to create a music that was highly individual, reserved for those in the "in" crowd. The usual practice of sitting in with groups was relatively difficult with bebop tunes, because most likely the casual player who was not a member of the group could not follow what they were doing.

Bebop was a style that was elitist from a musical point of view. Regardless of the racial overtones, which certainly existed, there was an attempt to exclude simple music, insisting on high speeds, melodic pyrotechnics, and obscure chord changes. Also, a high premium was placed on the melody players starting with ornamented musical lines that were based on original melodies but were highly embellished and played at the speed of light.

These musicians departed from the norm in their dress also. Much as contemporary Afro Americans wear African garb to identify themselves, beboppers tried their efforts by dressing in Bohemian ways—such as Dizzy Gillespie did when he donned his beret. It was as if they were trying to create a form of music that white people could not steal. And although a few white musicians did assimilate the style, this was not to happen for quite some time.

Although many influences led to bebop, such as the Coleman Hawkins' solo "Body and Soul," there can be little question that Charlie Parker and Dizzy Gillespie were the two leaders. Both worked their way to New York, playing in small ensembles and in big bands; Gillespie led his own big band prior to starting the bebop revolution. Parker played with Jay McShann and sat in with the big bands of Gillespie and Woody Herman. Gillespie played with Cab Calloway. They both played with Earl Hines and Billy Eckstine. Parker first played in a combo with Gillespie as the leader and then they traded leadership through the mid-1940s.

Dizzy Gillespie, 1946

The instruments usually employed in bebop were piano, bass, drums, saxophone, and trumpet, although other instruments were occasionally used. Clarinet was seldom used. Most tunes were head charts in the sense that the members of the group knew the melodies, which they played at the beginning. After that, solos filled out the rest of the performance until the group came back together to play the melody or the "head." Bebop and combo jazz in general after 1940 did not use written arrangements.

Musicians tended to improvise in a style that created long phrases which lapped over four- and eight-measure units, so the action never seemed to stop. As well, musicians quite often began and ended their solos in the middle of a section rather than playing to the end of a sixteen- or thirty-two-measure unit and then quitting neatly. The melodies which they created and the solos were much more diverse, with more notes and more skips in the melodies. The harmonies are very complicated and featured all altered chords and dominant seventh chains. Generally in bebop, the rhythm section plays very different roles, sometimes playing continuous and regular accompaniment and other times playing very sparse accompaniment.

Bebop is aggressive and hard edged, although interestingly, the technical demands required players to occasionally cut corners in getting from one place to another. Bebop represented a new technique and introduced a new musical vocabulary; it also created additional technical demands, and it extended the range of instruments used. The tempo was so fast that players in general—regardless of the instrument they played—had to have their fingers closer to the keys. Elements of surprise and sudden change were very popular in the bebop style because that made the music that much harder to play for the uninitiated. As well, many of the melodic and harmonic devices created tremendous tension which made the resolution into the head and the closing all that much more satisfying.

To fully appreciate bebop, one must understand harmonic variations, since beboppers tended to employ this almost as a matter of course. Dating back to New Orleans, many musicians had experimented with harmonic variation. Harmonic variation is a change in the basic harmonic unit (like the blues progression) each time it is produced, for example:

Original blues progression

C	C	C	C	F	F	C	C	G	G	C	C
1	2	3	4	5	6	7	8	9	10	11	12

Harmonic variation of above

C F7	C	C7	F	Fo7C	A7	d	G7	C a	d	G7
1 2	3	4	5 6	7	8	9	10	11	12	

Art Tatum, in particular, was very fond of employing altered chords in his improvisations. Of course, you could find plenty of examples of harmonic variation of a basic idea just by looking at the analyses in this book.

Many bebop tunes are based upon popular chord progressions, such as the "I Got Rhythm" chord progressions (called, in jazz slang, "changes"). However, when beboppers created a tune, they took the changes and did one of two things: (1) They created a brand new melody for the old changes and speeded it up three or four times; or (2) they created a new melody and altered changes. A good example of the first idea is the tune "How High the Moon," which was given a new melody by Charlie Parker and became "Ornithology." Parker's "KoKo" does the same thing.

Bebop musicians also wrote original compositions that usually used altered chords to a great extent, such as a dominant chord with a flatted fifth or sharp ninth. Ultimately, these altered chords caused the improvisers to create melodies which took advantage of altered tonal concepts and scales, which of course eventually led to modal improvisation, which uses scales or modes different from traditional major and minor scales, such as Renaissance church modes, Oriental, or Indian scales.

Charlie Parker's influence on bebop is paramount because he was the one who raised saxophone playing to a new level of technical virtuosity. He also created a body of solo works that have been transcribed and imitated by other musicians. His work still influences people today, thirty years after his death. Some modern saxophone

Charlie Parker

players, like Richie Cole, play in a style called neobop, a 1970s and 1980s version of bebop, characterized by an even slightly faster tempo and increased pyrotechnics than the 1940s style.

Although he had legal and personal problems because of drug addiction, Charlie Parker ("Bird" or "Yardbird") inspired and influenced an entire generation of jazz musicians. His legacy is his continued influence, a body of solos and compositions that people still play, and records that are still readily available.

Dizzy Gillespie has also been paramount to the development of jazz. A prolific composer, he has written many tunes, some of which are jazz standards. And he had complete technical mastery of his instrument, playing with incredible speed, nuance, and range. He has also been an ambassador for jazz throughout the world, somewhat like Louis Armstrong.

Another very important musician in the bebop revolution was pianist and arranger Thelonius Monk. Monk was also a prolific composer who wrote some popular slow tunes such as "'Round Midnight." Not really a fast player in the same vein as Parker and Gillespie, Monk was influential with the unusual combinations of notes (called voicings) he played on the piano. Essentially a spartan player (he often created solos that had very few notes), during most of his early career he created complex tone clusters with clashing notes. He was also an expert at the unexpected, creating "hanging dissonance" (clashing chords) which somehow seemed to resolve at the end. In some senses a stride pianist gone modern, he was a master of rhythmic variation.

Bud Powell is the pianist most often credited with translating Charlie Parker's style to the piano. The most significant change Powell made was deemphasizing the use of the left hand. Instead of playing stride bass with the left hand, he played closed position chords in the mid-range of the keyboard every once in a while, thus freeing his mental activity for right-hand work. As a result, like Charlie Parker and Gillespie, he was able to play long, flowing lines and display flashy technique.

Kenny Clarke and Max Roach were the leaders of the bebop drummers. Roach, in particular, led the way in emphasizing the use of the cymbals for time rather than the bass and snare drums. Both players used spontaneous offbeat hits on various drums and cymbals as a method of breaking up the constant rhythmic activity. They played both more aggressively and more efficiently. Their playing style tended to leave the playing of regular beats to the bass player.

Significant bass players included Ray Brown, Oscar Pettiford, Tommy Potter, and Curly Russell, with Russell appearing on most of the recordings of bebop in the Smithsonian collection. Bass players developed double-fast technique, solo ability, singing while playing, double stops, and the offbeat accents and surprises common to the style.

Max Roach

Other musicians who were significant in this style are the following: trumpet—Conte Candoli, Miles Davis, Howard McGhee, Fats Navarro, and Clark Terry; saxophone—Stan Getz, Dexter Gordon, James Moody, Sonny Rollins, Sonny Stitt, Zoot Sims; trombone—J. J. Johnson, Kai Winding; piano—Hank Jones, Tadd Dameron, Ahmad Jamal, John Lewis, Oscar Peterson, and Billy Taylor; bass—Red Callender and Chubby Jackson; drums—Joe Harris and Roy Haynes; vibraphone—Terry Gibbs and Milt Jackson; guitar—Bill DeArango and Jimmy Raney; and arranger-composer—Gil Evans, Neal Hefti and Gerry Mulligan. These are certainly not all of the significant beboppers, but it is a good representative list. Many of the significant musician-players were also composer-arrangers.

ALIENATION OF BEBOP

One of the chief issues with bebop was the relative alienation of the musicians from the general public. The bebop audience was relatively small by comparison to previous jazz styles. Without a doubt, this was double-edged sword. Musicians became embittered and often aloof, separate from the crowd. On the other hand, that very same isolation allowed them to mature and develop their art to a high degree because they no longer had the practical obligation of pleasing the public.

One of the most intriguing subjects in any discussion of popular music is precisely the relationship between the development and evolution of the technique itself and the need to satisfy the audience.

The progressive quality of bebop jazz drove the style practically underground, and the admiration of fans became almost cultlike. Commercial interest in jazz waned after the demise of big bands. However, in one sense, bebop profited by this—certainly not financially, but artistically. By no longer being slaves to commercial success, beboppers were able to work at perfecting their singular craft. This newfound freedom, however, came at a high economic price to some of the most talented and adventuresome bebop artists.

"Night in Tunisia"
Bud Powell Trio (SCCJ F-5)

MUSICAL ANALYSIS

Originally composed by Dizzy Gillespie, this piece is performed with Powell on piano, Curly Russell on bass, and Max Roach on drums. It was recorded in 1951. With a 165 tempo, this piece is slower than previous tunes we have analyzed. The key is d, and the chief rhythmic character of the tune is the switch from a Latin feel to a swing beat; note where this is indicated on the chart. The piano solo is all swing, but that Latin-swing shift is an important part of both the original composition and this performance.

The musicians involved were the premium rhythm section used by New York beboppers. The first to translate bebop style to the piano, Bud Powell blazes across the keyboard, translating the Charlie Parker style to the piano. The chord changes are basically a shift back and forth between Eb7 and dm and are therefore easy to hear. Notice the way that the B section shifts to swing to emphasize the change. Also notice that the sections are switched a bit toward the end.

Drums

	Bass/Drums				Bass/Drums/Piano			
	Eb7	d	Eb7	d	Eb7	d	Eb7	d
1 2 3 4	1	2	3	4	1	2	3	4

A1
Piano melody

Latin					Swing			A2 Latin					Swing		
Eb7d	Eb7d	Eb7	d		e	A7	d	Eb7d	Eb7d	Eb	d		e A		d
1	2	3	4	5	6	7	8	1	2	3	4	5	6	7	8

B
Swing

								A3							
a	D7	g	D7g		C7	F	e	A Eb	d	Eb	d	Eb	d	e A7	d
1	2	3	4 5	6	7		8	1	2	3	4	5	6	7	8

Transition

e		Eb7		d		G7		g		Gb7	
1	2	3	4	5	6	7	8	9	10	11	12

Piano
Lead in to Solo

F

1   2   3   4

A1   **A2**
Piano Solo
Swing

Eb7 d   Eb7 d   Eb7   d   e A7   d   Eb7 d   Eb7 d   Eb   d   e A   d
1   2   3   4   5   6   7   8   1   2   3   4   5   6   7   8

B   **A3**
Piano Solo Continued

a   D7 g   D7 g   C7 F   e   A   Eb   d   Eb   d   Eb   d   e A7   d
1   2   3   4 5   6   7   8   1   2   3   4   5   6   7   8

A1   **B**
Piano Solo Continued

Eb7 d   Eb7 d   Eb7   d   e A7   d   a   D7 g   D7 g   C7 F   e   A
1   2   3   4   5   6   7   8   1   2   3   4   5   6   7   8

A3   **A1**
                                          Returning to Melody

Eb   d   Eb   d   Eb   d   e A7   d   Eb7 d   Eb7 d   Eb7   d   e A7   d
1   2   3   4   5   6   7   8   1   2   3   4   5   6   7   8

A2   **B (Solo)**

Eb7 d   Eb7 d   Eb   d   e A   d   a   D7 g   D7 g   C7   F   e   A
1   2   3   4   5   6   7   8   1   2   3   4   5   6   7   8

A3

Eb   d   Eb   d   Eb   d   e   A7   d
1   2   3   4   5   6   7   8

A   **A**
Rhythmic Variation of Melody   **Cadenza**   **Cadenza**

Eb7 d   Eb7 d   Eb7   d   e A7   d   Eb7 d   Eb7 d   Eb   d   e A   ‖
1   2   3   4   5   6   7   8   1   2   3   4   5   6   7   8

d Held Chord ‖

Charlie Parker

Charles Christopher (Charlie, Bird, or Yardbird) Parker Jr. was born in Kansas City on August 29, 1920 and died in New York on March 12, 1955. He started playing alto sax in 1931 and quit school four years later. He worked with a variety of local bands until 1939 (including Jay McShann) when he went to New York. He made his first records with McShann in New York in 1941; he met Dizzy Gillespie that year. He played with the Noble Sissle band in 1942 and with Earl Hines on Tenor Sax in 1943. He went on the road with the Billy Eckstine band in 1944, where he played in a style which would later be called bebop.

He made his first combo recording in September of 1944 and the first one with Gillespie in May of 1945. He continued working with Gillespie, with whom he moved to California in 1946. From 1946 on, he worked occasionally and at times with incredible brilliance, including other people such as Miles Davis and Max Roach. He toured Europe in 1949, playing at the Paris Jazz Festival. A week before he died he played at Birdland.

The legacy of Charlie Parker is that every alto sax player at one time or another wants to play like Bird. His compositions (Yardbird Suite, Ornithology, etc.) are staples. The chord changes were innovative then as they still are today. The combination of Parker and Gillespie was electrifying and unique in the way that they played rapid-fire lines in unison. Bebop was probably one of the most intellectualized developments in jazz and certainly Charlie Parker was both an important ingredient in its development and in its mysticism.

Dizzy Gillespie

John Birks (Dizzy) Gillespie was born in Cheraw, South Carolina, on October 21, 1917. He studied trombone at the age of 14 and trumpet one year later. He also studied harmony and music theory in North Carolina. In 1935 he moved to Philadelphia, where he played his first jobs. He joined the Teddy Hill band in 1937 and took his first trip to Europe. He was a free-lance musician in New York when he started with the Cab Calloway band in 1939. He worked in succession with Ella Fitzgerald, Benny Carter, Charlie Barnett, and Les Hite. In 1943, he was with Earl Hines and in 1944 with Billy Eckstine. He formed his own small combo in 1945 and then a big band in the same year. He has played with small combos from five to seven musicians since the big band broke up in 1950. He was the first jazz musician to tour for the U.S. State Department in 1956.

Dizzy Gillespie was innovative as early as 1939 in that he created trumpet lines that were continuous melodies; typically the trumpet had not been used to play melodic lines. The acoustic property of the trumpet suggests skipping melodies rather than continuous scalar melodies, as in bebop. Gillespie and Parker met in New York City in 1945, having traveled the same evolutionary path, but on different instruments.

There are, of course, "Diz" tunes as there are "Bird" tunes. As well, Gillespie is a classic entertainer, in some ways resembling Louis Armstrong; he was always a charismatic performer. One of Gillespie's trademarks is a special trumpet with a turned-up bell.

Suggested Listening

1. "Dizzy Gillespie: Development of an American Artist 1940–1946"   Smithsonian P213455
2. "Rollins/Stitt Session"   Verve 2505
3. "One Night in Birdland"   COL. JG-34808

Chapter 13
Cool Jazz

"Cool jazz" is one of the more intriguing terms in jazz history. Although the general style has many similarities to bebop playing, most cool jazz pieces do not sound like bebop. The term was chosen to describe music which was relaxed by comparison to bebop, but in reality "cool" was used to classify many diversified styles. Although there were a number of musicians who played in what would be called cool style prior to the use of the term, such as Lester Young, tenor sax, and Dave Brubeck, piano, the Miles Davis' recording "Birth of the Cool" (1949–1950) would ultimately name this style of playing. Cool started on the East Coast with the Davis recording and with East Coast ensembles, but in the 1950s a West Coast style of playing developed which was perhaps more cool in characteristics than subsequent developments by players in the East, many of whom evolved into hard bop and funky (see chapter 14). Probably the best way to define cool is in relationship to bebop, which has always had a certain "hot" quality to it.

The word "cool," when used to describe a person, refers to someone who is "hip" and relaxed, someone who does not show much emotion. The difference between this and someone who is "hot" is obvious. Bebop is often described as "hot" music.

The characteristics that define cool jazz are as follows: (1) greater emphasis on arrangements and unusual textures, (2) melodic counterpoint, (3) less use of high notes on melody instruments, (4) subdued tonal quality, and (5) slower tempos than in bebop. West coast jazz characteristics as separate from cool jazz carried the digression from bebop one step further. Although they continued to use the harmonic changes of bebop, they developed smoother solo lines without the angularity and surprise elements of bebop.

My preference is to lump cool and West Coast together into one style and to see cool jazz in general as a logical extension of bebop, similar in many ways but different in others. If one accepts the notion that cool jazz is simply a development of bebop, then it becomes possible to see its invention in practical terms.

However, there is another point of view that deserves representation. Cool jazz can be seen as an academic musical activity. In fact, college and university music departments grew demonstrably after World War II, and an interest on the part of "serious" or orchestral composers in the wealth of jazz materials increased. Cool jazz also contains musical compositions that were primarily orchestrations, many of which depended on the use of traditional orchestral instruments, such as the french horn and strings. Some of the first schools to recognize jazz as a legitimate new style were the City College of Los Angeles, North Texas State University, and the Berklee College of Music in Boston. Others would follow later.

This was not the first time that jazz musicians showed an interest in classical music. Bix Beiderbecke and his colleagues explored French Impressionism in the 1920s, and Duke Ellington wrote orchestral-type arrangements prior to the emergence of cool jazz. However, jazz concerts began to be presented at Carnegie Hall and on college campuses in the 1940s. If one accepts the point of view that cool jazz sprang from a more intellectual approach to music, then one would probably also assert that cool jazz logically led to third-stream music, which is jazz in a classical or orchestral setting.

Bebop changes the relationship between the musician and the audience; at least, it caused audiences to become smaller. In many ways, cool jazz as it was practiced by East Coast musicians, like Miles Davis (Chicago) and Lennie Tristano (New York), and by Tristano's student, Lee Konitz, was simply an extension of the jazz player's bohemian image, but in a slightly more relaxed style. These East Coast players performed bebop tunes and cool tunes one right after another. They were not thought of as different styles, but rather simply contrast pieces.

What separates the two styles is the practice of arranging some bebop tunes so that the instruments blend to create unusual textures, in a sense, like big band music. "Boplicity" is a good example of this. A bebop tune has a fast-paced melodic "head" at the beginning, which is played in unison, and then the solos begin. Cool has a well-constructed ensemble playing the melody in harmonies at the beginning before the solos. Speed and the arrangement of the beginning melody are the two primary differences between the bebop and cool jazz on the East Coast. The analyzed tune, "Subconscious Lee," is an excellent example of a piece that is somewhere in between. It has cool aspects to it, but it is fast enough to be considered a bebop tune.

One of the significant impacts of early cool jazz was a slight expansion of the jazz audience. In some senses, although probably not intended by the musicians who created the style, cool jazz was more pleasing to the average listener because of its softer nature and its lower intensity level. West Coast jazz, in particular, did have popular appeal and regained some of the audience which bebop had lost.

East Coast cool music was produced by Miles Davis, George Shearing, the Modern Jazz Quartet, Tristano, and Konitz. Konitz in particular became a model for alto players; his tone is very breathy and light textured, very unlike alto players Johnny Hodges and Benny Carter, or even Charlie Parker, for that matter. Lennie Tristano influenced other pianists and musicians as well because he taught privately. One major influence he had was on Bill Evans.

Of course, the arrangers for the nine-piece ensembles that played on the Miles Davis "Birth of the Cool" session were very significant in that they represented for that concept the very best of the available arrangers: Johnny Carisi, Miles Davis, Gil Evans, John Lewis, and Gerry Mulligan. My opinion is that Gil Evans was the real genius, but all of them wrote fine pieces. Beginning in the 1950s, Mulligan became the premier baritone sax player, until Mulligan Harry Carney of the Ellington band and Serge Chalof (of Woody Herman's band, Second Herd) were the only baritone sax players of any fame. Mulligan played in a variety of styles, moving from swing to cool and bebop with great ease.

Like bebop a few years earlier, East Coast cool was a group effort, albeit a small group. Certain musicians, the foremost of which was Miles Davis, worked toward a new mode of communication. Although cool had strong roots in bebop, there was something new about it, primarily the genius of the arrangements and the relaxation of the

Gil Evans

music. Miles had first been important during the bebop time, although he was still quite young at the time. With cool, he began to assert his musical leadership. Interestingly enough, he was also the prime mover for the creation of jazz/rock in the late 1960s (see chapter 16). Davis emerged as a strong, influential, and assertive soloist when he teamed up with John Coltrane, Red Garland, Paul Chambers, and Philly Joe Jones in the mid-1950s.

WEST COAST INFLUENCES

Although for purposes of this chapter, we are considering West Coast jazz a part of cool, in some senses it is slightly different. West Coast jazz is more relaxed than cool jazz of the East Coast variety, and, generally speaking, some West Coast musicians carried the principle further away from bebop. However, for all practical purposes, they are part of a continuum of evolution moving further from bebop.

At first, the significant West Coast musicians centered around Dave Brubeck, who had already created a type of cool music as early as 1946, and around Gerry Mulligan, who had been involved in Davis's experiments. Interestingly, Brubeck and Mulligan would continue to work together for some time. The prototype alto player for West Coast jazz was Paul Desmond, who played with the Brubeck quartet. Desmond had a very distinctive tone, even drier in character

Gerry Mulligan

than that of Lee Konitz. And when he played, he seemed to pick melodic snatches of melody out of the air; he used silence very effectively. Yet his improvisations were extremely pleasing and also had popular appeal. As well, Brubeck's experimentation with unusual time meters, such as 5/4 and 7/4, gave the Brubeck group a unique sound.

There was a variety of significant musicians who played more or less in the cool, West Coast jazz style. These included the following: trumpet, Chet Baker, Conte Candoli, Shorty Rogers; trombone, Bob Brookmeyer; tenor sax, Stan Getz, Jimmy Giuffre (who wrote "Four Brothers" for Woody Herman), Dave Pell, Zoot Sims; alto sax, Lennie Niehaus (Kenton), Art Pepper, Bud Shank; guitar, Barney Kessel, piano, Vince Guaraldi, Andre Previn; bass, Carson Smith, Eugene Wright; and drums, Chico Hamilton, Mel Lewis, Shelly Manne, and Joe Morello.

A number of California-based musicians became interested in using music from other countries, in particular Dave Brubeck, as shown in his series of jazz albums based on music from Mexico, Japan, and other countries, and Stan Kenton. Later examples certainly include the Toshiko Akiyoshi/Lew Tabackin Big Band with its Japanese influences. Cool jazz as it was practiced on the West Coast began to broaden the definition of jazz materials, also including Western art music and contemporary "serious" compositions. For instance, Dave Brubeck has also written concert choral works.

Paul Desmond

In conclusion, cool jazz is a logical and diversified extension of bebop. The West Coast variant on this style was even more relaxed and at times more ethereal than the East Coast version, which was actually closer to bebop, except in arranging style. Probably the most important developments of cool or West Coat jazz was the arranging concept and its implications, the use of other types of music, and the creation of new bridges to the audience.

MUSICAL
ANALYSIS

"Body and Soul"
Gene Norman's "Just Jazz" Featuring Red Norvo and Stan Getz (SCCJ F-10)

This composition uses trumpet, alto sax, tenor sax, vibraphone, piano, electric guitar, bass, and drums. The featured soloists are Stan Getz on tenor sax, Red Norvo on vibraphone and Nat "King" Cole on piano; Louis Bellson is the drummer. Recorded in 1947 in Pasadena, California, this example of West Coast jazz has definite cool musical traits, especially in the styles of Norvo and Getz. In the key of Db, the tempo is a slow 78. This piece also gives a rare glimpse of Nat "King" Cole playing jazz piano; he is primarily known as a pop singer, starting in the late 1940s.

Stan Getz

The recording on the Smithsonian Collection is an excerpt of a longer piece; it starts with the back half of the vibraphone solo and continues through to the end. The chord changes suggest a thirty-two-measure unit, which is repeated twice. Note the double-time feel in the B section of the piano solo.

A1
Xylophone

```
eb Bb7 eb D7 Db eb    f  Eo    eb  F7      bb Eb7eb  Ab7 DbBb7
// /!  // // // //     // //    ////////    /  /  /    /   ////
1      2   3           4        5   6       7          8
```

A2

```
eb  Bb7  bb  D7 Db eb    f  Eo   eb  F7      bb eb Ab7  DbA7
// /!    //  // // //     // //   ////////    //  /  /    ////
1        2   3           4   5   6           7          8
```

B
Tenor Sax

D	e	f♯	g	D	A7	D		d	G7	e	eb	d	G7	C7B7Bb7
//	//	//	//	//	//	////	//	//	//	//	//	//	////
1		2		3		4	5		6		7		8	

A3
Piano

eb	Bb7	bb	D7	Db	eb	f	Eo	eb	F7		bb	eb	Ab7	DbBb7
//	//	//	//	//	//	// //	////////	//	/	/	////
1		2		3		4	5	6		7		8	

A1
Piano

eb	Bb7	eb	D7	Db	eb	f	Eo	eb	F7		bb	Eb7	eb	Ab7	DbBb7
//	//	//	// //	//	// //	////////	/	/	/	/	////
1		2		3		4	5	6	7			8	

A2

eb	Bb7	bb	D7	Db	eb	f	Eo	eb	F7		bb	eb	Ab7	DbA7
//	//	//	// //	//	// //	////////	//	/	/	////
1		2		3		4	5	6		7		8	

B
Piano (Double-Time Feel)

D	e	f♯	g	D	A7	D	d	G7	e	eb	d	G7	C7B7Bb7
//	//	//	//	//	//	////	// //	//	//	//	//	/ / //
1		2		3		4	5		6		7		8	

A3   **Trp. Cadenza to**
Group   **Chord**

eb	Bb7	bb	D7	Db	eb	f	Eo	eb	F7		bb	D9	Db
//	//	//	// //	//	//	//	////////	//	held	held
	2		3		4		5	6		7		8	

SIDE-NOTES

Lennie Tristano

Leonard Joseph (Lennie) Tristano was born in Chicago on March 19, 1919, and died in New York on November 18, 1978. As a youth he had weak vision and was blind by the age of 9. He played woodwind instruments and the piano. He attended the American Conservatory of Music and began playing piano professionally in clubs at the age of 12. He moved to New York in 1946, where he ultimately hooked up with Lee Konitz (alto sax), Billy Bauer (guitar), and others. Originally influenced by Earl Hines, Tristano developed a tonally rich yet thin style of playing the piano, in short the personification of cool.

Tristano opened a teaching studio in 1951, and, besides the occasional club or concert appearance he primarily taught. However, Tristano's lasting influence was his revelation that the piano could be used to impart moods and not just function as a rhythm or solo instrument. His influence on modal improvisation is especially important; this style, which Tristano and his group developed, allowed the sonorities of the piano to be heard.

Miles Davis

Miles Dewey Davis Jr. was born in Alton, Illinois, on May 25, 1926; he moved to St. Louis when he was 1 year old. His parents were well off, as his father was a dentist. He played trumpet in his high school band. He played locally from 1941 through 1944 and was influenced early by Clark Terry. When the Eckstine band played in St. Louis in 1944, Davis met Parker and Gillespie. His father sent him to study at Juilliard in 1945, and he was soon working with Gillespie and Parker in small clubs. He toured with Benny Carter, and in 1946–1947 he spent time touring with the Eckstine band. Back in New York, he began leading his own groups.

In 1948 he put together a nine-piece ensemble made up of trumpet, trombone, tuba, alto sax, baritone sax, French horn, piano, bass, and drums. Gil Evans and Gerry Mulligan wrote arrangements for this unusual sound, and this band was responsible for the invention of the cool sound. Although this particular ensemble and its recordings were not commercially successful, their influence was vast. Davis then played with a variety of small groups and a nineteen-piece reunion group in the late 1950s that had more far-reaching popularity. In the late 1960s Davis moved into fusion and rock-influenced music. In the 1970s he became reclusive and made few public appearances. He returned in the 1980s to make recordings and motor scooter television commercials, and to win awards.

Miles Davis was one of the most popular jazz musicians of the 1950s and was also extremely important to the development of jazz/rock. The list of his band members over the years is formidable, and his style of playing continues to influence other players. The continuing development of his style from bebop to cool to modal to fusion is an intriguing case study in jazz development in general.

Suggested Listening

1. "The Complete Birth of the Cool"   Capitol N-16168
2. "Crosscurrents"   Capitol M-11060
3. "Genius of Gerry Mulligan"   Pacific Jazz PJ-8
4. "Time Out"   COL. CS-8192

Chapter 14
Hard Bop

BASIC STYLE

Hard Bop is primarily a Midwest and East Coast playing style that followed directly from bebop. It is also called simply bebop, bop, or occasionally funky, which is in fact one of its traits. However, the use of the term *funky* is confusing because of the appearance of a rock style called "funk" a decade later. Fortunately, hard bop can be defined fairly precisely, although clearly it has many bebop characteristics.

Unlike cool jazz and West Coast jazz, which follow bebop tangentially, hard bop evolved directly out of bebop style. And many hard bop (funky) style musicians were in fact beboppers before the term "hard bop" came into existence. The main charcteristics of hard bop are as follows: (1) tone colors used by melody instruments are hard edged and heavy in texture; (2) improvisations are melodically complicated with massive density (almost like a sheet of sound); (3) some hard bop used blueslike elements that conveyed Afro-American (funky) characteristics. In particular, blues became popular again, especially the use of flatted thirds, fifths, and other altered notes. The funky aspect of hard bop comes from the use of these altered tones and the tendency for funky players to emphasize those notes by accents or length. Also, the rhythm section and the horn players emphasize a laid-back beat 2 and 4 in four-beat measures; the second and fourth beats are actually played a little late.

Hard bop melody players accepted as role models the alto sax style of Charlie Parker, who had a very raw-edged alto sound, the tenor sax sound of Don Byas, Dexter Gordon, and Sonny Stitt, the trumpet sound of Clifford Brown, and, to an extent, Miles Davis, the trombone

Donald Byrd

sound of J. J. Johnson. The major bebop rhythm players were the inspirations for hard bop rhythm players, particularly Max Roach (drums); in many cases, the rhythm players were beboppers first and became hard boppers later.

Interestingly, Philadelphia and Detroit seemed to be the centers for developing hard bop players, with a few exceptions. Philadelphia contributed Clifford Brown (trumpet), McCoy Tyner (piano), Philly Joe Jones (drums), and John Coltrane (tenor and soprano sax), among others. Cannonball Adderley was from Philadelphia, as were Michael and Randy Brecker (see chapter 19). Detroit produced the Jones brothers (Thad, Elvin, and Hank), Ron Carter (bass), Yusef Lateef, Donald Byrd, and Pepper Adams, among others.

Hard bop was played throughout the United States, but it had the least influence on the West Coast. Hard bop was more organized than bebop and less organized than cool jazz was. The typical ensemble would use piano, bass, and drums with two melody instruments, usually sax and piano, although there were other combinations. In the funky style, the main melody was played by the horn players, either in unison or in fourths, and then they proceeded to solo, usually including the pianist.

The funky style was actually present in hard bop, although players like John Coltrane seemed to balance the scales. In funky style, the ensembles quite often used Latin beats (such as many tunes by Horace Silver). There also existed a sense of working out the way the

John Coltrane

melody would be played in advance. There were no hard bop arrangements, as there was in cool jazz, but the pieces were played in an organized fashion and were somewhat predictable. A major influence on funky style was gospel piano playing; in turn, funky style influenced contemporary gospel piano playing of the 1970s and 1980s.

Generally speaking hard bop had more variety in its organizational structures than funky. Bebop used either the blues progression or a ballad AABA over thirty-two measures (sometimes simply doubled to sixty-four). Hard bop used all sorts of combinations of eight-, twelve-, and sixteen-measure phrases (see analyses for examples). As a result, hard bop players, in their improvised solos, tended to rely somewhat less on standard formulas and to play more extended solos, overlapping phrases, and nonharmonic tones. Hard bop is hard to play, but it is also very flexible in its materials.

Some of the important hard bop musicians are as follows: trumpet, Nat Adderley, Clifford Brown, Donald Byrd, Freddie Hubbard, Thad Jones; tenor saxophone, John Coltrane, Joe Henderson, Yusef Lateef, Sonny Rollins, Wayne Shorter (see chapter 17), and Stanley Turrentine; alto sax, Cannonball Adderley, Jackie McLean, Phil Woods; trombone, Curtis Fuller, J. J. Johnson; piano, Ramsey Lewis, Horace Silver; bass, Paul Chambers, Percy Heath, Sam Jones; guitar, Kenny Burrell, Wes Montgomery; drums, Art Blakey (and his jazz messengers), Al Heath, Elvin Jones, Philly Joe Jones, Max Roach. The significance of Art Blakey and his Jazz Messengers cannot be overstated; some have said that he held the hard bop movement together through his group.

CHAPTER 14

Horace Silver

Hard bop as a style had its greatest impact on other musicians and a fairly small listening audience (analagous to bebop in the 40s). Funkier tunes, like Horace Silver's "Song for My Father," enjoyed greater popularity with listening audiences, primarily because of the catchy tune.

Hard bop has contributed many jazz standards, because most of the pieces that hard boppers recorded were original songs written for that style. That logically follows from the fact that hard bop is a fairly organized style in performance. There is, of course, improvisation, but the ensemble presented structured, rather than free, experimentation.

The career of John Coltrane clearly began in the hard bop era, although he played everything from cool (in "So What") in the fifties to a somewhat free-form rhapsody style in the sixties. Two tunes that clearly fit the hard bop style were "Pristine," which Coltrane recorded with Art Blakey, and "Grand Central," which he recorded with Cannonball Adderley. He developed a number of techniques that influenced many other saxophonists, including: (1) a very powerful and hard-edged sound; (2) an improvisational style that, in the early period, was filled with tension and many notes; (3) a tendency to leave the harmonic implications, and play sheets of sound in a melodic fashion; (4) extensive use of high register and "altissimo" register (notes above the traditional range of the instrument); (5) screeches and honks that made use of multiphonics (pitches consisting of more

Art Blakey

than one note or harmonics); (6) extended harmonies or early bitonality; (7) the use of pedal points in Latin American or non-Western pieces (one long held note as the central harmony rather than a moving bass line); (8) increased emphasis on soprano saxophone; and (9) in later work, increased interest in spirituality and mystical communication. Many of the later characteristics are present in the pieces he performed in the modal jazz style (based on historical scales from the Middle Ages and Renaissance or church modes as well as Indian and Oriental scales).

Sonny Rollins is also a prototype hard bopper, with more funky overtones. Horace Silver is everybody's hard bop piano player, and Clifford Brown is the trumpet player. Although Dizzy Gillespie had introduced the concept of using Latin rhythms in original jazz compositions, hard boppers codified the practice.

Hard bop has had tremendous influence in jazz if for no other reason than the experimentation in the use of tone color. The comparison between the tone color of hard bop players and West Coast players describes the gamut of possible tone variation. Hard bop also influenced the development of jazz/rock and the ultimate use of electronics in jazz and rock. Some hard bop musicians went on to make significant contributions to jazz in later years in other styles.

"Watermelon Man"
Herbie Hancock

This piece uses tenor sax (Dexter Gordon), trumpet (Freddie Hubbard), piano (Hancock), bass (Butch Warren), and drums (Billy Higgins) and was recorded in 1961. The tempo is 130, and the piece is in F. The trumpet and tenor solos are the best, as Herbie Hancock was fairly young at this point. The piece itself is a sixteen-bar blues progression with an eight-measure introduction.

The chord changes are 1,1,1,1,4,4,1,1,5,4,5,4,5,4,1,1. The regular twelve-bar progression is extended by repeating measures 9 and 10. It is obviously a solo vehicle in funky style. Listen carefully to the rhythm section introduction, as that particular figure has been stolen by countless rock musicians.

Rhythm (Introduction)

```
F7
1    2    3    4    5    6    7    8
```

A
Melody—Tenor/Trumpet   brk.

```
||: F7          Bb7      F7      C7  Bb7  C7  Bb7  C7  Bb7  F7   :||
   1   2    3  4 5    6   7   8 9    10    11   12   13   14   15  16
```

A
Three Times
Trumpet Solo   brk.

```
||: F7          Bb7      F7      C7  Bb7  C7  Bb7  C7  Bb7  F7   :||
   1   2    3  4 5    6   7   8 9    10    11   12   13   14   15  16
```

A
Four Times
Tenor Solo   brk.

```
||: F7          Bb7      F7      C7  Bb7  C7  Bb7  C7  Bb7  F7   :||
   1   2    3  4 5    6   7   8 9    10    11   12   13   14   15  16
```

A
Piano Solo   brk.

```
||: F7          Bb7      F7      C7  Bb7  C7  Bb7  C7  Bb7  F7   :||
   1   2    3  4 5    6   7   8 9    10    11   12   13   14   15  16
```

A
Melody—Tenor/Trumpet   brk.

```
||: F7          Bb7      F7      C7  Bb7  C7  Bb7  C7  Bb7  F7 :||
   1   2    3  4 5    6   7   8 9    10    11   12   13   14   15 16
```

Rhythm (Introduction)

F7   to fade out ....

1   2   3   4   5   6   7   8   9   10   11   12   13   14   15   16

SIDE-NOTES   ### Horace Silver

Horace Ward Martin Tavares Silver was born in Norwalk, Connecticut, on September 2, 1928. He played sax in the high school band and studied piano privately. He played local jobs while in high school and after graduation. Stan Getz heard Silver and took him on the road with him in 1950–1951. Silver then moved to New York City, where he worked with Art Blakey in 1951–1952, Terry Gibbs and Coleman Hawkins in 1952, and Oscar Pettiford and Lester Young in 1953. In September of 1956 he formed his own ensemble, with which he achieved fame as a funky/hard bop player. In the 1960s he moved into soul, and in the 1970s into Latin American music. Always a composer and songwriter, he has written a number of original compositions; he has been known primarily for songwriting since the mid-1970s.

An explosive player, Silver has evolved through various stages. Although most of his standards, including "Song for My Father" and "Nica's Dream," are clearly in the funky style, his solos have changed over time. Early in his career, he played clearly in late bebop style. Later he turned to more angular and percussive phrasing, and finally, in the 1950s, to the funky style, using lowered fifths and blues notes. In some senses a fusion player, the influences of soul and Latin American music affected his playing technique later in the sixties and seventies. He also showed great versatility.

SIDE-NOTES   ### Max Roach

Maxwell Roach was born in Brooklyn on January 10, 1925. He began working with Charlie Parker in 1942 and made his first recording, with Coleman Hawkins, in 1944. Also in 1944 he worked with Dizzy Gillespie in New York and in California with Benny Carter. From 1947 to 1949, Roach was the drummer with the Charlie Parker quintet and while still quite a young man became the premiere bebop drummer. His trademark became the use of the cymbal rather than the bass drum, for fluidity, speed, and lightness in drumming style. This choice of instrument fits bebop, since a heavy feel should be avoided.

In the 1950s, Roach moved easily into the hard bop style of playing, mostly with Clifford Brown until Brown's death in 1956. Roach has been on the international music scene since he first accompanied Bird and Diz in 1949 to the Paris Jazz Festival. He continued to perform through the 1960s in small combos, began a percussion ensemble for recordings, and began teaching at the University of Massachusetts in 1972. A very warm-hearted individual, he has been extensively involved in jazz education and in doing clinic work. Stylistically, he undoubtedly is one of the most significant jazz drummers in influence and impact.

Suggested Listening

1. "Clifford Brown—The Quintet"   Emarcy EMS2 403
2. "Saxophone Colossus and More"   Prestige 24050
3. "Best of Horace Silver"   Blue Note 84325
4. "My Favorite Things"   Atlantic SD 1361
5. "Giant Steps"   Atlantic SD 1311
6. "Soultrane"   Prestige 7531

Chapter 15
Free Jazz

Free jazz is a conscious attempt by a fairly small number of musicians to create music that breaks with traditional practice, in particular the practice of controlling improvisation through specific chord changes and progressions. In some senses, free jazz in the 1950s and 1960s was a logical extension of bebop, in its art music conception of musical function. Beboppers consciously tried to create music that was artistically elite; free jazz musicians carried that conception one step further. Whereas first beboppers, then cool and later hard bop and funky musicians purposefully made chord changes more complex and further divergent from the original sources, free jazz musicians broke with tradition completely.

Free jazz was an attempt to make a sociological statement; many of its earliest practitioners were black musicians on the edge of black power elitism. Free was similar to bebop in its musical separatism. A significant amount of black pride is evident in the work of Don Ayler, Archie Shepp and John Coltrane, as well as in the music of Ornette Coleman, Eric Dolphy, and Don Cherry. But aside from the black issue, free jazz was progressive music that attempted to find new methods by which to communicate and improvise. Free jazz altered the standards for judging jazz performance, and it has had a deeply felt influence on jazz that followed the invention of free jazz models in the early sixties.

The theory behind free jazz is complete freedom in improvisation. Of course, complete freedom is humanly impossible, but the idea is for the improvisor to play whatever he or she desires without respect to chord changes or a previously conceived melody. Free jazz also implies collective free improvisation in which every member of the ensemble simply plays whatever comes into his or her head. In practice, free jazz does have an inherent logic to it. Normally it has an underlying pulse that is fairly regular. In the Ornette Coleman

Bobby McFerrin. Photo used by permission of Dr. John Kuzmich, photographer. Taken at the 1988 meeting of the National Association of Jazz Educators, Detroit, MI.

Art Ensemble of Chicago. Photo used by permission of Dr. John Kuzmich, photographer. Taken at the 1988 meeting of the National Association of Jazz Educators, Detroit, MI.

Wayne Shorter. Photo used by permission of John Sobczak, Lorien Studio, Bloomfield Hills, MI 48013, John Sobczak, photographer. Taken at Montreux-Detroit Jazz Festival, 1987.

Sheila Jordan. Photo used by permission of John Sobczak, Lorien Studio, Bloomfield Hills, MI 48013, John Sobczak, photographer. Taken at Montreux-Detroit Jazz Festival, 1987.

David Balker. Permission granted by David Balker.

Sonny Rollins. Photo used by permission of John Sobczak, Lorien Studio, Bloomfield Hills, MI 48013, John Sobczak, photographer. Taken at Montreux-Detroit Jazz Festival, 1987.

Maynard Ferguson. Photo
used by permission of
John Sobczak, Lorien
Studio, Bloomfield Hills,
MI 48013, John Sobczak,
photographer. Taken at
Montreux-Detroit Jazz
Festival, 1986.

Wynton Marsalis. Photo
used by permission of
John Sobczak, Lorien
Studio, Bloomfield Hills,
MI 48013, John Sobczak,
photographer. Taken at
Montreux-Detroit Jazz
Festival, 1987.

Bunky Green, Chicago State University. Photo taken at North Sea Jazz Festival, Summer 1987. Permission granted by Bunky Green.

Sundiata, *left,* and Dizzy Gillespie. Photo used by permission of John Sobczak, Lorien Studio, Bloomfield Hills, MI 48013, John Sobczak, photographer. Taken at Montreux-Detroit Jazz Festival, 1987.

Ernie Rodgers. Photo used by permission of John Sobczak, Lorien Studio, Bloomfield Hills, MI 48013, John Sobczak, photographer. Taken at Montreux-Detroit Jazz Festival, 1987.

Dizzy Gillespie. Photo used by permission of John Sobczak, Lorien Studio, Bloomfield Hills, MI 48013, John Sobczak, photographer. Taken at Montreux-Detroit Jazz Festival, 1987.

J. C. Heard. Photo used
by permission of John
Sobczak, Lorien Studio,
Bloomfield Hills, MI
48013, John Sobczak,
photographer. Taken at
Montreux-Detroit Jazz
Festival, 1987.

groups, for example, the bass player tends to play a continuous bass line. There are no preset chord changes, and for the most part there are few implied chords, even by chance. Players tend to play recognizable pieces of melodies, but the musicians tend to feel quite free to play continuous collective improvisations (see analysis of a piece by the World Saxophone Quartet in the Appendix).

We will be discussing jazz that does not conform to traditional organizational logic. Theoretically, there are no blues or ballad progressions in free jazz, no regular structure, phrases, or measures, although one will hear quite often brief suggestions of blues melodies or recognizable tunes. Free jazz is not random, nor is it completely chaotic.

There have been very few players of true free jazz. John Coltrane is often mentioned as a significant free player, and in fact some of his pieces from the sixties have great flexibility in their harmonic conception. However, most of those pieces are actually free rhapsodic playing on top of one chord or a note played by bass or piano; many of the same pieces can be described as modal jazz. In that sense, they are really not free jazz, although we have used as an analysis piece for this chapter a piece that is a free rhapsody based upon a mode.

Some of the major figures in free jazz are as follows: tenor sax, Albert Ayler, Pharoah Sanders; alto sax, Eric Dolphy, Ornette Coleman; woodwinds, Anthony Braxton, Archie Shepp; trumpet, Don Ayler, Don

Cherry, Freddie Hubbard; piano, Keith Jarrett, Sun Ra (and his Arkestra), Cecil Taylor; drums, Sunny Murray (Cecil Taylor), Andrew Cyrille (Cecil Taylor), Elvin Jones, Jack DeJohnette; and bass, Charlie Haden, Scott LaFaro, Charles Mingus.

Some people have claimed that Eric Dolphy, had he lived longer, would have been one of the most important players in modern jazz. A very innovative woodwind player on a variety of instruments including bass clarinet, Dolphy indeed had mammoth playing technique. He played in a straight ahead bluesy alto style and in free form. Unfortunately, however, he died at the early age of 36 in 1964. However, the two most significant musician-composer-leaders were Ornette Coleman and Cecil Taylor. The music created by these two is actually quite different and manifests two different aspects of relatively controlled freedom.

The music of Cecil Taylor is organized around group arrangements that take over when two musicians play a preconceived signal to trigger the return. In this sense, Cecil Taylor used concepts found in chance music of the late 1950s; chance music is an aspect of "classical art" music. In between the preconceived sections, the orchestra improvises with no sense of traditional timekeeping. In particular, the drummer plays all parts of the drum set in rapid-fire and nonrhythmic style. Most of the improvisation is collective and is based on creating sheets of constant sound.

As a pianist, Taylor created long, jagged melodies that are constantly unresolved, in some senses like a progressive Theolonius Monk. The general purpose of his music seems to be to create textures that happen as a result of constant activity on the part of the players. This is very high energy music and although it is not free in the true sense of the word, it does produce nonharmonic and nontempoed music.

Ornette Coleman is the musician around whom the entire free jazz movement seems to have been built; Coleman has continued to play in that style into the 1980s. An alto sax player, Ornette Coleman created a style based on no harmonic changes. He eliminated the use of piano and guitar because they generally play harmonies. Also a prolific composer, he has written original tunes, many of which have been used as melodic material in free jazz composition performances.

Free jazz does contain recognizable melodies, but they are used somewhat spontaneously. Recognizable melodies are sometimes preconceived in particular pieces, although their exact position within the piece is not planned, nor is the key or rhythmic configuration. In that sense, preconceived or recognizable melodies function as organizational events for the musicians, and they also function as material from which musical responses and variations spring during the production of free jazz. The musicians are also controlled to a certain extent by their musical training and environment, as well as by physical limitations of the fingers and body to produce certain tones in combination. Therefore, there is a predictability about free jazz. Each player tends to fall into certain patterns; one can hear the bass player, Charlie Haden, do this in "Free Jazz" (see analysis).

Ornette Coleman

Occasionally, one can hear quotes from other pieces of music, such as popular songs. Free jazz musicians also tend to use altered scales to confuse or destroy tonality. This has prompted some critics to suggest that the use of non-Western classical music has a third-stream quality. There can be no question that free jazz players, especially Coleman and Taylor, had philosophical reasons for doing the things they did. They did use other sources, which might partially justify the use of the term "third-stream" for free jazz, but the term is not specific enough to describe what Coleman did.

The main point of free jazz in general and Ornette Coleman's music in particular is that melody is primary and harmony is almost nonexistent. In traditional chord-based jazz, the relationship is about equal. But within the melodically conceived organization, both improvised and precomposed, key relationships exist that are consciously and unconsciously ordered by the soloists or the interaction of soloists.

The general commandment of free jazz is that musicians are compelled to listen to one another and to respond appropriately to what they hear. Of course, that is generally true of jazz, but the functions are normally well defined. That is, the bass player plays a walking bass; the piano player plays chords; the saxophone plays solos. In free jazz, each idea played by one musician has a chance to become the focal point for all the musicians to treat collectively, and for an indeterminate time.

Don Cherry

Perhaps this term, "indeterminate," best explains free jazz. The music is allowed to last as long as the idea sustains it, rather than a certain number of times through the progression. Musicians who play this style constantly try out new ideas or sample melodies. If they are picked up, then other people will join in, interpreting or varying the idea. If one idea does not work, then that musician will try another one. In short, free jazz is open elaboration and collaboration rather than complete random chaos.

In this sense, "Free Jazz" by Ornette Coleman (see analysis in Appendix B) is a very controlled piece. It is not without key feeling; you can sing one-chord notes if you try. It does have a definite tempo from time to time. It has sections of solo material, collective improvisation, structured melodies, and tension and release. The example in the Smithsonian collection is only one example, but it has all the elements of the free jazz style.

It is important to realize that Ornette Coleman was influenced by bebop musicians, particularly Charlie Parker. His alto sound is very unusual; at one time, he used a plastic saxophone. He has gone to great lengths to avoid any control from established musical practices, yet his music does show clear influence from both bebop and the blues. Coleman once said that his playing improved "the minute he learned that it was all right to make mistakes."

Charlie Mingus

One influential musician who played with Ornette Coleman was Don Cherry (trumpet). In his playing, he exemplified the technique of free jazz, playing brief outbursts and long melodic lines that were not based on previous models (see analysis of "Congeniality"). Starting in the mid-1960s, Cherry spent much of his time in Europe, recording music that was influenced by East Indian and Oriental scales; thus, he has been a legitimate third-stream composer and musician.

A fair number of later musicians were influenced by free jazz. Good examples are Pat Metheny (guitar) and groups like the World Saxophone Quartet (see chapter 19). But even musicians who do not play in a definitive free jazz style have been influenced by Cherry's technique. The hard-edged tone he employed has been picked up by both jazz and rock players.

In conclusion, free jazz represented a logical development from bebop, although it was clearly rooted in that style. It was not popular music at all and in fact it still is not; this eclectic style is appreciated by only a very small audience. However, one has to appreciate its philosophical construct.

Free jazz musicians were specifically trying to expand the range of musical communication and to explore new methods of artistic interaction. Remembering that the primary responsibility of the

Eric Dolphy
(Woodwinds), playing
Bass Clarinet

free jazz musician was to listen and respond to other ideas presented by fellow musicians, one can see that a high degree of respect and comradery developed in free jazz. And although it had little commercial appeal, it did have quite an influence on future musicians.

MUSICAL
ANALYSIS

"Alabama"
John Coltrane Quartet (SCCJ I-3)

Coltrane's quartet was made up of piano, bass, drums, and tenor sax. This recording was made in 1963. Sounding almost like a spiritual incantation, the piece is composed of a fairly free opening and closing, with a middle section that is countable. The chart form is given for only the beginning and end, with references to the concluding chord changes. For more complicated examples of Ornette Coleman's free jazz, see the analyses in Appendix B.

The middle section uses one set of chords over four measures again and again. The soloist plays in C Dorian scale, which is C D Eb F G A Bb C. Again, the relative freedom of the piece makes standard analysis tough, if not impossible. The bass player uses several unusual "roots" against the basic chord. Listen to the kinds of emotions and sounds John Coltrane evokes, rather than trying to count the beats; by this time, you should be listening for musical quality, not just quantification.

Tenor Sax
Free Opening
Opening Motive   A A B A
Piano/Sax Together C C; the Chord Changes to C' Occur Over
Four Free Measures as Follows:

g7	Ab g7	c7	Ab	c
1		2	3	4

Sax Solo with Pickups (Tempo is 108)
Rhythm Section Enters Playing Time
Three Times   **Fade Out**

‖: Eb7		Abo	c7	Eb7		Abo	c7 ‖:		:‖
1	2	3	4	5	6	7	8		

Free Section Based on Opening
Opening Motive A A B A
Piano/Sax Together C C'
Free Opening with Drum and Cymbol Crashes ‖

John Coltrane

John William Coltrane was born in North Carolina on September 23, 1926, and died in New York on July 17, 1967. Coltrane's father was an amateur musician. The young Coltrane learned to play several instruments in high school. Upon graduation, he moved to Philadelphia, where he went to the Combs Broadstreet Conservatory of Music; Michael Guerra was his saxophone teacher. Coltrane played his first professional job in 1945 and was in a navy band in 1946–1947. His first touring job with a professional group was a rhythm and blues band led by Eddie Vinson. Other groups he played in are as follows: Dizzy (1949–1951), Earl Bostic (1952–1953), Johnny Hodges (1953–1954), Miles Davis (1955–1957), Theolonius Monk, Red Garland, Donald Byrd, and then again with Davis. In 1960, Coltrane founded his own quartet. He experimented with Indian music, modality, and spiritually inspired music until his death in 1967.

Coltrane played in at least two distinctly different stylistic periods before 1960 and after 1960. Before 1960, when he was a member of other ensembles, he almost always played under the direction of other people. And although his style in these early periods is obvious in his strong tone and angular improvisations, he was not the focal point of the groups. In fact, he played conservatively for the time, perhaps owing to his shyness. After 1960, with his own ensemble, he moved much more toward experimentation, longer tunes, free improvisation, and other musical influences. Coltrane was influenced by other people and also has had massive influence on players who followed him. There is no question that he was a technical master and a major inventor. In terms of overall impact on jazz, John Coltrane certainly is one of the most important.

SIDE-NOTES

Ornette Coleman

Ornette Coleman was born in Fort Worth, Texas, on March 19, 1930. He started playing saxophone in high school and began playing in public in the late 1940s. He left home in 1949 and joined the carnival; he then toured with a rhythm-and-blues band, ultimately ending up in New Orleans. Returning to Fort Worth in 1950, he took another job with a rhythm-and-blues band and left that band in Los Angeles. After returning to Fort Worth for two years, he went back to Los Angeles, where he worked as an elevator operator. He also studied music theory and harmony.

Coleman developed an entirely new theory of improvisation based on free tonality, that is, no apparent chord changes. He signed with Atlantic Records, which paid his tuition for School of Jazz in Lenox, Massachusetts in 1959. He then moved to New York City, where he began to be heard by jazz audiences. At first, Ornette Coleman was rejected by jazz enthusiasts; he used a plastic saxophone from which he purposely extracted unusual sounds. However, slowly people realized that he was developing something that was actually inventive and brand new.

Moving further and further away from conscious tonality, he had achieved as complete a freedom as possible by the mid-1960s. He continues to play in the same style today, with more and more recognition. Although not financially successful, Coleman has performed at many jazz festivals. In 1983, he was recognized as being the spiritual godfather of what some rock critics called punk-jazz. While nothing like that was in Ornette Coleman's mind, he did achieve some popularity as a result of it. In the mid-1980s, he collaborated with Pat Methany.

Suggested Listening

1. "Ascension"   MCA 29020
2. "Crescent"   MCA 29016
3. "Cosmic"   MCA 29025
4. "Free Jazz"   Atlantic SD-1364
5. "Song X"   Geffen GHS-24096

Part V
Fusion Jazz

Chapter 16
The Fusion Concept: Funk, Rock, and Disco

JAZZ/ROCK

Chapters 16 through 19 are about jazz styles after the mid-1960s. Many of these styles—at least, elements of them—have been used together to create fusion music. While the term "fusion" is sometimes used to describe a particular musical style, in the context of this book it should be understood as a general term that simply describes any combination of musical styles.

This particular chapter is about a type of fusion music we will call jazz/rock, which has had a major impact on both jazz and rock styles of music since about 1965. The phenomenon seems to have two origins: (1) rock musicians who have developed a jazz sound; and (2) jazz musicians who began using rock devices. Both types are important to the development of jazz/rock and ultimately to the improvement of each form separately. Although some may not agree that jazz has been improved as a result of this melding, there is no question that rock has been improved.

Origins in Rock

Rock and jazz are both, of course, very broad terms. In trying to be specific about the basis for the development of jazz/rock, we should probably limit our discussion to funk and early funk, that is, to groups that play in a black style, first rhythm-and-blues, then soul and gospel, and finally funk. Interestingly, the kinds of rock bands that finally contributed to the development of jazz/rock were riff-oriented bands. Although the popular jazz/rock ensembles were not all black, the origins of the style were.

In the 1950s, James Brown had his first big hit, with "Please, Please, Please," singing with a gospel group called the Famous Flames. He put together the first touring rhythm and blues show, the James Brown Revue, in the late 1950s; this became the model for the Motown Revue and others. This large show featured a big stage band called the JBs. Reminiscent of the types of bands that backed up Ray Charles in the 1950s, the JBs were essentially a riff band with a rock rhythm section. The horns punctuated the singing style with accented and clipped melodic riffs. Stronger than Basie riffs, this style became the predecessor of soul and funk. The bands of James Brown and Ray Charles both played rhythms just slightly behind the beat, which became a characteristic of funk and also jazz/rock.

In the 1960s, Motown was a significant part of the black recording industry. And although many of the Motown hits were patterned after white pop music, the backup musicians, The Funk Brothers, as the rhythm section for Motown was called, played in a very tight and jazz-oriented style. The bass lines were very complicated, which became a trademark of the funk style.

Soul also contributed music influenced by jazz/black gospel, for instance, the recordings of Aretha Franklin (Lady Soul), Otis Redding, and Wilson Pickett. Many of the soul musicians recorded in Memphis, Tennessee, at the Atlantic Records Stax/Volt studio, whose house band was very jazz oriented. Atlantic had done the Ray Charles recordings in New York in the 1950s. Soul music from Memphis, which was an important center for the blues going back into the early 1900s, was stronger than Motown music; some have said that it was more black as well. The studio musicians who backed up soul singers in Memphis in the 1960s were significant in their own right; the Mar-Keys, in 1957, was the first quartet formed out of those musicians. The group that followed them was Booker T (Jones) and the MGs (for Memphis Group). Booker T and the MGs recorded major hits of their own, including one hit from the sound track for "Hang 'Em High."

One example of a technical virtuoso is King Curtis (Curtis Ousley), who was a popular tenor sax player known primarily as the "honking" saxophone player in tunes he recorded with the Coasters and as a singer. He was a session player in Memphis and New York and was also responsible for the backup band for most of Aretha Franklin's early New York work. However, he was also a jazz player with a rich deep tenor sound and very fast technique. He easily could have been another Coltrane or Rollins had he chosen to emphasize that style.

A few Motown artists who developed directly through the lineage of rhythm and blues, and soul to funk also had impact on jazz. Singer Marvin Gaye is certainly one example, as is Stevie Wonder as both a singer and an instrumentalist-arranger. In particular, Stevie Wonder has had a significant impact on jazz players, if for only some of the tunes he has written.

The roots of jazz/rock groups that developed out of the rock or funk tradition are essentially in black-oriented style music that used a riff-oriented backup band. This usually meant an expanded rock band with additional melody instruments; in fact, this tendency to use expanded instrumentation is one characteristic of jazz/rock.

The first really popular band to develop was Blood, Sweat and Tears, a New York group. They formed in New York in 1967 around keyboardist Al Kooper and included the following instruments: keyboards, guitar, bass, drums, saxophone, trombone, and two trumpets. One of the trumpet players was Randy Brecker. The group was conceived as a rock band with touches of jazz, blues, classical, and folk music, although it became essentially a rhythm and blues band with brass. A relatively soft example of jazz/rock, Blood, Sweat and Tears has been extremely popular over time and has released numerous hit records.

The next band to develop was Chicago Transit Authority (later, simply Chicago), which also formed in 1967. Also an eight-piece ensemble, the band often used only one trumpet in arrangements, although Walt Perry played both trumpet and trombone. Chicago was an unusual group in that most of its players were highly trained musicians, some with degrees from music conservatories. Some believe that their music is somewhat mechanical; nonetheless, they have been very successful over a long period (see the analyses).

Earth, Wind and Fire is a black group that normally falls into a funk or Latin/funk classification. However, its roots are clearly in jazz and black/gospel. Started in 1969 in Chicago, the group had as its leader Maurice White, who was the grandson of a New Orleans honky-tonk piano player. Using a varying ensemble that always featured at least two horn players, Earth, Wind and Fire is another jazz/rock-oriented ensemble that was very successful.

Other important bands include the Commodores (jazz/rock disco band of the mid-1970s which included Lionel Richie); Electric Flag (which established itself at the Monterey Pop Festival of 1967); Kool and the Gang (East Coast group that used horns successfully in hits such as "Celebration," "Funky Stuff," and "Jungle Boogie"); the Parliament/Funkadelic group (which is hard-core funk bordering on rap); Santana (whose Mexican guitar player did Latin/rock and also played with John McLaughlin); and Ten Wheel Drive (a ten-piece jazz/rock ensemble that started in 1970).

Origins in Jazz

The distinction between musicians who play rock and jazz and musicians who play fusion jazz/rock is rather arbitrary; this section gives examples of representative jazz musicians who used rock devices in playing jazz and ultimately jazz/rock. Clearly some of these musicians were more influenced by rock than others were, but they have all been recognized for their significance within the jazz/rock movement.

From 1964 to 1968, Miles Davis led a quintet responsible for occasional dips into rock material, although clearly he used rock influences from the soul/gospel and funk evolutionary tree. Some of the musicians he used contributed the following general characteristics of rock. Ron Carter (bass) played repeating bass figures rather than straight walking bass. Tony Williams (drums) played straight eighth notes (even division) rather than the long-short swing feel; his keyboard players of that era—Herbie Hancock (Head Hunters), Josef Zawinul (Weather Report), Chick Corea (Return to Forever)—used electric pianos.

By the time Davis made his "Bitches Brew" album in 1969, he had experimented fully with rock devices, often using young jazz musicians who would later have a major impact on jazz/rock. Davis's band became a meeting ground for several musicians who formed other bands out of those associations.

One of the more overt rock devices that Davis used was multiple drummers, something traditional jazz did not use. Also, Davis's players started using the electric bass guitar rather than the stand-up bass. Electric guitar was used extensively by George Benson and John McLaughlin. Electric piano and organ were also used; both instruments were common in rock and gospel music. But the most significant generalization that one could make was that the Davis bands of that era generally supported the movement toward electronics, a movement atypical of jazz musicians.

When electronics first became available to musicians in the 1930s, they were used sparingly. Of course, amplification was used for radio broadcasting and for television, but generally, acoustic instruments were thought to be better, except for solo-oriented guitar players like Charlie Christian. In other words, musicians through big band and bebop generally felt that the natural sound was better. When rockabilly started in the 1950s, most jazz musicians attempted to move as far away from it as possible. As a result, amplification and electronic instruments were shunned by many serious jazz musicians. In a very important sense, Miles Davis changed that by encouraging young musicians to use electrified instruments.

The use of electronics caused some changes as well. After the mid-sixties, Davis created compositions and recordings that did not rely on extensive chord changes but rather on few harmonic changes. Much of the improvisation (of which there was a great deal) was based on tonal expansion of basic scales. He also used non-Western influences and unusual electronic effects in his own playing. He used an electronic pickup on his trumpet mouthpiece and ran his sound through special equipment to create special electronic effects (see Appendix A—Technical Electronic Terms and Definitions). In short, Miles Davis remained contemporary on a consistent basis. The style of playing had generally changed, and in one very important sense, jazz/rock did create an entirely new improvisational and musical vocabulary and technique.

There are numerous other jazz musicians who were highly significant to the development of jazz/rock from the jazz style. One of the first groups to come out of the Miles Davis association was Lifetime, featuring Tony Williams (drums) and John McLaughlin (guitar); John McLaughlin would eventually form the Mahavishnu Orchestra, which featured electric effects and rapid-fire pyrotechnics plus mysticism (see analysis of "Love Supreme" with McLaughlin and Santana). The Mahavishnu Orchestra included Billy Cobham (Panamanian-born power drummer who influenced hard rock, jazz/rock,

John McLaughlin

Chick Corea

Stanley Clarke

and heavy metal drummers) and violinist Jean-Luc Ponty. A band called the Free Spirits was formed in 1966 and featured Larry Coryell (guitar) and Gary Burton (vibraphone). Chick Corea, another Davis alumnus, formed a group called Return to Forever, which had both artistic and popular success; that group included Stanley Clarke (a premium jazz/rock bass player with phenomenal speed and technique), and guitarist Al DiMeola. The group Spyro Gyra is also worthy of note.

Weather Report is a jazz/rock ensemble that also came out of the Davis organization. Keyboardist and composer Josef Zawinul had played with Cannonball Adderley and then joined Davis. He joined with veteran sax player, Wayne Shorter, who had also played with Davis, to form a highly successful jazz group that had enormous popularity, especially for "Birdland" (see analysis). Weather Report is a prototype jazz/rock ensemble, using a rock rhythm section with jazz-oriented solos. The synthesizer work of Zawinul is most impressive and illustrates the use of electronic devices in jazz.

Interestingly, Zawinul was born in Vienna, Austria and moved to the United States in 1959. He played with Maynard Ferguson, accompanied Dinah Washington, and played with Cannonball Adderly and Miles Davis. In short, he was a fully accomplished and experienced jazz musician, as was Shorter by the time Weather Report was

Weather Report, late
1970's. From left to right:
Josef Zawinul
(Synthesizers and
Keyboards), Wayne
Shorter (Saxophones),
Peter Erskine (Drums),
and Jaco Pastorius (Bass).

formed. Unlike many new phases in musical history, jazz/rock musicians generally had a strong foundation in previous jazz styles before they contributed to the development of a new form. They all seemed to follow the example of Miles Davis, who, after all, was the child prodigy of the beboppers.

INFLUENCES OF JAZZ/ROCK

Jazz/rock fusion continued to influence both jazz and rock; it was also successful in attracting more and more people from the purist ranks as its techniques became more solid. Jazz musicians as pure as Dizzy Gillespie used some rock elements, especially the electric bass. Rock groups were increasingly influenced by the soloistic lines created by jazz and jazz/rock groups.

Probably the biggest influence jazz had on rock was melodic improvisation. Rock, generally speaking, used improvisational techniques that created skipping lines or harmonically conceived variations rather than melodies. Generally, rock melodies were measured in even phrase lengths (that is, four or eight measures). Jazz lines and melodies tend to overlap those units. As a result of jazz/rock, we began to hear rock lines that overlapped those simple phrases, and we also began to hear longer melodies. The compositions of Elton John represent that concept.

Rock had a big influence on jazz through jazz/rock. First of all, the rock rhythm section was functionally different from a jazz rhythm section. Generally it was more homogeneous and less complementary in playing style (remember the Basie rhythm section explanation). Rock bass players tended to play repeating patterns rather than a walking bass pattern. And rock drummers, not the bass player, are in charge of the tempo. The use of rock rhythm style gave jazz/rock ensembles two different styles, which they could use for contrast or in combination.

Jazz/rock created a larger market for records because it appeals to both jazz and rock aficionados. In a sense, it legitimized rock by giving it credibility. It also massively improved the technique necessary to play contemporary rock, as there is no question that the intricate melodic and rhythmic figures which jazz rock musicians play require skill. Careful listening to the bass lines of Stanley Clarke or to some of the horn riffs in Chicago's tunes will illustrate that point.

Perhaps the most important contribution of jazz/rock has been the increasing use of electronics. Jazz has always been slightly elitist, and until Miles Davis and Don Ellis (a big band trumpet player who experimented with rock figures and very unusual meter signatures) and others, electronics was not, for the most part, acceptable in jazz. Jazz/rock made it acceptable to use electronics for emotional and creative effects. While some might disagree, the lasting legacy of jazz/rock may be its reintroduction of jazz to the modern world.

The most obvious impact of jazz/rock has been its popularity. Jazz/rock, unlike free jazz, is viable commercial music. Since jazz is a part of the American popular and art tradition, anything that happens to enhance its popularity is significant (see analysis of 1987 Michael Brecker piece in Chapter 19).

| MUSICAL ANALYSIS | **Watermelon Man** |

MUSICAL ANALYSIS

Watermelon Man
Herbie Hancock

The instrumentation on this piece is electric piano, soprano sax, bass, drums and countless rhythm, and Latin American and African percussion instruments (played by Bill Summers). It was recorded in 1973. The piece is in the standard key of F, and the tempo is 160. An ethereal-sounding piece, it is jazz/rock in style, although it has major African influences in its use of percussion instruments, especially at the beginning and end.

One reason this piece was done was for comparison with the original. The melody and chord changes are the same, but this piece is more mature, more African, and perhaps less jazzy than the original. The electric piano solos are more interesting than Hancock's solo in the original, and the use of synthesizers is interesting.

Introduction				**Yelp**		**Other Whistles**			**C Pedal**		
1	2	3	4	5	6	7	8	9	10	11	12

	Bass				**Drums**						
13	14	15	16	17	18	19	20	21	22	23	24

Herbie Hancock

Synthesizer   **Melody (Electric Piano and Soprano)**

F7								C7B7Bb7B7	C7		Bb7B7
1	2	3	4	5	6	7	8	9	10	11	12

Break

C7B7	Bb7	Ab7							Ab7G7Gb7	
13	14	15	16	17	18	19	20	21	22

Soprano Sax Melody

F7			Bb7		F7		C7B7Bb7		B7C7B7	Bb7B7
1	2	3	4	5	6	7	8	9	10	11	12

Break

C7B7	Bb7	Ab	A		Ab7		Ab7G7Gb7	
13	14	15			16			

F7			Bb7		F7		C7B7Bb7B7C7		Bb7B7	

1	2	3	4	5	6	7	8	9	10	11	12

Break

C7B7	Bb7	Ab7						Ab7G7Gb7	
13	14	15	16	17	18	19	20	21	22

Synthesizer

//F7

1	2	3	4	5	6	7	8

Whistle (as in Intro) Other Whistles + Yelps

F7 ....

1	2	3	4	5	6	7	8	9	10	11	12

Drums Out   Bass Out   Fade Out

F7 ....

13	14	15	16	17	18	19	20	21	22	23	24	25	26

SIDE-NOTES

Herbie Hancock

Herbie Hancock was born April 12, 1940, in Chicago. He was known to the public first as a member of a Miles Davis Quintet. While he was attending Grinnell College in Iowa, working on an engineering degree, he played in a quintet. By 1963, he was working with Donald Byrd, at whose suggestion he made his first solo album, which included "Watermelon Man." This attracted the attention of Miles Davis, with whom he spent the years 1963–1968. In 1968, he wrote the film score for Michelangelo Antonioni's film "Blow-up." He left the Miles Davis group to form a new group called Mwandishi. The "Head-hunters" album, which also later became the group's new name, cat-apulted him to commercial success and solidified his reputation for doing funk/jazz.

In the late 1970s, Hancock worked extensively with Chick Corea. In the 1980s he made several forays into pop-oriented music, to great financial success. In 1981, he toured with a jazz quartet, which featured young Wynton Marsalis on trumpet. His part in the film *Round Midnight* was quite memorable. He also very tastefully backed up Dexter Gordon, who played saxophone on the original recording of "Watermelon Man." Hancock's association with popular music has been important in that he has probably raised the artistic level of pop-ular music, assisting the careers of musicians such as Stanley Clarke and even Michael Jackson.

Hancock is, first and foremost, a fine acoustic piano player who has become expert in the use of electronic synthesizers, fusion music through African influences, and funk. Perhaps no individual musician represents jazz/rock better, although jazz fans disclaim Hancock when he plays rock, and many rock fans probably do not even know that he is a jazz player.

Wayne Shorter

Wayne Shorter was born in Newark, New Jersey, on August 25, 1933. He went to New York University to study music education, after which he served in the army. He first worked in New York with Horace Silver, then Maynard Ferguson in the summer of 1959, and finally Art Blakey. Heavily influenced by Sonny Rollins, he was considered one of the finest young tenor players of that era. He did session work behind Joe Williams, Yusef Lateef, and Ben Webster. He also did backup work for Aretha Franklin before she went to Memphis, where she became famous. Shorter played in the Cannonball Adderly Quintet from 1961 to 1969.

He also played in the Miles Davis Quintet while Herbie Hancock was a member and wrote "Nefertiti," the title track on a 1967 Davis album. On the historic "Bitches Brew" album, both Shorter and Josef Zawinul were members of the Davis congregation. In 1970, Zawinul and Shorter combined with Miroslav Vitous from Czechoslovakia, Alphonse Mouzon from South Carolina, and Airto Moreira from Brazil to form Weather Report.

In some senses, Weather Report is the reason Wayne Shorter is mentioned in this chapter. Shorter is a superb saxophonist who could easily have contributed greatly to straight neo-bop playing and, in fact, has. His soprano playing is also reminiscent of Coltrane's soprano work. However, it is a unique combination of playing styles that pits his Rollin/Coltrane tone on tenor against the jazz/rock fusion of Weather Report. Weather Report has had a great deal of popularity and success, yet it retains the jazz edge even in popular tunes like "Birdland." Shorter represents the best of jazz/rock musicians in that he is essentially a jazz player who plays with a rock rhythm ensemble.

Suggested Listening

1.	"VSOP"	COL. C2-34976
2.	"Monster"	COL. PC-36415
3.	"Mr. Gone"	COL. PC-35358
4.	"Children of Forever"	Pol. 827559-1
5.	"Modern Man"	Nemp. PZ-35303

Chapter 17
International Influences

Jazz has become more and more an international language, shared among American and non-American musicians alike. In recent years, especially, a healthy mixture of non-U.S. musical materials which has made its way into American jazz.

In 1919, Sidney Bechet, with Will Marion Cook's Southern Syncopated Orchestra, made a European tour with a concert jazz band. Bechet so impressed European audiences that the first piece of jazz criticism was written about his talent by Ernest Ansermet, an orchestra director and composer. In 1933, Louis Armstrong and Duke Ellington, and later Joe Venuti (violin), pianist Fats Waller, and Dizzy Gillespie made historic tours which further established jazz style in Europe. In fact, in Paris, jazz was a viable part of night-life entertainment in the 1920s and 1930s.

In the fifties and sixties, many black jazz musicians migrated to Paris to escape what they viewed as artistic and personal bigotry; 'Round Midnight, a 1986 film, is about those musicians and how they lived. Other jazz musicians, like Gary Burton and Phil Woods, have regularly performed in Europe; interviews on a lively videotape called *Jazz in Exile* illustrate how sophisticated and knowledgeable European audiences are about jazz. In fact, some of the best discographic, bibliographic, and critical work on jazz is European, especially German.

A major influence on jazz in general has been European classical music, from the reported interest of Bix Beiderbecke to the symphonic compositions of Duke Ellington, Stan Kenton (Wagner and Bach), and "jazzing" of the classics (the Swingle Singers and others).

European music in the form of dance pieces and suites has been an influence in jazz from ragtime through free form. In some senses, many free-form pieces rely heavily on atonality and advanced compositional techniques first established in Europe, especially Austria and France. Some of the composers who have had a profound effect on American jazz have been Claude Debussy, Arnold Schoenberg, and Karlheinz Stockhausen.

European compositional orchestration techniques have been constantly influential in U.S. music in general, and jazz is no exception. Although many people have tried to break with European traditions, European techniques in music are constantly there, as a given. But more interestingly, a number of European musicians have been influential in jazz, artists such as Stephane Grappelli, Jean-Luc Ponty, and Django Reinhardt (a French guitarist). European jazz festivals have continued to draw huge numbers of musicians who are very convincing in their talent, musicians from all over western Europe, Russia, Poland, and other eastern European countries. Some of the important festivals are India's Jazz Yatra, Germany's Jazzfest Berlin, London's Camden Jazz Festival, Norway's Kongsberg Jazz Festival, Portugal's Cascals Jazz Festival, and Switzerland's Montreux Jazz Festival. Probably the best known, the Montreux festival features jazz, rock, and country.

Other significant European jazz musicians are Michel Legrand (piano), Peter Brotzmann (alto sax), Albert Mangelsdorff (trombone), and pianists Friedrich Gulda and Joachim Kuhn. Alexander von Schlippenbach is one of the best free jazz players from Europe. Lars Guillin was a Scandanavian baritone sax player. Other reed players include Hacke Bjorksten, Arne Domnerus, Bjarne Nerem, and Eero Koivistoinene. A significant bass player from Czechoslovakia is Georg Riedel. Oerstad Pederson (bass) is from Denmark. One Danish-born trombone player who moved to the United States is Kai Winding.

There are, as well, numerous jazz musicians and festivals throughout Canada and Latin America. Of course, Latin American music has been very influential in jazz since the big band era; Dizzy Gillespie and Horace Silver are just two of the many artists who have been influenced. Latin American music in general has also been very influential in the development of American popular music. Creole culture was heavily influenced by the Latin population of New Orleans, and many forms have been influenced by Mexican influences—especially western swing and jazz/rock, among them Chick Corea, and Santana, who was born in Mexico.

There are also significant oriental influences, in particular nonwestern scales as adapted by modal improvisors. As well, oriental tunes, especially Japanese, have influenced free form, third-stream, big band, and West Coast–style players, such as Dave Brubeck, who created impressions of Japanese pieces. Oriental music probably first influenced American musicians through musical plays and through Gilbert and Sullivan. Through the work of Toshiko Akiyoshi, Japanese melodies have made their way into current big band literature.

Kai Winding, Trombone

Numerous jazz festivals are held in Japan, where many significant jazz musicians have played, Sadao Watanabe among others. Musicians Tiger Okoshi on trumpet and Yoshaki Masuo on guitar have also been featured. At the Montreux Festival, a Japanese University band usually is present, and they frequently outplay everyone else. Jazz in Japan can be found in all forms, from Dixieland to more contemporary styles. Japanese audiences are very conversant in jazz styles and jazz greats.

The importance of African influence in jazz goes almost without saying; the original African influences that created the blues, ragtime, stomps, gospel/soul, funk, and jazz/rock are pivotal to the existence of jazz. More contemporary influences from Africa can be found in African-based jazz/rock ensembles such as the Art Ensemble of Chicago and Sun Ra and the use of African instruments, such as the African drums present in the Head Hunters' version of Hancock's "Watermelon Man." In short, African influence is pervasive in jazz in general, but it also can be found in ensembles that try to communicate black African images. Many contemporary black Americans are returning to African instruments and techniques, similar to the way in which New Wave rock ensembles such as the Talking Heads have used African musical techniques. Significant African musicians include Louis Moholo (drums), Dudu Puckwana (alto sax), Mongezi Feza (trumpet), and Harvey Miller (bass).

Toshiko Akiyoshi   Lew Tabackin

The internationalization of jazz has therefore occurred through the importation of the form to other places, through tours and festivals, and through independent development. For instance, a Polish tenor player named Jan Wroblonski plays incredibly well, though he has had almost no western contact. At a National Association of Jazz Educator's Conference in the late 1970's, the audience was stunned by his originality and uniqueness. His quartet swung, and his improvisations were very well developed. But he showed almost no similarity to other styles. In short, jazz in Poland seems to have developed without reference to players in America.

Materials for jazz can come from anywhere. Whereas at one time, jazz musicians tried to work against influence from European-based music, composers and arrangers now strive to use materials that will invoke other values and cultures. In a sense, the internationalization of jazz has created a multitude of new materials for jazz musicians to manipulate; as well, it has provided the possibility of exploring new structures, textures, and instruments.

"Koto Song"
Dave Brubeck Quartet

MUSICAL ANALYSIS

The instrumentation of the Dave Brubeck Quartet is alto sax (Paul Desmond), piano (Dave Brubeck), bass (Eugene Wright), and drums (Joe Morello). This piece was recorded for an album entitled "Jazz

Sadao Watanabe

Impressions of Japan," which resulted from a tour of Japan by the quartet in the spring of 1964. The piece is in the key of B-minor, and the tempo is 110.

It is a fairly straight minor blues tune, with Bm being 1, Em being 4, and F♯7 being 5; the result is 1,1,1,1,4,4,1,1,2,5,1,5 (minor variation at the end). Notice that the opening and closing melody has a slightly different progression at the end. The reason for this variation is that Brubeck is trying to imitate the sound of a Japanese koto, a thirteen-string zither, which is tuned in a minor scale and emphasizes the fifth relationship; Brubeck therefore hangs the end of the melody up on the fifth.

Notice the way Brubeck uses the piano to evoke tonal colors of Japanese music and the way he imitates the koto at the beginning, especially with the glissandos. Also notice that Desmond's alto tone produces the subtlety of Japanese music. The general style of the Brubeck quartet fits into the West Coast or cool approach, even though they are also known for unusual meters. This piece is not unusual in that respect; it is in 4/4 meter. There are several chords that have alterations beyond the chord symbols represented below.

Opening

Tremelo   Tremelo   Glissando down   Glissando down
Unmeasured

Melody

b				e		b		c♯7	F♯7		
1	2	3	4	5	6	7	8	9	10	11	12

Alto Sax Solo

‖: b ... e ... b ... c♯7 F♯7 ... b ... F♯7 :‖

	b			e		b		c♯7	F♯7	b		F♯7
	1	2	3	4	5	6	7	8	9	10	11	12

Piano Solo

‖: b ... e ... b ... c♯7 F♯7 ... b ... F♯7 :‖

	b			e		b		c♯7	F♯7	b		F♯7
1	2	3	4	5	6	7	8	9	10	11	12

Melody

b				e		b		c♯7	F♯7		
1	2	3	4	5	6	7	8	9	10	11	12

Drum Tremelo

b

Chick Corea

Armando Anthony Corea was born in Chelsea, Massachusetts, on June 12, 1941, the son of a Puerto Rican family. He started studying classical music at the age of 4; when he was a teen-ager, he played with his father's band and was also in a Latin band. He went to both Columbia University and the Juilliard School of Music but soon quit to become a professional musician. His first job was with Mongo Santamaria in 1962. He worked later with Stan Getz, Herbie Mann, and Sarah Vaughn. In 1968, he started playing with Miles Davis and was the electric piano player on "Bitches Brew" in 1969. In 1971, he formed an avant-garde band called Circle that included Anthony Braxton on multiple reeds. He recorded three albums in Europe, and in 1972 he returned to the United States to form the group Return to Forever.

Stanley Clarke was another charter member of Return to Forever, as were Airto Moreira (charter member of Weather Report) and singer Flora Purim, Moreira's wife. Return to Forever produced an album of the same name as well as "Light As a Feather." Both albums were commercial successes, with tunes like "La Fiesta" and "Spain." Latin influence and popular overtunes colored that first period of Return to Forever, a group whose work is still sold in record stores.

Return to Forever expanded in 1973 to use more electronic instruments, patterning itself after the Mahavishnu Orchestra of John McLaughlin, who had been in the Miles Davis band at one point. In the mid-1970s, Al DiMeola joined the band as guitarist, and the ensemble became even more popular, especially on the rock circuit.

Return to Forever formally disbanded in 1976, although Clarke, Lenny White, DiMeola, and Corea performed together during a reunion tour in 1983.

Chick Corea remains a significant force on the fusion style jazz keyboard, having done concerts with Herbie Hancock and with Gary Burton on vibes. He also does critical writing for numerous magazines.

SIDE-NOTES

Toshiko Akiyoshi

Toshiko Akiyoshi was born in Dalren, Manchuria (now China), on December 12, 1929. She studied classical piano and music until she moved to Japan in 1947, where she took up jazz piano. In the 1950s she formed her own jazz group, which included Sadao Watanabe on reeds. Visiting American jazz musicians encouraged her to come to the United States, which she finally did in 1956, attending the Berklee College of Music in Boston; she became an alumnus in 1957. Watanabe took over leadership of her group in Japan, which ultimately led to his name being well known.

While at Berklee she married one of her instructors, Charlie Mariano, who plays alto sax. She played in a group with her husband, where she became known as a fine bop piano player. Later, in 1962, she worked with Charlie Mingus. After her divorce from Mariano, she moved to Los Angeles, where she eventually founded a big band with Lew Tabackin (saxophonist and flutist); the two then married. Their first album, "Kogun," was quite successful for RCA in 1974, and subsequent albums did fairly well for contemporary big band jazz.

Akiyoshi is a fine composer and arranger, who writes very subtle and powerful charts for big bands. Her music—a delightful combination of Thad Jones/Mel Lewis, cool jazz, and Japanese style—is unusual and very satisfying at the same time. Most contemporary critics agree that the Akiyoshi/Tabackin Big Band may well be the best big band in America, although the "Tonight Show" band wins more awards. The band moved to New York in the mid-1980s.

Suggested Listening

1. "Kogun"   RCA JPL1–0236
2. "My Spanish Heart"   Pol. 825657-2
3. "500 Miles High"   Mile. 9070
4. "Afternoon in Paris" (Grappelli)   Verve-MPS 821865-2

Chapter 18
Big Band Revival

TRADITIONAL BIG BAND MUSIC IN THE SEVENTIES AND EIGHTIES

Some of the big bands popular in the 1930s and 1940s continued past the 1940s, in particular, the bands of Count Basie, Duke Ellington, Woody Herman, and Stan Kenton. However, these were rare exceptions, as most of the older-style big bands simply could not compete financially. From the late 1960s and into the 1970s, many of the original bands went back out on the road, quite often under the directorship of a former band member or a completely new director; Glenn Miller's band has often toured without Glenn Miller, who died in 1944. The Guy Lombardo band, the Dorsey band, and the Harry James band were others that toured. However, it is important to understand that many of the bands that reestablished road activity and concerts were in fact recreating their old sound, as a nostalgia phenomenon.

The Count Basie and Duke Ellington bands continued to tour right through the 1950s, although they were greatly diminished in public visibility. Only the Herman and Kenton bands had highly visible road tours, and that is an interesting story in itself. One of the substantial reasons for the success of these bands, as opposed to that of other big bands, was that their music changed with the times. Neither Woody Herman nor Stan Kenton was satisfied with sitting still.

SIDE-NOTES

Woody Herman

Woodrow Charles Herman was born in Milwaukee on May 16, 1913, and died on October 29, 1987. He sang and danced in theaters from the age of 6 and began playing the saxophone when he was 11. He played local jobs while in high school, and left home when he was 17 to go on the road (Tony Martin was in the reed section). He traveled with Isham Jones Juniors from 1934 to 1936, playing tenor sax and clarinet and singing. He then started his own group, which became successful; he had tried this in 1933, but failed. His first band was known as a blues band, with his first big hit coming in 1939, "Woodchopper's Ball."

In the early 1940s, he changed the sound of the band by adding modern arrangements, somewhat copying Ellington, and he also hired several arrangers, one being Neal Hefti.

The first "herd" (the informal title that Herman gave to each of his bands when he changed personnel) was very popular and had its own sponsored radio show; it was voted the best swing band in the 1945 Down Beat poll. His second important big band lasted from 1947 through 1949; this band included such luminaries as Stan Getz, Urbie Green, Milt Jackson, and Zoot Sims. The second herd band included the four brothers, tenor saxophonists Stan Getz, Herbie Steward, and Zoot Sims, plus baritone sax player Serge Chaloff; Jimmy Giuffre wrote a composition for the band called "The Four Brothers," which featured the four saxophonists. His third herd was active in the early 1950s, making a European tour in 1954. Since that time, Herman has led countless herds all the way through 1987, when he was hospitalized.

The significance of the Herman band is that it is constantly modernizing. While his "Four Brothers," "Early Autumn," and "Woodchopper's Ball" still are played regularly, he has also done much more modern tunes, including tunes like "Blues for Poland," "America Drinks and Goes Home" (Frank Zappa), "Naima" (John Coltrane) and "Bass Folk Song" (Stanley Clarke), from his 1974 album called the "Thundering Herd." Herman's music is a delightful combination of contemporary sounds with fairly young musicians playing tunes like "Caledonia." The significance of Herman himself is his charisma as a bandleader, a force that holds the group together. Like Kenton, he is perhaps less important for his playing, although, like Kenton, he is an excellent player.

I once tried to order some old big band stocks of Woody Herman by writing directly to him through his agent. The response I got from Herman's agent was that Mr. Herman was really not interested in the past, and therefore they could not supply old arrangements.

If you were to trace the Woody Herman herds, starting in the late 1930s, you would see wave after wave of essentially new bands and new musical concepts. The Woody Herman band has gone through many transitions through the ages, from the four brothers concept of the forties, through the "cool" linear jazz approach of the fifties, to the funk sound of the seventies. Although the sound changed, Herman did have some players who remained with the band for some time, providing stability.

Woody Herman, 1947–
1948

Stan Kenton

In a sense, Stan Kenton was a similar type of bandleader, but with some important differences. Kenton put together a big band and went on tour to make enough money so that he could relax and work out new ideas, such as the Neophonic Orchestra of the 1960s. The Neophonic Orchestra was located primarily in southern California because of its size; it used augmented brass and string sections. Definitely a third-stream type of music because of the symphonic dimensions it developed and because of the transcriptions of western European classical music, among others, the Neophonic Orchestra was not the kind of organization that could easily be taken out on the road. However, Kenton was successful in retaining an active road life until his death, although it was somewhat more sporadic than the road schedule of Woody Herman.

THE SCHOOL JAZZ BAND MOVEMENT

I have always been convinced that one of the significant factors in the revitalized interest in big band music has been jazz education over a period from the mid-fifties to the mid-seventies. By the mid-1970s, big bands were definitely back, both old ones and new ones. However, that twenty-year period from 1955 to 1975 or so is the time when the school jazz movement developed. I believe that it was a catalyst for other big band activities, or at least it filled in the gaps between the two major periods of interest in big band activity.

At least in California in the mid-fifties, high school band directors were starting dance bands. There were high school jazz festivals in California in the fifties as well as the Camp Pacific Dance Band Camp put on in Carlsbad, California, and sponsored by Art Dedrick, a leading arranger for school dance bands. These activities were led primarily by big band musicians who had become high school band directors, although ultimately the ranks of jazz educators would include those who were university trained. College and university programs developed slowly in the sixties but have gained great momentum in the seventies and eighties.

In a sense, big band music is perfect for beginning jazz players because much of the music is written down, even the solos. One of the downsides to a jazz program centered on big bands is that musicians tend to avoid breaking with the security of a big band, but as a beginning point it makes perfect sense. Obviously, stage bands of the fifties and sixties played older big band pieces, but they also played Stan Kenton and Marshall Brown material. That has continued unabated through the eighties, with high school and college big bands and combos achieving incredible success and phenomenal musicianship. However, the crux of our interest here is how the high school stage band (dance band) program ultimately provided a catalyst for reemerging interest in big band music in general.

CONTEMPORARY BIG BANDS

Big band music thrives in virtually all cities in the United States and in many parts of Europe. One can find big bands in smaller American towns, made up of older and younger musicians who essentially re-create the past. However, one can also find good big bands that create modern sounds.

Probably the first new style of big band was that of Mel Lewis and Thad Jones. In the mid-1960s, these two players who were in New York at the time, decided to form a big band of session and professional musicians to read big band charts and to encourage new composition. They formed a band that met one night each week at a New York club, where they played for the fun of it. Obviously they were good because they were all professionals, many with road and recording experience. They recorded their first album in 1966; charts or arrangements that have been created for the band or by band members have been made available in print (see analysis); and they have been accepted as one of the best big bands on the scene.

Maynard Ferguson formed his first big band straight out of playing with Stan Kenton, with whom he got his start as a child. Ferguson has followed the Herman pattern of keeping up with the times, but even more so than Herman. Ferguson constantly uses younger musicians; now they are twenty to thirty years younger than he is. Many of his players are straight out of college and university jazz programs.

He plays primarily jazz/rock, although he will occasionally do a straight jazz tune, like his incredibly technical version of "Airegen." A screech trumpet player (he plays very high notes), he is not always well respected by jazz snobs, but nevertheless he is a fine player and has had a positive impact on the popularity of jazz (for instance his version of the theme song from the film *Rocky* or the theme from "Star Trek").

The Akiyoshi/Tabackin Big Band is highly respected, especially because of the Japanese undertone of many of the pieces and the unusual time meters. The solo work of Tabackin, especially on flute, is delightful. The band was made up of studio musicians and professionals from the Los Angeles area; the band moved to New York in the mid-1980s. Their arrangements are available in print (see analysis).

Another band that is highly respected and wins awards is The Tonight Show Band. Unfortunately, we seldom get to hear more than twenty-three seconds of that band's music. Their arrangements are rather short because of time limitations imposed by the program, but they are solid compositions performed by excellent players. Doc Severinson is one of the finest trumpet players alive, but like many studio musicians he plays everything perfectly without the bravado of a road musician.

One of the most intriguing qualities of contemporary big bands in general is the increased fascination with unusual tonal colors and textures, that is, unusual mixtures of and use of musical instruments. Of course, this was begun back in the 1930s, but the experimentation of many big bands has gone quite a bit farther than what was common in those days. There is also increased emphasis on original improvisation within the big band context. Performing musicians who travel on the road and use pickup bands (local musicians who are hired to fill out a big band, reading the professionals' written arrangements) often function as accompaniment for solos by the professionals. These same musicians often do clinics in high schools, colleges, and universities, where the band prepares the arrangements in advance; the soloist comes in for the concert only. There are many other excellent big bands, including lesser-known ones such as the J. C. Heard (drummer) Big Band from Detroit.

The big band concept has been shaped to the seventies and eighties, both by financial and physical changes and by changes in musical taste. Big bands play a great deal of rock and funk because it is popular; high school bands, especially, tend to overload on this type of music. However, big band music generally runs the gamut from traditional to highly experimental.

There has been a great deal of big band activity in the seventies and even more in the eighties. Some people have argued that with the "yuppie" movement of the eighties, the relatively conservative times have renewed interest in formal types of activity, and that big band somehow seems to fit that. I prefer to think that big band music is exciting, and that is what accounts for the renewed interest in it.

"Blues for Poland"
Woody Herman

Recorded in 1974 on the "Thundering Herd" album, this composition is for a full big band; this tune is also available in printed form. In the key of Eb the tempo is 136, it is actually a sixteen-bar blues form with some minor chord variations. The main melody is quite obviously repeated three times at the beginning of the piece, followed by a brass section, then baritone sax solo, ensemble transition, flügelhorn solo, a tutti section in which the meter shifts from 5/4 to 4/4 (watch for that), a brief piano solo, opening melody, a grand pause (silence), and one quarter-note chord in the key of E, for a surprise. Eb is 1, Ab is 4, and Bb7 is 5.

Main Melody with Three Notes as Pickups
Three times

‖:EbAb Eb   Ab7 Ao Eb   Ab7Ao Eb C7 f Bb7 g GFBb:‖
1   2   3   4   5   6   7   8   9 10   11 12 13 14 15 16

Brass Section

Eb E bb Eb7a D AbAo Eb Eb7 Ab Ao EbD Dbc f   Bb7 EbCCbBb
1 2 3   4   5   6   7   8   9   10 11 12   13   14 15 16

Baritone Solo

Eb   Eb7   Ab7 Ao Eb7   Ab7 Ao EbD G C f Bb EbGbf Bb

Flügelhorn Solo Continued with Background Figures

Eb Ab Eb   Ab7 Ao Eb   Ab Ao Eb C7 f Bb EbC f Bb
1 2 3   4   5   6   7 8   9 10 11 12 13 14 15   16

Tutti Section
5/4 4/4 5/4 4/4   All 7ths

N.C.   Ab7 Ao Eb Eb7 Ab Ao Eb7 C7 f   Bb g   Gb b e
1 2 3 4 5   6   7   8   9 10 11 12 13 14 15   16

Chord Falloff to
Piano Solo   Opening Melody   Silence

Eb7 Ab Eb Eb7 Ab7 Ao Eb Eb7 Ab Ao Eb C7 f7 Bb Eb   E
1   2   3   4   5   6   7   8   9   10 11 12 13 14 15   16

SIDE-NOTES

Stan Kenton

Stanley Newcomb Kenton was born in Wichita, Kansas, on February 19, 1912, and died in Los Angeles on August 25, 1979. He was raised in Los Angeles, studying piano with his mother and other teachers. He wrote his first arrangement at the age of 16 and played with local bands before joining the Everett Hoagland band as pianist and arranger in 1934. He worked with others, including Vido Musso, prior to starting his own band in 1941 on Balboa Island; he recorded for Decca Records in the same year. The band's theme song was "Artistry in Rhythm."

By 1944 Kenton had achieved a national reputation based on the band's rather unusual style; his reed section played in a clipped and widely orchestrated style, as opposed to the closer-position, even reed sound incorporated by most big bands of that era. Although Kenton's music was always innovative in a variety of ways, a healthy argument could be made for the notion that it was the unusual reed sound which made Kenton's band truly unique. From the end of 1944 through 1946, the band recorded primarily vocals, featuring Anita O'Day, Gene Howard, and June Christy. In 1946, Pete Rugolo joined the band as arranger, and Kenton discontinued most of his arranging activities. He dissolved the band for the first time in 1947, setting up a pattern of many generations of the Kenton band.

In 1950, he went on the road with a forty-piece ensemble, including strings, which was called "Innovations in Modern Music." In 1955 he had a weekly TV series in New York, and in 1956 he toured England. In the late 1950s, he alternated between commercial recordings and live concerts with more modern and esoteric music. In the 1960s, he experimented with what he called the Neophonic Orchestra, an expanded ensemble that often played orchestral transcriptions, such as his amazing transcriptions of Wagner opera segments. He also did a variety of recordings that used music from different cultures; an interesting example are the jazz settings of national anthems from many different countries, as arranged by Bob Curnow.

Kenton's music can be divided into three basic categories: (1) orchestral works in the Duke Ellington vein; (2) commerical pieces; and (3) riff-oriented swing pieces with improvised solos. Of course, numerous excellent musicians have been in the Kenton organization at one time or another; a young Maynard Ferguson, for instance, got his start with Kenton. Although his music lives on in the lives of musicians who played with him, and in his arrangements and records, available through Creative World, his record and publishing company, the band stopped playing upon Kenton's death. Actually, Kenton had arranged things so that there would be no road band without him.

Kenton continued to tour until his death, although he personally devoted a great deal of his time to jazz education, especially in the form of his summer jazz camps. An extremely important force in modern jazz, his band was innovative from the beginning and remained so always.

Suggested Listening

1. "Thundering Herd"   Fan. 9452
2. "Greatest Hits" (Kenton)   Cap. N-16182
3. "Kenton/Wagner"   Cre. W. 1033
4. "Live in Munich" (Thad Jones/Mel   Hori. 724
   Lewis)
5. "The Tonight Show Band"   Amherst AMH-3311

Chapter 19
Overview of the Eighties: Players and Singers

This chapter will present a short discussion of some musicians who are considered significant, without meaning to suggest that these are the only musicians who are playing jazz during the 1980s. One of the most striking characteristics of eighties players and singers in general is the healthy mixture of styles. Jazz musicians of the 1980s have a marvelous panorama of jazz styles from which to choose, and generally they combine styles from the past with contemporary practice.

Musicians like Miles Davis, Dexter Gordon, and Sonny Rollins are still actively recording and creating new sounds, especially Miles Davis, who in 1987 was selected BMI (Broadcast Music Incorporated) Jazz Musician and Jazz Trumpet Player of the Year. The film *'Round Midnight* expresses the continuing spirit of jazz activity in the 1980s, even though its setting was the late 1950s. Various sound tracks and special recordings have been made since that film was made, all based on Thelonius Monk's immortal tune of the same name. This suggests the meaningful impact of jazz standards in a continuing tradition of reinterpretation.

JAZZ IN NEW YORK

New York continues to be an active center for jazz, both live performance and the recording industry. A number of major jazz stars are still recording and performing actively in New York, including many musicians discussed in this book. In New York City in the 1980s, numerous modern stars have emerged who play in a variety of styles, essentially mixing all the jazz styles available to them in the viable New York City scene.

Black musician Steve Coleman (alto), originally from Chicago, studied with Bunky Green at Chicago State University. He has played with Oliver Lake, Don Cherry, and Arthur Blythe. He also plays with the Dave Holland Quintet (a strong example of three horns, bass, and drums, hard bop, Mingus-influenced, free improvisational group). Marvin Smith and Geri Allen (originally from Detroit) are also important in the same collaborative group. These musicians and their colleagues do a lot of recording for European labels. Lester Bowie lives in New York but spends most of his time in Europe.

White New York musicians include Marc Johnson (bass), a session player from Texas, who recorded with John Abercrombie and Bill Evans. He worked with Peter Erskine, a drummer from Indiana University, who played with Maynard Ferguson and Weather Report. Erskine recently moved from New York to Los Angeles. David Murray (woodwinds) leads an octet and big band in the Mingus tradition. Murray works throughout the New York area, with James Blood Ulmer (guitar) from Texas. He is a hot player from the late seventies who is still quite vibrant. Bill Frissell is a significant guitar player who is having an impact.

New Haven, Connecticut, has produced a number of fine jazz players who have worked on the east coast and in New York. Some representatives of the New Haven connection are as follows: Anthony Davis (piano), a very technical jazz player who recently had an opera performed called "X," at the Met, Mark Helis (bass), and Jerry Hemingway (drums). All three of the above play in straight tonal and melodic style; they all play free form. Also from the New Haven area is Ray Anderson (trombone).

JAZZ IN CHICAGO

The most vibrant avant garde (progressive) group in Chicago was the Art Ensemble of Chicago. Although it is not as influential in the 1980s as it was in the 1970s, the Art Ensemble is still alive and well, under the leadership of Ed Wilkerson (tenor sax/arranger). Kahil El-Zabar (drums) is also active in the Art Ensemble. Other musicians not connected with the Art Ensemble are Howard Johnson (guitar), who plays mostly pop-oriented jazz in the vein of George Benson, who, incidentally was a significant jazz guitarist before going to pop recently. The rhythm section duo of Steve Rodby (bass) and Paul Wertico (drums) is very active in Chicago. They play many recording dates and concerts when they are not touring with Pat Metheny (guitar). Joseph Jarman, formerly from Chicago, is playing with Richie Workman.

Art Ensemble of Chicago

JAZZ IN DETROIT

Detroit has a very viable jazz scene in the 1980s. Musicians like Marcus Belgrave (trumpet) and J. C. Heard (drums) and his big band continue to play provocative tonal music, often in a slightly funk vein. Eddie Harris and Wendell Harrison (both sax players) have joined with pianist Pamela Weiss to form a booking agency and record company called Rebirth; they are creating very modern music that often sounds like late Coltrane. Detroit now has the Detroit/Montreux Festival, which is a mini-version of the Swiss festival; the Detroit version features primarily jazz, with most professional groups coming from Detroit.

JAZZ IN TEXAS

There is a relatively hot scene in Fort Worth, Texas, which comes from Caravan of Dreams, a nightclub where live recordings are done. Ornette Coleman, James Blood Ulmer, and Ronald Shannon Jackson (drummer with a melodic/funk band called Decoding Society) all produce recordings from this center of activity. Ornette Coleman, in particular, has made several returns to popularity in the 1980s.

Wynton Marsalis

JAZZ IN OTHER LOCATIONS

Viable jazz in the 1980s exists in many towns, including Cleveland, Denver, Los Angeles, San Francisco, and Atlanta. There are school and area jazz festivals on a regular basis, and although other forms of popular music get much more radio airplay and space in record store bins, jazz gets public attention when it happens. There are some university and college music departments that support jazz education and jazz experimentation. Obvious examples include the Eastman School of Music, the Berklee College of Music, the University of Miami, and North Texas State University, although music departments like Indiana University have produced major players such as Pete Erskine. The University of Massachusetts has had Archie Shepp on its faculty (lately he has been into Coltrane's 1950s music, recording very little except for gospel albums with Horace Parlan on piano); similarly, other schools have given jazz musicians that aura of respect.

As well, notable musicians like Wynton Marsalis and Michael Brecker (see biographies and analyses) were not from New York, Chicago, or the other locations. Marsalis was from New Orleans, a reasonably important town in jazz history, and Brecker was from Philadelphia, also a city of some significance. Marsalis, in particular,

Michael Brecker

has had a great impact on other jazz and classical musicians, for he is expert in both areas. As one of the bright young stars in jazz today, Marsalis illustrates that a musician does not need to be from a hotbed of progressive jazz to become progressive and influential.

SINGERS

A number of fine vocalists are connected with jazz, although jazz vocalists generally do not get the same kind of press that instrumentalists do. Older singers who are still around, like Ella Fitzgerald, continue a tradition of the past, although of course they do it with great skill. One must think of people like Mel Torme in that respect. Basically a big band stylist who carried scat singing further in his solo career, Mel Torme sings with a beautiful vocal control and lovely styling. He is a very good vocal improvisor, although generally speaking he is not always considered mainstream.

Newer singers include some of the following. Laurel Masse, from Chicago and originally a singer with Manhattan Transfer, began a solo career in the early 1980s. A beautiful jazz stylist, she sings both sensitive ballads, almost in a Billie Holiday style, and Manhattan Transfer–type fast tunes. Bobby McFerrin, from San Francisco, is everyone's jazz singer of the year in the mid-eighties. Carman Lundy, from Miami, is also influential. Al Jarreau was the most significant new

Bobby McFerrin

singer of the 1970s, although in the eighties he has moved toward a more pop orientation. One is reminded of the fence-sitting style of Marvin Gaye in the 1970s, who could have gone either pop, or jazz in singing style. Cassandra Wilson sings with Steve Coleman, currently with Henry Treadgill's trio "Air" and a sextet. DeeDee Bridgewater is a pop singer fron the 1970s; in 1987 she did a show on Billie Holiday in Paris and club dates in a contemporary jazz style.

Jazz vocal style in the last thirty years has moved more toward free improvisation, with the primary influences being Billie Holiday and Ella Fitzgerald. However, there is also a very viable jazz vocal movement in schools, led by musicians who are creating all sorts of interesting improvisational opportunities within solo groups, small vocal ensembles, and large jazz/show choirs. Some of the most interesting jazz vocals are really being created in schools.

PUNK AND NEW WAVE ATTITUDES EXPRESSED IN JAZZ

One of the more interesting phenomena in the 1980s has been the little-known relationship between punk/new wave rock and jazz. Terms such as punk/jazz, new wave jazz, and techno-punk/funk have been used by writers from magazines like *Rolling Stone* and *Playboy* to describe new music. Historical accuracy aside, these terms suggest an interesting phenomenon—the relationship between jazz and rock.

Al Jarreau

Jazz is often thought to be on the cutting edge of new ideas, and jazz also legitimizes musical styles that are not thought to be intellectually respectable.

Interestingly enough, the proclaimed leader of punk/jazz became Ornette Coleman, although Rick James had held the title before him. While it is still not clear that the term means anything, it was applied to Coleman for his free-form ideas over a reiterative pattern supplied by the rhythm section. Coleman has gone through two renaissances of interest in his style—one in the late-seventies to early eighties, and ultimately connected with the Playboy Jazz Festivals. The other occurred in the mid-eighties and was especially in connection with his work with Pat Metheny. In some senses, this can be seen as the ultimate in fusion music. When a free-form and noncommercial musician like Ornette Coleman becomes popular with progressive rock fans, that is a very clear indication that some very interesting interrelationships are coming into play. The mere existence of the concept of new wave jazz or the other concepts suggests a new kind of interchange between the various forms of American "popular" music.

In conclusion, we have seen in this chapter and in the book that jazz has progressed through many stages and has drawn upon many techniques to create its complex fabric. Jazz is like other forms of music in that it is a mirror of its culture. We have seen in jazz in general and the 1980s in specific that society has been mirrored in the creative expressions of the players and singers who have created it. Jazz has been called the only truly American art form. While it is certainly an American art form and well deserves that recognition, we must also credit other cultures—in particular the African culture—for its inception and constant revitalization. However, as an expression of American culture, jazz is a creation which well deserves national pride.

"Original Rays"
Michael Brecker

This piece features Brecker on tenor saxophone and electronic wind instrument, Jack DeJohnette on drums, Charlie Haden (Ornette Coleman's bass player) on bass, Kenny Kirkland on keyboards, and Pat Metheny on guitar. Recorded in 1987, I hear the beginning of the piece in Bb and the middle section in F at a tempo of 110 throughout. Although the beginning section is quite difficult to count, it does fit into clear sections. The middle section, where he plays acoustic tenor sax is very easy to follow, breaking into nice eight-measure phrases.

Notice the slight allusion to "La Cucaracha" in the beginning. The use of the electronic wind instrument is very tasty; the saxophone solo evokes Coltrane and funk at the same time; and the Metheny guitar solo is nice also. A very satisfying example of contemporary jazz, this piece draws on the best of old and new.

Electric Wind Instrument Introduction, based on Bb, Brecker plays in time, but it is essentially free improvisation without chord changes. Note reference to "La Cucaracha."

A Tempo (110 Per Minute) EWI
Drums Enter

N.C.								CBbA	DGCFBbEbDGC		
1	2	3	4	5	6	7	8	9	10	11	12
FD		BbBOF	G		BB	EB	Db	g	C7	F	
13		14	15			16					

Transition (EWI Out)
F Pedal with g7 and C7 Chords Over   15/4 Time-1 Measure

1 2 3 4 5   6   7 8 9 10

Main Melody
Sax Enters/Bass Continues Pedal F

11 12 13 14 15 16 17 18

Transition

C	Bb	A	D	G	C	F	Bb	EbD	G	C
1		2		3			4			

Main Theme

||:F   d BbBo F A d Bb g a Bb C7 F d F Bb g E a Bb F C#odC:||
  1   2   3   4   5 6   7   8

Transition (Sax Out)

F
1   2   3   4

Guitar Solo (Base-C Pedal)

||:C Bb A D G   C F Bb EbD G C :||
  1   2   3   4

Guitar Solo Continued

||:F   d BbBo F A d Bb g a Bb C7   F d F Bb g E a Bb F C#odC:||
  1   2   3   4   5 6   7   8

Transition

F
1 2 3 3 4

Sax Solo
Three Times

||:A   d   C   a   Bb   eb   g7   C7   :||
  1   2   3   4   5   6   7   8

Transition

F
1 2 3 4

Sax and Guitar Melody

||:F d BbBo F A d Bb   g a Bb C7 F d   F Bb g E a Bb F C#odC:||
  1 2   3   4   5   6   7   8

Sax Improvisation

F d   BbBo F A d Bb g a Bb C7 F d F Bb g E a Bb   F C#odC
1 2   3   4   5 6   7   8

Sax and Guitar Melody   EWI Free Improv. to Fade Out

F d BbBoF A d Bb g a Bb C7   F
1   2   3   4   5...

Michael Brecker

Michael Brecker was born in Philadelphia on March 29, 1949. He grew up listening to Cannonball Adderly, Miles Davis, Clifford Brown, and John Coltrane (who was also from Philadelphia). Studying clarinet first, he switched to alto and then to tenor saxophone. He attended Indiana University for one semester and then moved to New York at the age of 18. Working as a sideman and eventually as a session man on recordings in New York, he was in the ensemble Dreams, which included Billy Cobham. This ensemble used a horn section on top of a powerhouse rock rhythm section.

He played with Horace Silver in the 1970s and also with Billy Cobham. In 1975, he joined with his brother Randy (trumpet) to form the Brecker Brothers, which lasted for six years. At Seventh Avenue South, a Manhattan club where he and brother Randy were co-headliners from 1977 through 1985, he formed a group in 1979 that was specifically designed to tour Japan. It was in this group that he developed strong interest in synthesizers, in particular the Electronic Wind Instrument, which he made extensive use of in his solo album of 1987.

A strong player, who has overtones of many other players, in particular John Coltrane, Brecker is esoteric and pop oriented at the same time. Capable of playing a variety of styles, he has been a very active studio musician in New York since the early 1970s, backing up musicians like Bruce Springsteen, the Funkadelic, Frank Sinatra, John Lennon, Dire Straits, and Billy Joel. In short, he is very diverse. But in his jazz style, especially as represented by the six Brecker Brothers' albums and his solo album, he illustrates that he can play straight jazz and fusion music all at the same time. In short, he is an excellent representative of what is happening in the mid-1980s and the excellence of the mid-1980s in jazz.

Wynton Marsalis

If you had to include only one musician as an example of excellence in the 1980s, it would have to be Wynton Marsalis. Born in New Orleans on October 18, 1961, Marsalis was a child prodigy. Given his first trumpet lesson at the age of 6 by Al Hirt, Wynton was associated with professional musicians of all types from an early age. His father, Ellis, is a widely respected pianist, composer, and educator from New Orleans. Although Marsalis claims that he did not take the trumpet seriously until he was 12, his early accomplishments suggest otherwise.

He won a citywide competition at the age of 14, which led him to perform the Haydn "Trumpet Concerto" with the New Orleans Philharmonic; two years later he played Bach's "Brandenburg Concerto #2." Through high school he played first chair with the New Orleans Civic Orchestra. At the age of 17, he attended the Berkshire Music Center Summer Program at Tanglewood, where he won the award for outstanding brass player. Normally students are not allowed to attend until they are 18.

When he was 18, he entered Juilliard and after one year joined Art Blakey and his Jazz Messengers. In 1981, Marsalis got a recording contract with CBS Records. He formed a quartet which consisted of himself, Herbie Hancock, Ron Carter, and Tony Williams, touring the world and culminating at the Kool Jazz Festival. He has continued to win numerous awards as both a classical and jazz trumpet player, a relatively rare combination; his teacher, Al Hirt, also played jazz and classical music. He toured with the Eastman School of Music in 1986 and is clearly the major young trumpet player of the 1980s.

His style is a combination of older styles, with a definite contemporary leaning. He plays cleanly, yet with soul. He is a very mature individual and keenly intelligent. In high school he was a National Achievement Scholar, but he also played in the school marching band. The 1982 Downbeat Jazz Musician of the Year and Best Trumpeter has a short biography that puts him right up there with the best music has to offer.

Suggested Listening

1. "Wynton Marsalis" COL. FC-37574
2. "Michael Brecker" MCAC-5980(Cassette)
3. "3 Compositions" Del. 415
   (Anthony Braxton)
4. "Live at Brooklyn Academy Black Saint BSR-0096
   of Music—World Saxophone
   Quartet"
5. " 'Round Midnight" COL. SC-40464

Appendix A
Technological
Electronic Terms
and Definitions

The changes in electronic technology over the last thirty years have been phenomenal. Scientific change in general has had a major influence on society, both in its viewpoint and in its physical life. Technological change has always had a massive effect on human society. No matter what the technological advancement, there is always a corresponding reaction to it, sometimes positive and sometimes negative.

However, since World War II, the world has experienced technological change at a seemingly impossible rate. Although it is certain that other eras felt the change as much as we have, somehow our reaction to it has been stronger, if for no other reason than the speed of change. We have had less time to get used to change before the next advancement is upon us.

Although technology has affected everything in our society, it has been especially important in music. Music in general has become an electronic art in the last thirty to forty years; jazz and rock have been leaders in that movement. In this appendix, electronic devices and terms are defined. An understanding of these devices is important to grasping the technique by which jazz musicians have created their music.

It should also be understood that many nonelectronic devices were significant in their ability to proliferate. An example of this would be the invention of high-speed record-producing machines, whereby thousands of records could be produced quickly to meet the demand created by marketing techniques.

A-B test: Testing performance of two or more amplifiers and/or speaker systems by switching back and forth between devices.

Absorption: The ability of a room to absorb acoustic energy.

AC power: In the United States 110–120 volts of alternating current.

Acoustic: The science of sound, sound heard, hearing ability, and the production of sound.

Active: Circuitry that can increase the amplitude of a signal.

Additive synthesis: see *Synthesis*.

Ampere: A unit of measurement of electrical current.

Amplifier: A device that accepts a sound source and increases the loudness or power level of a wave form without distorting the original sound source. It raises the sound level so that it can be driven through speakers.

Attenuation: Reduction in level of a signal.

Audio chain: The order of connecting components for reproduction of sound, typically sound source, microphone, preamplifier, special effects, graphic equalizer, amplifier, and speaker.

Audio range: The frequency response spectrum of sound perceptible by humans, 20 c.p.s. (cycles per second or hertz) to 20,000 c.p.s.

Baffle: The panel on which a speaker is mounted in a speaker box.

Balanced cable: A shielded cable.

Balanced line: A transmission line (cable) capable of being operated so that the voltage of both ends is equal.

Bandwidth: The definition of a range of sound frequency that can be controlled by one switch. See also *Graphic equalizer*.

Bass reflex: A speaker enclosure in which the speaker's rear sound wave comes from an opening that reinforces the bass sounds.

Bi-amp: An amplifier that sends two bands of frequencies to a crossover unit, which divides the sounds into high and low bands, sending the high signals to a high-range speaker or horn (sometimes called a tweeter) and the low signals to a low-range bass speaker or woofer.

Boost: Indicates an increase in gain of a band of frequencies to equalize the entire sound spectrum presented through a speaker system.

Bus: A conductor that services two or more signal sources, used in a mixer board.

Capacitor: An electrical part that reduces heat loss in the conducting of electrical energy. It blocks direct current and allows the passage of alternating current.

Cardoid: A unidimensional microphone whose construction picks up sound from the front rather than the back.

Chorus: A pedal device that makes the sound bigger through a simple flanger without regeneration control. See also *Flanger*.

Clipping: Amplifier overload that causes a change in the wave form, resulting in distortion.

Compression: Reduction in amplifier gain at one level which allows for increase of gain at another level.

Compressor: A type of pedal that aids in sustaining the signal by taking some of the signal from the initial sound and reproducing that sound at the normal decay point.

Conductor: A wire or cable that carries electrical current.

Continuous power: The power rating of an amplifier, measured at 1,000 Hz for a specific amount of time. Rated in amps.

CPS: Cycles per second, the measurement historically used to describe a simple tone and the number of sine waves per second which it produces. Measured in hertz.

Critical distance: The point in a room where the sound level produced by the speaker equals the reverberation field of the acoustic properties of the room.

Crossover: An electronic device that divides electrical power sent to speakers from amplifiers into various bandwidths corresponding to different-sized speakers. See also *Bi-amp* and *Bandwidth*.

Current: The rate of flow (measured in amps) of electricity in a circuit.

Cut: A reduction in gain of a band of frequencies when an equalizer is used.

Decibel: Relative strength, power, or loudness of a sound source.

Digital delay: Also referred to as echo (or the more complicated echoplex), this is a pedal-controlled device that allows for a controlled repeat of original sound from 1 millisecond to 2 seconds. On some devices, one can also control the number of repeats.

Digital sampling: See *Synthesis*.

Dip: A reduction in gain at certain frequencies.

Directivity: Area of coverage of a speaker or microphone.

Dispersion: The spread or distribution of sound coverage produced by a speaker. If the sound decreases in volume as the listener moves away from a point directly in front of the speaker, it is a directional speaker.

Distortion: Change in wave form.

Dynamic range: The decibel range capable of being produced by an instrument or the range of acceptable volumes produced by electrical equipment.

Echo: See *Digital delay*.

Efficiency: The relationship between power usage and power output.

Electronic drums: A reasonably recent development, electronic drums are essentially membranes or drum heads that have built-in sensors which trigger individual circuits. This allows for a variety of electronic drum sounds and also can be used in connection with a drum synthesizer.

Enclosure: An acoustically designed housing for a speaker.

Equalization: Control of various bands of frequency so as to enhance or modify the total sound. See also *Graphic equalizer*.

Excursion: Movement of the cone of a loudspeaker.

Exponential horn: A high-range speaker shaped like a horn.

Feedback: In electronic terms, a return of some of the signal back to the circuit; in acoustic terms, the return of signal to the original microphone.

Filter: A device that allows certain frequencies to pass through the circuit while blocking others.

Flanger: A pedal device that creates a millisecond delay or a moving sine wave. It is not the same as a phaser but rather creates a chorus effect. The delay rate is controllable by a knob on the pedal, as is the regeneration control, which controls a change in intensity of harmonic structure. The flanger is a very popular device.

Frequency: The number of cycles per second produced by an oscillator or instrument and which determines the high or low quality of the sound.

Frequency response: A measure of the effectiveness of a circuit, device (microphone, amplifier, or speaker) or electronic system to produce equal intensity across the frequency bands between a lower and upper limit.

Fuzz: Another pedal effect, the fuzz pedal produces distortion by introducing a square wave, a wave in which positive energy peaks and then immediately becomes negative.

Gain: Increase in strength of a signal, usually expressed in ratio of input to output voltage or power increase in decibels.

Graphic equalizer: A set of controls which allows one to lower or raise the decibel level of specific bands of frequencies, typically built into mixer units and power amplifiers. See also *Equalization*.

Ground: A wire in an electric circuit that does not carry power but is connected to a metal part of the frame or to the junction box.

Harmonic: Describes particular frequencies in relation to a fundamental pitch. These frequencies are determined by the harmonic series of a fundamental pitch or sine wave. Harmonics and their relative intensity determine the timbre or tone quality of a complex sound. Harmonics can also be produced on acoustic instruments by lightly stopping the string or overblowing.

Headroom: The difference between optimal power level and the level at which clipping or distortion occurs.

Hertz: A unit of measurement of sound frequency which replaced the older term, cycles per second (cps).

High pass: Signals above a certain frequency.

Hum: Distortion of the power line which typically impedes listening to the sound source.

Impedence: Opposition to alternating current flow from a circuit, expressed in ohms. High- and low-impedence cords and microphones are used to match the resistances of various devices.

Inductance: Generated force of a circuit or two circuits which creates electrical force by virtue of change within the circuit(s).

Input overload: Distortion created by too strong a signal.

Integrated: Multiple components or functions combined into one unit.

Jack: A receptacle into which something is plugged.

Kilohertz (kilocycles): 1,000 hertz or 1,000 cps (kcps).

LED: Diode or small bulb which emits light when a specific current is applied to it.

Limiter: A circuit that limits the amplitude of a waveform from exceeding a certain preset limit and also maintains waveform shape.

Line out: An output connection which will drive an amplifier or allow reproduction.

Low pass: Frequencies below a certain frequency.

Loudness control: Controls the volume of the output of an amplifier.

Loudspeaker: A reproduction device which translates electrical energy into acoustic energy after the original sound source has been amplified and sometimes modified through the audio chain. See also *Tweeter* and *Woofer.*

Loudspeaker efficiency: The ratio of signal input to signal output.

Master: Main control for gain or volume level.

Microphone: A transducer which receives acoustic energy and transmits it as electrical energy through wires to the rest of the audio chain. See also *Unidimensional* and *Omnidirectional.*

MIDI: A universal connection used on many contemporary electronic keyboard units and synthesizers which allows computer control of multiple keyboard and synthesizer units.

Mono: Monophonic sound, which creates one single source emitting from speakers.

Noise: Any signal that adds distortion, hum, or other undesired signals to sound output.

Notch filter: A filter that substantially lowers the gain of a specific spectrum of sounds.

Octave: The interval between two frequencies with a ratio of 1:2, for example, low C and the C above it.

Octave divider: Usually, a small unit hung on the belt of the musician and controlled by a pedal. It creates an octave below the basic miked sound sent through it and/or two octaves below. The relative intensity of the reproduced sound can be adjusted by a volume control on the unit.

Ohm: A unit of electrical resistance. It takes 1 volt of potential to drive 1 amp of current through 1 ohm of resistance.

Omnidirectional: Microphones that pick up sound from all directions.

Overtone harmonic: Multiples of fundamental waveform.

Palm pedal: A lever screwed into the side of a guitar, not a food pedal. Popularized by Duane Eddy, the palm pedal is an adaption of the knee pedal used by steel guitarists; it has been adapted to the organ (Farfisa). The palm pedal is a mechanical device in that it stretches the strings, thus raising the pitch. In some senses, it is the predecessor of the electronic pedal.

Phaser: This particular pedal device actually creates an opposite sine wave to the basic sound being sent through the pedal.

Power: Electrical energy in watts.

Power amplifier: The final amplification of the audio chain, just prior to the speakers.

Preamp: An amplifier that increases the total gain of a source from a microphone so that it is at a level sufficient to be driven by a power amplifier.

Real-time analyzer: An instrument which measures the response of a system to the room in which it is operating.

Reflection: Bouncing of sound waves from walls and other obstacles.

Resistance: Opposition to flow of current (ohms).

Resistor: An electrical component designed to create resistance or to provide a voltage drop.

Resonance: Tendency of all electronic parts to vibrate.

Response: The range of frequencies at which an amplifier or speaker will respond and the relative intensity of those frequencies.

Return: An input which accepts a signal after it has been sent to special effects.

Parallel: Devices connected directly to a circuit; current flows from each device back to the circuit rather than in series.

Peak: Maximum value of a signal amplitude.

Pedal devices: Electronic circuits which create various effects and can be controlled by a foot pedal, which often turns them on or off and, less occasionally, allows one to control the actual device. They are plugged between the instrument and/or microphone and the preamplifier. See *Chorus,* *Compressor, Digital delay (Echo), Flanger, Fuzz (Distortion), Octave Divider, Phaser, Wah-wah.* See also *Palm Pedal.*

Phase: Time interval between two events. Two signals are in phase when their waveforms overlap exactly. When sine waves or other waves are separated by part of the entire wave, they are out of phase.

Polarity: Opposite magnetic poles, plus and minus.

Reverb: Sound that continues after source has ceased to produce sound. Sometimes understood as echo, reverb is actually a continuation of the sound rather than a repetition of all or parts of it.

Ring mode: Sound which lies just below the threshold or occurrence of feedback.

Roll off: Attenuation or reduction in sound level above or below certain frequencies, measured in decibels per octave.

Send: An output to an external processor or effect.

Sensitivity: Minimum input signal required to produce output.

Series: A series of circuits forming one signal path for current, the opposite of parallel.

Sine wave: A wave which follows the mathematical sine of time in shift from positive polarity to negative polarity and back again.

Solid state: A type of circuitry in which all components are placed on circuit boards rather than being connected by wires. Typically using transistors to replace vacuum tubes, solid state circuitry is the technique for miniaturization, and it avoids the bane of electronics—heat buildup.

Snake: A multiconductor-shielded input cable which allows for the connection of many microphones to a mixer-amplifier at some distance from the stage.

Speaker: See *Loudspeaker.* See also *Tweeter,* and *Woofer.*

Splitter: A box or connector with which one sound input can be broken into two or more output signals.

Stereo: A system in which two separate power amplifiers create control over different inputs so that the speaker effect reproduces the original sound more accurately than monophonic reproduction. See also *Bi-amp*.

Synthesis: The process by which sounds are created. Essentially a collection of interconnected oscillators (sound producers). Filters and envelope controls were added later to primitive synthesizers. Synthesizers were first designed for studio production of electronic music and later were adapted for live performance and pop music.

Subtractive synthesis was the first type of synthesis used, in which a basic wave form created by an oscillator was modified by notching out harmonics and articulating the sound over time. Filters were used to control harmonics and to vary the intensity of various harmonics. Envelopes were used to control the attack of the sound (starting of a pitch), the sustain (over time), the decay (the dropping intensity or ending of a sound) and the release.

Additive synthesis is relatively new, since about 1982, in which a pure sine wave is modified by a carrier modulator, i.e., sounds were added. Envelope was used in a manner similar to the earlier process of subtractive synthesis.

Digital sampling is perhaps the newest and most exciting development in synthesis. By using standard binary storage techniques of computer technology, one takes a basic sound through a direct connection to an instrument, a microphone or recorded sources, and then reduces it to 256 units per page of material, determined by the type and sophistication of the sampling device. This allows for looping and control of sampled sounds through traditional subtractive synthesis techniques. Most units are essentially a computer within a keyboard unit. Usually a MIDI-connected device, this allows for computer control, storage, reproduction through a printer, and overdubbing by the basic device up to studio overdubbing through external computer storage and manipulation.

Subtractive synthesis: See *Synthesis*.

Timbre: The complex waveform of sound, including the basic pitch (pure sine wave) and the harmonics produced by the instrument and/or sound producer, i.e., sound quality.

Transistor: A nonvacuum electronic device which replaces vacuum tubes in function. Non-heat-producing, they are very small and are used in solid state circuitry. See also *Solid state*.

Transducer: A device which changes energy from one form to another, such as acoustic energy to electrical energy.

Transformer: A component that features a coiled wire to transfer alternating current from one circuit to another. It can increase or decrease the voltage according to the ratio of turns of the wire to diameter of the coils.

Tweeter: A high-range speaker.

Unidimensional: A term normally applied to microphones, although it can be associated with speakers, it defines a narrow spectrum of sound reception. Unidimensional microphones pick up only in one direction and therefore do not pick up crowd sounds and other interference.

Voltage: Measure of electrical pressure.

Volts: The unit of electromotive force.

Volume: Intensity or loudness of sound.

VU Meter: A test unit which indicates the frequency power level or volume of a complex waveform.

Wah-wah: A pedal device that has been around for some time, the Wah-wah pedal is also called a cry-baby because of the sound it creates. Most often used by blues musicians, the wah-wah creates full treble sound by moving the pedal forward, and full bass by moving it back (toe is treble and heel is bass). Moving it back and forth creates its plaintive and at times funk sound.

Watt: A unit of power. The electrical wattage of an amp describes the power with which it can drive a speaker.

Woofer: A low-range speaker for bass notes.

Appendix B
Analyses

CHAPTER THREE

"Lost Your Head Blues"—BESSIE SMITH
(SCCJ A-4)

The instrumentation of this ensemble is cornet, piano, and vocalist; it was recorded in 1926. The meter signature is 4/4 and the tempo is 96. The key of the piece is Eb, so Eb is 1, Ab is 4, and Bb is 5.

This piece has a simple four-measure introduction, followed by five sung verses, all in a fairly standard blues progression, although you will notice that there are some small variations throughout. Notice the use of the trumpet obligatto (countermelody) which sometimes fills in space and at other times accompanies the singer. In some senses, this piece is made easier by the lyrics, which can also be analyzed in terms of structure.

Notice Smith's strong voice and blues singing style. The piano player is a young Fletcher Henderson, who later became important as one of the first big band arrangers and leaders. The cornet player is Joe Smith, who did not play in the forceful style of Louis Armstrong, which perhaps made him more appropriate for accompaniment work. However, Louis Armstrong made a number of recordings with Bessie Smith as well.

Intro (Trumpet)

```
Bb7      Eb   Bb   Eb
         //   //   ////
1     2   3         4
```

Verse 1 (Sung) **Trumpet Obligatto**

Eb	Bb7	Eb	Eb7	Ab		Eb		Bb		Eb	EbEb7
1	2	3	4	5	6	7	8	9	10	11	12

Verse 2 (Sung) Trumpet Obligatto

Eb	f	Bb	Eb	Eb7	Ab		Eb		Bb7		Eb	EbBb7
1	2		3	4	5	6	7	8	9	10	11	12

Verse 3 (Sung)

Eb	Bb7	Eb	Eb7	Ab		Eb		Bb		Eb	
1	2	3	4	5	6	7	8	9	10	11	12

Verse 4 (Sung)

Eb			Eb7	Ab		Eb		Bb7		Eb	EbBb7
1	2	3	4	5	6	7	8	9	10	11	12

Verse 5 (Sung) **Hold**

Eb			Eb7	Ab		Eb		Bb7		Eb	Eb
1	2	3	4	5	6	7	8	9	10	11	12

"Honky Tonk Train Blues"—MEADE "LUX" LEWIS (SCCJ C-4)

This composition is for solo piano and is in boogie-woogie style; it was recorded in 1937. The meter signature is 4/4 and the tempo is 170 beats per minute. The piece is in G major with G being 1, C being 4, and D7 being 5. With a short introduction of two measures, the straight blues progression is repeated nine times with a concluding unit that has some slight changes in chord progressions at the end. I have used the symbols ‖: and :‖; those are repeat signs indicating that the material inside the repeat signs is to be repeated once. Writing nine times above the unit indicates nine repetitions. Normally I would not use repeat signs unless the repetition was exact and the entire piece fairly similar.

However, this is not to suggest that there are not differences between the statements other than structural. The boogie-woogie pattern is an ostinato base figure; the left hand plays the chords in broken fashion using the same pattern. That pattern in boogie-woogie accents a short and long pattern over and over again. First listen for that left-hand figure so that you can recognize it and count it.

Once you understand the underlying structural device of the left hand, then you should try to analyze what the right hand is doing, essentially a set of variations or rhythmic riffs (short melodies). At times, Lewis sets up an interesting cross rhythm; the right hand does something rhythmically different from the left-hand figure. This is a very important quality in jazz. To analyze this, you might want to write out nine lines so that you can write different notes on top of each progression.

Intro

D	NC												
1	2												

G			C	G		D7				G D7 G D7 G D7 GD7G
1	2	3	4	5	6	7	8	9	10	11 12 13 14

Nine Times

‖: G   C   G   D7   G   :‖

    1 2   3   4   5   6   7   8   9   10   11   12

CHAPTER FOUR

"Cake Walking Babies from Home"—RED ONION JAZZ BABIES (SCCJ A-10)

The instrumentation of this ensemble is cornet (Louis Armstrong), soprano sax (Sidney Bechet), trombone, piano (Lil Armstrong), banjo, and vocal duo; it was recorded in 1924. The meter signature is 4/4 and the tempo is 120 (two beats per second); one could count this at 240 beats per minute, but I prefer the half-time count. The key is Ab, and the piece is not a blues progression at all. An excellent example of New Orleans style playing in that the group is essentially the improvisational unit, this piece also features a central section with a vocal duo.

The formal structure of this piece is made up of two melodies with an interlude. Melody A takes eight measures; melody B takes twelve measures; and the interlude covers eight measures. However, the interlude is only used once to set up the vocal section. The chord changes are standard song form, and they fit into two- and four-measure units within the larger melody. Melody A starts on a 5 chord and ends on a 5 chord; melody B starts on a 5 (Eb7) chord and ends on a 1 (Ab). Probably the best way to listen to this piece is by counting the beats and phrases and trying to memorize the different melodies; they are repeated throughout the piece.

Also of interest are the solo cadenzas or short expositions by the trumpet and the soprano sax. Some have suggested that the soprano playing in this piece helped to establish Bechet's dominance on that instrument. Also you should listen for the way the three melody instruments (trombone, soprano sax, and trumpet) play as one unit.

**Group
A Melody**

Eb7		AB	F7	Bb7			bb	Eb7
1	2	3	4	5	6	7	8	

**Group
B Melody**

Eb7		Ab	f	Db	DbDo	AbEb7Ab	Eb7		Bb Eb	Ab
1	2	3	4	5	6	7	8	9	10	11 12

Group
Interlude

Ab			Bb	EbC	f	C	f	Bb7	Bb	Eb
1	2	3	4	5		6		7	8	

Vocal
A Melody

Eb7		Ab	F7	Bb7			Eb7
1	2	3	4	5	6	7	8

Vocal
B Melody

Eb7		Ab	f	Db		Ab		Eb7		Bb	Eb Ab
1	2	3	4	5	6	7	8	9	10	11	12

Group   **Sax**
A Melody

Eb7		Ab	F7	Bb7			Eb7
1	2	3	4	5	6	7	8

Group   **Trumpet**
B Melody

Eb7		Ab	f	Db		Ab		Eb7		Bb Eb	Ab
1	2	3	4	5	6	7	8	9	10	11	12

Group   **Trombone**
A Melody

Eb7		Ab	F7	Bb7			Eb7
1	2	3	4	5	6	7	8

Group   **Sax**
B Melody

Eb7		Ab	f	Db		Ab		Eb7		Bb Eb	Ab
1	2	3	4	5	6	7	8	9	10	11	12

"Dead Man Blues"—JELLY ROLL MORTON'S RED HOT PEPPERS (SCCJ A-7)

The instrumentation of this ensemble is piano, trumpet, trombone, clarinet, guitar, banjo, bass, and drums; it was recorded in 1926. The meter signature is 4/4; the tempo starts at 74 during the slow introduction and speeds up to 124 for the main part of the piece. The key of the piece is Bb, although the introduction starts in g. Another clear example of the blues, the chord progression goes as follows: 1,1,1,1,4,4,1,6,2,5,1,5. With the exception of the back half, the first seven measures of each twelve-measure unit follows the standard progression; the last five measures imply the same sound as the standard progression but actually are a variation of the blues progression.

Probably the most interesting feature of the piece is the orchestrated way in which the three clarinets play together and the rather distinctive rhythmic passage in which there is a sharp accent on beat 3 of measures 2, 4, and so on. It is precisely devices like this which have been truly memorable in jazz. Although a blues, there are clearly three distinct melodies, beginning with the trombone intro suggesting a funeral march by Frederic Chopin.

You will notice the slash symbol (/) used underneath some chord changes in this piece. Each slash stands for a beat in the measure to which it is associated. In this manner, you can tell exactly how many beats each chord gets. For instance, in measure 4 of the introduction, each chord gets one beat, while in measure 1 the g chord occurs on all four beats.

Intro   Slow   74 Beats Per Minute

g		D g D	g c g F7
/ / / /	/ / / /	/ / / /	/ / /
1	2	3	4

Speeds up to 124
Group

Bb				Eb			Bb	G7	C7	F7	Bb	F7
1	2	3	4	5	6		7	8	9	10	11	12

Clarinet

Bb	BboF	Bb7		Eb			Bb	G7	C7	F7	BbF7	BbF7
1	2	3	4	5	6	7	8	9	10	11	12	

Trumpet

Bb			Bb7	Eb		Bb	G7	C7	F7	BbF7	BbF7
1	2	3	4	5	6	7	8	9	10	11	12

Trumpet

Bb			Bb7	Eb		Bb	G7	C7	F7	Bb	F7
1	2	3	4	5	6	7	8	9	10	11	12

Three Clarinets in Harmony with Stop-Time Rhythm

BB			Eb		Bb	G7	C7	F7	BbF7	BbF7
1	2	3	4	5	6	7	8	9	10	11	12

Three Clarinets in Harmony with Trombone Obligatto

Bb				Eb		Bb	G7	C7	F7	BbF7	BbF7
1	2	3	4	5	6	7	8	9	10	11	12

Group

Bb			Bb7	Eb	Eo	Bb7	G7	C7	F7	BbF7	BbFBb
										////	/ ///
1	2	3	4	5	6	7	8	9	10	11	12

CHAPTER FIVE

"Singing the Blues"—Frankie Trumbauer and his Orchestra (SCCJ B-8)

The instrumentation of this piece is cornet, C-melody sax, trombone, clarinet and alto sax, piano, guitar, and drums; the piece was recorded in 1927. The meter signature is 4/4 and the tempo is 132. The key is Eb. This is an excellent example of a piece that has the word "blues" in the title but is not a blues progression at all; in fact, the piece has very few blues qualities to it.

The composition is an example of Chicago Dixieland, in its reliance on individual solos, especially the Beiderbecke cornet solo. However, there also is group activity at the end. Note the Jimmy Dorsey clarinet solo and the guitar breaks at the end. The piece divides very easily into eight-measure units. Therefore, you should not find it difficult to follow.

Intro
Clarinet/Sax

Ab	g	Bb7EbBbEb	
1	2	3	4

C Melody Sax Solo   **Sax Break**

f	Bb7	Eb		f	Bb7	Eb		G7		C7		F7		Bb7	
1	2	3	4	5	6	7	8	1	2	3	4	5	6	7	8

C Melody Sax Solo Continued   **Break**

f	Bb7	Eb		C7		f C	f	Ab	Ao	Eb	C7	F7	Bb7Eb	
1	2	3	4	5	6	7	8	1	2	3	4	5	6 7	8

Trumpet   **Break**

f	Bb7	Eb		f	Bb7	Eb		G7		C7		F7		Bb7	
1	2	3	4	5	6	7	8	1	2	3	4	5	6	7 8	

Trumpet Continued

f	Bb7	Eb		C7		f C		f	Ab	Ao	Eb	C7	F7	Bb	Eb
1	2	3	4	5	6	7	8	1	2	3	4	5	6	7	8

Group
Clarinet   Break

f	Bb7	Eb		f	Bb7	Eb		G7	C7	F7		Bb7	
1	2	3	4	5	6	7	8	1 2	3 4	5	6	7 8	

Group   Group + Guitar Breaks

f	Bb7	Eb		C7		f C		f	Ab	Ao	Eb	C7	F7	Bb	Eb
1	2	3	4	5	6	7	8	1	2	3	4	5	6	7 8	

"Dinah"—Red Nichols and His Five Pennies (SCCJ C-1)

The instrumentation on this piece is three trumpets, two trombones, clarinet, tenor sax, piano, guitar, bass, and drums. Jack Teagarden is on trombone; Benny Goodman is on clarinet; and Gene Krupa is on drums. The piece was recorded in 1929. The meter is 4/4, the tempo is 134, and the key is Ab. The structure breaks down nicely into a thirty-two-measure unit, four units of eight each; the melody structure is AABA (see chart).

A familiar tune, the melody is presented first by trombones with reed backgrounds, then various solos completed by the group. This piece is an example of early big band style, with Dixieland improvisation and conclusion. Although not technically demanding like other Dixie tunes of the same era, it illustrates early big band style in transition.

Intro (Trombone)

Ab		Eb7	
1	2	3	4

Trombone Melody (Reed Background)   Trombone
A Melody   A Melody

AbGAb			bbEb	BbEbAbG	bbEb AbG	Ab		bb Eb	BbEbAb	
1 2	3 4	5	6	7	8	1	2 3 4	5	6 7	8

Trumpet Melody (Reed Background)   Trombone
B Melody   A Melody

f		Ab	Bb7	Eb7		AbG	Ab		bb	Eb	BbEbAb	
1 2 3	4	5	6	7	8	1	2	3 4	5	6 7	8

Trombone (Extension)

Db	CAb	Eb
1	2	

Clarinet Solo
A Melody   **Clarinet**
                          A Melody

Ab				BbEb	BbEb	Ab	Eb7	Ab				BbEbBbEbAb			
1	2	3	4	5	6	7	8	1	2	3	4	5	6	7	8

Tenor Sax Solo
B Melody   **Clarinet**
                          A Melody

f		Bb7		Ab	Bb7	Eb7		Ab		BbEb	BbEbAbc	AbEb
1	2	3	4	5	6	7	8	1	2 3 4	5	6	7	8

Trombone Solo
A Melody   **Trombone**
                          A Melody

Ab				BbEbBbEbAb	Eb7	Ab				BbEbBbEbAbDbAb			
1	2	3	4	5 6 7	8	1 2	3	4	5	6	7	8

Trombone
B Melody   **Group**
                          A Melody

Ab				BbEbBbEbAb	Eb7	Ab				BbEbBbEbAbDbAb			
1	2	3	4	5	6	7	8	1	2	3	4	5	6	7	8

CHAPTER SIX

"Maple Leaf Rag"—Scott Joplin (SCCJA-1)

A solo piano piece, this was recorded in 1916 from a piano roll. The meter signature is 4/4 and the tempo is 160, although one must realize that this simply refers to the speed with which the roll was played. The key of this version is Ab, which is the same as the printed versions. This piece is available in sheet music in most music stores.

The sections of this piece are very easy to hear, with four clear melodies, each repeated once. The chord progression is not a blues, but nevertheless it is fairly easy to hear. It fluctuates back and forth between the 1 chord (Ab) and the 5 chord (Eb7) in the first two melodies, and between 4 (Db) and 1 (Ab) in the last two. There are some stock cadences or ending formulas which you can hear at the end of most phrases; that is where there are many chord changes.

The playing style is very clean and mechanical, which probably has more to do with the piano roll than anything else. The actual performance of this piece by Scott Joplin is conjecture. Some people play Joplin rags very evenly, and others swing it a bit.

A Melody

Ab	Eb7	Ab	Eb7	FbEbFbEbab		Do	Ab	FbAb	Do	Ab	FbAb
1	2	3	4	5	6	7 8	1	2	3 4 5	6	7	8

A Melody

Ab	Eb7	Ab	Eb7	FbEbFbEbab			Do	Ab	FbAb	Do	Ab	FbAb
1	2	3	4	5	6	7 8	1	2	3 4 5	6	7	8

B Melody

Eb7		Ab		Eb7		Ab		Eb7		Ab	Ab	F7	bb	BbEbAb
1	2	3	4	5	6	7	8	1	2	3	4	5	6	7 8

B Melody

Eb7		Ab		Eb7		Ab		Eb7		Ab	Ab	F7	bb	BbEbAb
1	2	3	4	5	6	7	8	1	2	3	4	5	6	7 8

A Melody

Ab	Eb7	Ab	Eb7	FbEbFbEbab			Do	Ab	FbAb	Do	Ab	FbAb
1	2	3	4	5	6	7 8	1	2	3 4 5	6	7	8

C Melody

Ab7		Db	Bb7Ab7		Db		F7	Bb7		eb		Go	Bb7	EbAbDb
1	2	3	4	5	6	7	8	1	2	3 4	5	6	7	8

C Melody

Ab7		Db	Bb7Ab7		Db		F7	Bb7		eb		Go	Bb7	EbAbDb
1	2	3	4	5	6	7	8	1	2	3 4	5	6	7	8

D Melody

Db		Ab		Eb7		Ab		Db		Ab		Dbdb	Ab	BbEbAb
1	2	3	4	5	6	7	8	1	2	3 4	5	6	7	8

D Melody

Db		Ab		Eb7		Ab		Db		Ab		Dbdb	Ab	BbEbAb
1	2	3	4	5	6	7	8	1	2	3 4	5	6	7	8

"Carolina Shout"—James Johnson (SCCJ A-12)

The earliest recorded piece in the Smithsonian Collection (that is, recorded by a musician rather than a piano roll), this solo piano performance was recorded by Okeh Records in 1921. The meter signature is 4/4, the tempo is 176, and the key is G. The shout is an old black work song which became a religious piece in the nineteenth century. Although this piece is called a shout, it really is a rag with five distinct melodies.

The playing style is basically percussive and rhythmic rather than melodic. In that sense, the chord progression does not mean much. You should try to follow the progression while counting the beats, but you should write down your impressions of the changing rhythmic devices which the piano player uses. I make that suggestion partly because chord changes in this piece are very hard to analyze.

Intro

```
Ge    CA7    D7e    FoD7
1      2      3       4
```

A Melody

```
‖: GB7  e      G7      CD7 G    B7      e    Go      D7      Fo    D7
     1   2      3       4   5          6     7              8
```

A Melody (Part Two)

```
G   B7  e  G   C   D7  G   E7  a   D7   G :‖
1        2      3   4       5   6   7   8
```

B Melody

```
G   CG CG CC#oDG CG  CF#  b D7   G   CG  CG  CC#D G   Cc   D7  G
1    2   3   4      5   6    7   8    1    2    3    4     5    6    7   8
```

C Melody

```
G   D7  G   GD7 G   F#7  b  F#bD  G   D7  G   D7  G   Cc  D7  G
1    2   3      4   5   6    7     8    1   2   3   4   5   6   7   8
```

C Melody

```
G   D7  G   GD7 G   F#7  b  F#bD  G   D7  G   D7  G   Cc  D7  Go
1    2   3      4   5   6    7     8    1   2   3   4   5   6   7   8
```

D Melody

```
G  Go  G  Go  G  Go  C  D  G  Go  G  Go  G     A7  d  G7  C
1  2    3   4    5  6    7     8         1  2    3  4  5    6   7   8
```

E Melody

```
F   C   F   C   F   C   B7  e  G7  F   C   F   C A  A7  D7  G7 CGo
1    2   3   4   5   6   7    8       1   2   3   4    5    6    7   8
```

D Melody

```
G  Go  G  Go  G  Go  C  D  G  Go  G  Go  G     A7  d  G7  C
1  2    3   4    5  6    7     8         1  2    3  4  5    6   7   8
```

Ending Tag (Also New)

```
Eb    AB   G        C7
1      2    3        4
```

"I Ain't Got Nobody"—Fats Waller (SCCJ C-3)

This solo piano piece was recorded in 1937. Of the piano pieces illustrated in this chapter, this is the most progressive. Although Jelly Roll Morton recorded his Maple Leaf Rag in 1938, his playing is not nearly as advanced as Fats Waller's. The meter signature is 4/4, the tempo is a slow 92, and the key is F.

In this standard piece, Waller plays the melody once and then does one variation. However, before he finishes playing the melody, he is already interpreting the melody and providing alternative chord changes. You might try to follow the slashes, which indicate when chords change within measures. You will notice several rhythmic tricks, especially the boogie bass at the beginning of the variation and the stride piano style at the end of the second part of the melody. You might also write down how he uses dynamics, that is, loud and soft playing. This piece is very tasty in that respect.

Intro

1 2 3 4

A Melody (with Embellishment)

F7	F E EB	D G7		Db7	F	d	G7 C	C7 F	C7
////	/ / /	/ ////	//	//	//	//	// /	/ ////	////
1	2	3	4	5	6	7		8	

A Melody   Stride

F7	F7 E7 EB7 D7 G7	d	G7	d	G7	d	G7 C7 Co	C7
////	//// ////	//	//	//	//	//	// // //	////
1	2 3	4	5	6		7	8	

B Melody

F7		Bb F7	Bb	Eb	D	A	a	D G	C7
////	///	/ ///	/ //	//	//	//	//	/////	////
1	2	3	4	5	6	7		8	

A Melody

F		E EbD	G7	bb F	D7	G7 C7	F Bb7	F C7
////	/	////	// //	////	// //	// //	////	
1	2	3	4	5	6	7	8	

Variation (A Melody)
Boogie Bass at Beginning

F7	E	Eb	D	d	G7	bb	F	D G C	F Eo	d	C	b	a	Abo C7
////	/	/	//	// //	////	//	/////	//	/	/	/	/	/ //
1	2		3	4	5	6	7				8			

A Melody

F	C7	F	E	Eb	D	d		G7	d		G7	F		D7	G7	C7	Co	C7
////	/ /	/		/	/	//		//	//		//	//		////	//	//		////
1	2			3		4		5			6	7			8			

B Melody

F7		Bb7	F7	Bb	G7		C7	
1	2	3	4	5	6	7		8

A Melody   **Held**

F	C7	F	Eb	D	G7	g		bb	F	Abo	g	C7	F	C7	F	C	F
////	/	/ /	/		////	//		//	//	//		// //	////	/	/	//
1	2			3	4	5			6	7	8						

Ritard (slow down) ....

CHAPTER SEVEN

"St. Louis Blues"—Bessie Smith (SCCJ A-3)

The instrumentation of this classic recording from 1925 is vocalist, cornet, and reed organ. The meter is 4/4, the tempo is a very slow 75 beats per minute, and the key is Eb. The recording quality is not terribly good, but Louis Armstrong's background and Smith's singing are great early jazz performances. The blues progression of the first two sections is filled with alternate chords. However, the basic 1 (Eb),1,1,1,4(Ab),4,1,1,5,4,1,1 is preserved.

Be sure to try to distinguish between the two harmonic progressions represented in the first two twelve-measure phrases and the two eight-measure phrases. The first is in a major key and the second is in a minor. Of course, the eight-measure phrase is not blues but rather a different melody which functions as a transition or contrast phrase. Also pay careful attention to Armstrong's cornet work; in this case, he simply accompanies Smith.

Intro

Bb7

Vocal   **With Trumpet Obligatto**

Eb	AbBbEb		Ab	B	Bb	Eb	AbgGbof	Bb	Eb	Abab	EbGbo	f		Bb
////			////			////	////	//	/ /	////		//		//
1	2	3	4	5	6	7	8	9	10	11		12		

Vocal

Eb	AbBb	Eb	Eb7	Ab	B	Bb	Eb		f	F	Bb	Eb	AbabEbGbof	Bb
////				////					////	//	////	/ /		
1	2	3	4	5	6	7	8	9	10	11	12			

Vocal

eb		Bb7		Bb7		eb	
1	2	3	4	5	6	7	8

Vocal

eb		Bb7		Bb7		EbF	Bb7
1	2	3	4	5	6	7	8

Vocal   **Hold**

EbEboEbEboEbEboEbEboEb Ab Bb Eb   Bb F Bb Eb ab Eb
// // // //

1		2		3	4	5	6	7	8	9	10	11	12

"Hotter Than That"—Louis Armstrong and His Hot Peppers (SCCJ B-3)

The instrumentation of this piece is cornet, trombone, clarinet, piano, banjo, guitar, and vocalist. Armstrong both plays cornet and is the vocalist. Recorded in 1927, the meter is 4/4 and the tempo is 152. The key of the piece is Eb. Actually this piece is fairly simple to follow, with Eb being 1 and Bb7 being 5. The phrase structure is always broken into two eight-measure phrases, with occasional transition figures such as the piano break after the voice and guitar trading of two measures.

Of course, the vocal treatment of Armstrong is delightful, but I really think that the trumpet (cornet) and guitar trading at the end is the most exciting. This piece features quite a bit of imitation by two instrumentalists and also numerous breaks at the end of each sixteen-measure unit.

Intro   **Trumpet**

Ab	Ao	Eb	C7	F7	Bb7	Eb	
1	2	3	4	5	6	7	8

Trumpet

Eb				Bb7		Bb7					Eb		

1 2 3 4 5 6 7   8 1 2 3 4 5 6 7 8

Trumpet   **Clarinet**

Eb   Eb7 Ab   Ab Abo Eb C7 F7 Bb7 Eb

1 2 3 4   5 6 7 8 1   2   3   4   5   6   7 8

Clarinet   **Clarinet**

Eb   Bb7   Eb

1   2 3 4 5 6   7 8 1 2 3 4 5 6   7 8

Clarinet   **Vocal**

				Eb7	Ab		Ab	Ao	Eb		C7	F7	Bb7	Eb
1	2	3	4	5	6	7	8	1	2	3	4	5	6	7 8

Vocal and Guitar Only   **Vocal**

Eb						Bb7						Eb	
1	2	3	4	5	6	7	8	1	2	3	4	5	67 8

Eb			Eb7		Ab		Ab	Ao	Eb	C7	F7	Bb7	Eb
1	2	3 4	5	6	7	8	1	2	3	4	5	6	7 8

Voice   **Guitar**   **Voice**   **Guitar**   **Voice**   **Guitar**   **Voice**   **Guitar**

No chord (NC)

1	2	3	4	5	6	7	8	1	2	3	4	5	6	7	8

Piano

Eb			Bb7
1	2	3	4

Trombone   **Trumpet**

Eb						Bb7						Eb	
1	2	3	4	5	6	7	8	1 2 3 4 5 6	7	8			

Trumpet   **Breaks**   **Guitar**

Eb				Eb7		Ab		Ab	Ao	Eb	C7	F7	Bb7	Eb
1	2	3	4 5	6	7	8 1	2	3	4	5	6	7 8		

Trumpet   **Guitar**   **Held**

NC			Ebo	
1	2	3	4	5

"4 or 5 Times"—Jimmie Noone's Apex Club Orchestra (SCCJ B-10)

This piece is scored for clarinet, alto sax, piano, banjo/guitar, and drums. Both the clarinet and alto sax players sing the vocal parts, which consist of saying "four or five times" over and over. The meter signature is 4/4, the tempo is about 116, and the key is D.

The composition itself is a great example of maturing Dixieland style, with the vocal serving as crowd entertainment. In a sense, it was compositions like this which led to the vocal style of big band music, where the band sang the vocals. A good example of that would be "Pennsylvania 6-5000" by Glenn Miller. However, in this piece, the lyric is central, and the backup music simply supports that. Earl Hines is on piano in this recording; the clarinet and alto sax work are quite competent.

Intro (Piano)

Do		DB7	E7	A7
1	2	3	4	

Group

D		B7E7		A7		DFo	e	A D	D7	G	G#o	DB7	E7A7D A7
1	2	3	4	5	6	7	8	1	2	3	4	5	6 7 8

Piano

D		B7E7		A7		F# B E A	D		D7	G	G#oDBE A	DB E A
1	2	3	4	5	6	7	8	1	2	3	4 5	6 7 8

Vocal

D		B7E7		A7		F#B E A	D	D7	G	G#oDB E A	DFoA7
1	2	3	4	5	6	7	8	1	2	3 4 5	6 7 8

Vocal

D		B7E7		A7		F# B E A	D	D7	G	G#oDB E A	De	A7
1	2	3	4	5	6	7	8	1	2	3	4 5 6	7	8

Group (Alto Sax, Clarinet)

D		B7Eb		A7		DB	E A	D	D7	G	G#oDb E A	DFOe A7
1	2	3	4	5	6	7	8	1	2	3	4 5 6	7 8

Group   **Held D**

B7Eb		A7			DB7	E A	D D7	G	G#oDB	E A D	D
1	2 3	4 5 6	7		8	1	2	3	4 5	6	7 8

CHAPTER EIGHT

"Rockin' Chair"—Gene Krupa and His Orchestra" (SCCJ D-1)

The instrumentation of this recording is four trumpets, three trombones, four saxophones, piano, bass, guitar, and drums. Almost a complete big band, this recording was done in 1941 and is primarily a feature for Roy Eldridge; the arrangement was done by Benny Carter. The meter signature is 4/4, the tempo is 82 (slow ballad), and the key is Eb.

The basic composition is a thirty-two-measure ballad, divided into four eight-measure phrases: AABA. The chord progression is especially easy to hear, although you might have difficulty distinguishing particular chords. Eb is 1, Ab is 4, and Bb is 5. Of course, it is not a blues song, but a popular song. Notice the trumpet cadenzas, which Krupa shares with the clarinet at the end. Also notice the way the arranger uses the reeds to back up the soloist the first time through and the way in which Eldridge plays in screech trumpet style and repetition of B. A very satisfying arrangement, it illustrates the way a big band can be used to accompany a particular soloist or singer and also shows nice writing for woodwinds. Interestingly, the Krupa band was mainly known for showcasing Krupa, who was a hot drummer; however, this arrangement illustrates something different.

Trumpet Cadenza Trumpet Cadenza Trumpet Cadenza Trumpet Cadenza

Ab6	Db9	B9	Bb9

Unmeasured

A   **A'**

Trumpet Melody with Reed Background

Eb	Eb7	Ab	ab	EbDbC	F7	Bb7	Eb	a	D7	g	F	f	BbEb
1	2	3	4	5	6	7	8	1	2	3	4 5 6	7	8

B   **A'**   **Tutti**

Ab7	Eb	D	g	F	Bb7	Eb	Eb7	Ab	ab	EbEo	BbEb	A7
1	2 3	4	5	6 7 8		1	2	3	4	5	6 7	8

B   **A'**

Screech Trumpet   **Trumpet**   **Trumpet Free Piano Chord**

Ab7	Eb	D	g	F	Bb7	Eb	Eb7	Ab	ab	EbEoF7
1	2 3	4	5	6 7 8		1	2	3	4	5 6 7 8

Cadenzas

Trumpet   **Clarinet**   **Trumpet**   **Chord**

                                             Eb

Unmeasured

"In the Mood"—Glenn Miller

"In the Mood" is one of those pieces that just sticks out as a representative of big band music. Many musicians probably do not like the piece because they have played it so many times. Regardless of that bias, it remains one of the most popular pieces from that era, and for good reason. The instrumentation is a full big band, featuring alto and tenor sax solos and a trumpet solo; the original actually featured two tenors. The meter signature is 4/4, the tempo is 144, and the key is Ab.

The tune basically has two melodies to it, the first being the broken arpeggio (chord) right after the intro, marked A in my analysis. The second melody is marked B and features a reiterative chord sequence. The chord sequence is the one used for the sax solos. The trumpet solo uses a slightly different set of chord changes over sixteen measures.

Note particularly that the opening melody (A) is a blues progression: Ab is 1, Db is 4, and Eb is 5. The changes in measures 11 and 12 are a turnaround, but it does not alter the blues character. Melody B is not blueslike. There are several brass and ensemble interludes which move the piece from one section to another. The last four repetitions of melody A get softer and softer, and then loud for the conclusion. This is largely a riff-oriented piece, and although the solos are now played exactly the same way by everyone, it has a jazz quality to it.

Intro

Ab				Bb7		Eb7	
1	2	3	4	5	6	7	8

A

‖: Ab   Db   Ab   Eb   Ab Bo bb Eb7 :‖
    1   2   3   4   5   6   7   8   9   10 11   12

B

‖: AbBobb Eb AbBobb Eb AbBobb Eb7   EboEb Ab :‖
  /////   // //////   // ////// // // // /// /
  1 2   3   4   5   6   7   8

B
Tenor Solo   **Alto**   **Tenor**   **Tutti**

‖: AbBobb Eb AbBobb Eb AbBobb Eb   EboEb Ab :‖
  /////   // //////   // ////// // // // /// /
  1 2   3   4   5   6   7   8

Interlude

Ab	Eb7	Ab	
1	2	3	4

Trumpet Solo

Ab						Eb7Ab								Eb7	Ab
1	2	3	4	5	6	7	8	9	10	11	12	13	14	15	16

Brass Interlude

bb	Eb	Ab	Eb
1		2	

A
Soft/Very Soft

Trumpet Trombone x

‖: Ab				Db		Ab		Eb7		Ab			:‖
1	2	3	4	5	6	7	8	9	10	11	12	13	14

A
Extremely Soft

Trumpet Trombone x

Ab				Db		Ab		Eb7		Ab			
1	2	3	4	5	6	7	8	9	10	11	12	13	14

A
Loud

Ab				Db		Ab		Eb7
1	2	3	4	5	6	7	8	9

Trumpet

Trombone (off on beat 1)

Ab									
1	2	3	4	5	6	7	8	9	10

CHAPTER NINE

"Taxi War Dance"—Count Basie and His Orchestra (SCCJ D-6)

The instrumentation of this piece is four trumpets, three trombones, four saxophones, piano, guitar, bass, and drums; it was recorded in 1939. The meter signature is 4/4, the tempo is 192, and the key is G. The piece has the following structure: intro (8), tenor solo (32), interlude (2), trombone solo (32), trading eights (64), and conclusion (9). The basic unit of 32 is divided into four eights (A A B A). Except for the B section, the chord changes to A are simple. G is 1 and C is 4. The thirty-two-measure unit is a song form rather than a blues.

The Basie sound is obvious in this orchestration, and the riff orientation of the band basically supports solo work. The Lester Young tenor solo is exemplary, and the piece illustrates the arranging technique of Basie and Young, who wrote this piece together.

Piano   **Ensemble Interlude**

GG#oa	D	GG#oa	D	GG#oa	D	GG#oa	D7
1	2	3	4	5	6	7	8

A

Tenor Sax   **A**

```
G            C  c  G        G              C  c  G
1   2   3   4   5   6   7   8   1   2   3   4   5   6   7   8
```

B   **A**

```
c   g G c BbAbG     c  g G   c Bb   a D7   G          C   c  G
    ////////////
1   2   3   4        5  6    7       8      1  2  3 4  5   6 7 8
```

Ensemble Interlude

```
GG#o   a      D7
1      2
```

A

Trombone   **A**

```
G         C  c  G         G           C  c  G
1   2 3 4   5   6   7   8   1   2   3 4   5   6   7 8
```

B   **A**

```
c   g G c BbAbG     c   g G   c Bb  a D7 G           C   c   G
    ////////////
1   2   3   4        5   6     7     8    1   2   3 4 5   6   7 8
```

A

Ensemble Int. Tenor   **A**

Ensemble   Tenor

```
G            C  c  G         G           C  c  G
1   2 3 4   5   6   7   8   1   2   3 4   5   6   7 8
```

B   **A**

Piano   **Ensemble Tenor**

```
c   g G c BbAbG     c g G   c Bb   a D7   G          C   c  G
    ////////////
1   2   3   4        5 6    7       8      1  2  3 4  5   6 7 8
```

A

Ensemble   Tenor   **A**

Ensemble   Tenor

```
G            C  c  G         G           C  c  G
1   2 3 4   5   6   7   8   1   2   3 4   5   6   7 8
```

B									A							
Piano									**Ensemble Tenor**							

c	g G c BbAbG c		g G	c Bb	a D7	G		C	c G
	/////////////								
1	2 3 4	5 6	7	8	1 2	3 4	5	6 7 8	

Piano   Tenor Bass   Drums Ensemble Ext.

C	c	G		A D	G		a D G		||
1	2	3	4	5	6	7	8	9	

"Cottontail"—Duke Ellington and his Famous Orchestra (SCCJ E-2)

The instrumentation of this piece is three trumpets, three trombones, five saxes, piano, guitar, bass, and drums; it was recorded in 1940. The meter signature is 4/4, the tempo is 210, and the key is Bb. Essentially a solo vehicle, the piece is a series of variations based on the tune "I Got Rhythm" (see later analysis as well). The tenor sax solo by Ben Webster is the one which most people think highly of, but the entire composition is extremely well done. The baritone solo is worth mention, as are the Cootie Williams trumpet solo and Ellington's contribution.

The chord changes to the piece are actually quite easy to hear, once you get used to them. "I Got Rhythm" is based upon a 1, 6, 2, 5 set of changes. Several other tunes use the same progression, such as "Blue Moon," "Heart and Soul," and the "Shrimp Boat's Are A Comin'." But, in this song, the changes are pretty fast; see measures 1 and 2. Bb g7 c7 F7 or 1, 6, 2 5 in the key of Bb. The bridge section is quite different and very easy to hear.

The basic composition is thirty-two measures long and is first heard in its entirety for the tenor sax solo. Please notice that the first two lines of analysis are only twenty-eight measures in length. For some reason, they decided to cut off four measures at the end of the ensemble section. After that, the piece falls into thirty-two-measure units, essentially A A' B A'. Also note the super sax section toward the end, where the saxophones play in harmony and in quick melodic lines. This was another Ellington innovation, although this is clearly the work of Lester Young.

A1
Ensemble

A2
Ensemble

Bbg	c F	Bbg	c F	BbEbeb	Bbg	c	FBbgc F		Bbg	c F	Bb	EbebBb
1	2	3	4	5 6	7	8	9 10	11	12 13	14	15	16

B
Reeds/Trumpet

A' (transition)
Ensemble

D7		G7		C7		F7		Bb A	Ab G	Gb F	BbF
1	2	3	4	5	6	7	8	1	2	3	4

A1
Tenor Sax   **A2**

Bbg c F Bbg c F BbEbeb   Bbg   c   FBbgc F   Bbg   c F Bb EbebBb
1   2   3   4   5 6   7   8   9   10   11   12 13 14 15   16

B   **A2**
Tutti Chords

D7   G7   C7   F7   Bbgc F   Bbg   c F   Bb EbebBb
1   2   3   4   5 6 7   8   9   10   11   12   13 14   15   16

A1
Tenor Sax   **A2**

Bbg c F Bbg c F BbEbeb   Bbg   c   FBbgc F   Bbg   c F Bb EbebBb
1   2   3   4   5 6   7   8   9   10   11   12 13   14 15   16

B   **A2**
Tutti Chords

D7   G7   C7   F7   Bbgc F   Bbg   c F   Bb EbebBb
1   2   3   4   5 6 7   8   9   10   11   12   13 14   15   16

A1
Ensemble   **A2**

Bbg c F Bbg c F BbEbeb   Bbg   c   FBbgc F   Bbg   c F Bb EbebBb
1   2   3   4   5 6   7   8   9   10   11   12 13 14 15   16

B   **A2**
Baritone Sax   **Piano**

D7   G7   C7   F7   Bbgc F   Bbg   c F   Bb EbebBb
1   2   3   4   5 6 7   8   9   10   11   12   13 14   15   16

A1
Reed Soli (super sax)   **A2**

Bbg c F Bbg c F BbEbeb   Bbg   c   FBbgc F   Bbg   c F Bb EbebBb
1   2   3   4   5 6   7   8   9   10   11   12 13 14 15   16

B   **A2**
Continued Reed Soli

D7   G7   C7   F7   Bbgc F   Bbg   c F   Bb EbebBb
1   2   3   4   5 6 7   8   9   10   11   12   13 14   15   16

A1
Reeds with Brass Kicks   **A2**

Bbg	c F	Bbg	c F	BbEbeb	Bbg	c	FBbgc F	Bbg	c F	Bb	EbebBb	
1	2	3	4	5 6	7	8	9 10	11	12	13	14 15	16

B   **A2**
Trumpets   **Ensemble**   **Chord**

D7	G7	C7	F7	Bbgc F	Bbg	c F	Bb	EbebBb
1	2	3	4	5 6 7	8 9 10	11 12	13 14	15 16

CHAPTER TEN

"These Foolish Things"—Billie Holiday and Her Orchestra (SCCJ C-9)

The instrumentation on this piece features piano, guitar, bass, and drums backing Billie Holiday; the piece was recorded in 1952. The meter signature is 4/4, the tempo is 68, and the key is Eb. Although actually a fairly late recording for inclusion in this chapter, it represents many of the devices which Holiday developed during her career. Her earlier version of the same piece in 1938 is not as satisfying musically.

The structure of this piece is A A B A song form over thirty-two measures. As you can tell from the chart, the B and the A section are repeated to close out the piece. Note the rhythmic device employed at the end of the introduction. The rhythm section on this recording is quite good—Oscar Peterson on piano and Ray Brown on bass. From then on, the piece is all Holiday, who milks everything possible out of the original song. Don't bother trying to follow the chord changes; just pay attention to the nuances of sound that Billie Holiday gets out of a weak voice. By this time, her physical health was poor, but that did not stop her technique.

Piano—Very Free

Eb Pedal -

Eb7	Ab	Eb7	Ab	Eb7	Ab	Eb7	DbCBBbA
1	2	3	4	5	6	7	8

A
Vocal

Ab f	Bb Eb	c f	FBb e A	Ab	Dbc F	Bb	bb E A
1	2	3	4	5	6	7	8

A'
Vocal

Ab f	Bb Eb	c f	FBb e A	Ab	Dbc F	Bb Eb	Ab dG7
1	2	3	4	5	6	7	8

B

c	G c	F ab Db	Eb c	f Bb	Db F	bb Eb
1	2 3	4	5	6	7	8

A′
Vocal

Ab f	Bb Eb	c f	FBb e A	Ab	Dbc F	Bb Eb	Ab dG7
1	2	3	4	5	6	7	8

B

c	G c	F ab Db	Eb c	f Bb	Db F	bb Eb
1	2 3	4	5	6	7	8

A′
Vocal   **Slower**

Ab f Bb Eb	c f	FBb e A	Ab	Dbc F	Bb7	Eb7
1 2	3	4	5	6	7	8

Piano Extension

E A	Ab	
1	2	‖

"You'd Be So Nice to Come Home To"— Ella Fitzgerald (SCCJ C-10)

A small ensemble of trumpet, piano, bass, and drums backs up this quintessential singer; the recording was made in 1964. The meter is 4/4, the tempo is 190, and the key is F minor. This thirty-two measure song uses essentially the same chord progression over and over, with slight changes at the ends; for those who follow chord changes, this is based totally on 2 5 1. The actual form is ABAC over thirty-two measures.

In this piece, vocalist and trumpet player (Roy Eldridge) both take solos and then interact rather extensively. It is that interaction for which you should listen, especially the way Ella imitates the trumpet riff. She does not do scat singing, but she does change the melody of the tune during the vocal improvisation, which follows the trumpet and voice interaction.

Intro
Pickups

G7 C	f	G C	fG	C	f	g C7	f g C7
1	2	3	4	5	6	7	8

Vocal

f gC f gC eb Ab7 DbAbDb g C7 gC f d Db g C7
1 2 3 4 5 6 7 8 9 10 11 12 13 14 15 16

Vocal

f gC f gC eb Ab7 DbAbDb AboAb C7 Db FBb bbEbAb GC
1 2 3 4 5 6 7 8 9 10 11 12 13 14 15 16

Trumpet **Voice**

f gC f gC eb Ab7 DbAbDb g C7 gC f d Db g C7
1 2 3 4 5 6 7 8 9 10 11 12 13 14 15 16

Trumpet **Voice**

f gC f gC eb Ab7 DbAbDb AboAb C7 Db FBb bbEbAb GC
1 2 3 4 5 6 7 8 9 10 11 12 13 14 15 16

Vocal Improvisation

f gC f gC eb Ab7 DbAbDb g C7 gC f d Db g C7
1 2 3 4 5 6 7 8 9 10 11 12 13 14 15 16

Vocal Improvisation

f g Cf g Ceb Ab DbAbDbAboAb C7 Db d db Ab F bb gC
1 2 3 4 5 6 7 8 9 10 11 12 13 14 15 16 17 18

Vocal Breaks Up for Conclusion **Held chord**

G Cf G CfGCf g Cf g Cf d f d Db Gb f f|
1 2 3 4 5 6 7 8 9 10 11 12 13 14 15 16 17 18

CHAPTER ELEVEN

"Body and Soul"—Coleman Hawkins and His Orchestra (SCCJ C-6)

This nine-piece recording was made in 1939, with three saxes, two trumpets, trombone, piano, bass, and drums. The meter signature is 4/4, the tempo is 102, and the key is Db. The ensemble basically functions to play slow chord changes behind the soloist, which is the most important part.

Other than the four-measure piano introduction, the entire composition is dedicated to two times through the chord changes to Body and Soul (a thirty-two-measure song which breaks into four eight measure phrases—A A B A). While the chord changes may sound complex, they really are not that bad. However, you probably do not need to try to hear those changes, because the background sound makes each chord distinct. The important thing to listen to in this piece is what the soloist does with the melody.

Especially during the second rendition or variation, he really flows over the chord changes and leaves the melody completely. Many people have considered this the first modern saxophone solo. Hawkins double-times, he makes expansive leaps, and he expands the horizons of improvisation in the way he covers the entire dynamic and physical range of his instrument.

Inst. Intro (Piano)

bb	Db	A7	eb Ab
1	2	3	4

A1
Tenor Sax   **A2**

eb AbDb	f	Eoeb	c F	bb	AbDbBbeb	Ab	Db	f Eo	eb	c	FDbAbDbEA
1 2 3	4	5	6	7	8	9	10	11	12	13 14	15	16

B   **A1**
Tenor Sax

DA Dg DA D d G	eEbd	G	C Bbeb	AbDb	f Eo	eb	c	FbbAbDbBb
1 2 3 4 5 6	7 8	9	10 11	12	13 14	15	16

A1   **A2**
Tenor Sax Variation/Background

eb AbDb	f	Eoeb	c F	bb	AbDbBbeb	Ab	Db	f Eo	eb	c	FDbAbDbEA
1 2 3	4	5	6 7	8 9	10	11	12	13 14 15	16

B   **A2**   **Chord Cadenza**

DA Dg DA D d G	eEbd	G C Bbeb	Ab	Db	f Eo	eb c DbAb7	Db
1 2 3 4 5 6	7 8	9	10 11	12	13 14 15	16

"I Got Rhythm"—Don Byas and Slam Stewart (SCCJ E-5)

This is a great piece because of its very unusual instrumentation, tenor sax and bass, recorded live in 1945. This piece was improvised by Don Byas (tenor sax) and Slam Stewart (bass) when they were the only ones who showed up for a concert. The meter signature is 4/4, although this composition is easier to count in 2, that is two beats per measure. In 4/4 the tempo is 296 beats per minute, which is extremely fast. Counting just two beats per measure, the rate would be 148 per minute. It is in the standard key of Bb, and the chord progression is the same one you heard in Ellington's "Cotton tail." Notice that I have used repeat signs several times in the analysis.

The first thing you have to be amazed at is how fast these musicians played. Many New York players of that era thrived on playing at the speed of light. Also interesting is the way the bass player provides all the necessary tempo and rhythmic devices necessary to keep things going. The tenor work of Byas is very satisfying, and the bass solo with singing is a delightful technique which bass players still use. Listen also for the double stops Stewart uses in the second chorus of his solo. The ending shows that the piece was improvised.

Intro

```
Bb g   c    F7Bb g   c F7
1      2    3        4
```

A   **A**
Melody

```
Bbg  c F  Bbg c F  Bb  EbEoBbgc FBbg  c F  Bbg c F   Bb  EbEoBb
1    2    3   4     5   6     7  8 9    10   11  12    13  14  15 16
```

B   **A**

```
D7       G7       C7      F7       Bbg   c F  Bbg c F   Bb  EbEoBb
1    2   3    4    5   6  7 8      9     10   11  12    13  14  15 16
```

Sax Variations One through Four
Four Times

```
‖: Bbg c F  Bbg   c F  Bb  EbEoBbgc FBbg c F  Bbg c F  Bb  EbEoBb
   1   2    3     4    5   6      7  8  9  10  11  12   13  14  15 16
```

B   **A**

```
D7    G7    C7      F7    Bbg  c F   Bbg  c F   Bb  EbEoBb  :‖
1  2  3  4  5   6   7 8   9    10    11   12    13  14  15  16
```

Bass/Voice   **Double Stops Second Time**
A   **A**

```
‖: Bbg c F  Bbg   c F  Bb  EbEoBbgc FBbg c F  Bbg c F  Bb  EbEoBb
   1   2    3     4    5   6      7  8  9  10  11  12  13  14  15 16
```

B   **A**

```
D7    G7    C7      F7    Bbg  c F   Bbg  c F   Bb  EbEoBb  :‖
1  2  3  4  5   6   7 8   9    10    11   12    13  14  15  16
```

Sax Reenters
Three Times
A   **A**

‖ : Bbg c F Bbg c F Bb EbEoBbgc FBbg c F Bbg c F Bb EbEoBb
   1   2   3   4   5   6   7   8   9   10 11 12 13 14 15 16

B   **A**

D7   G7   C7   F7   Bbg c F Bbg c F   Bb EbEoBb   : ‖
1 2   3   4   5   6   7 8 9   10   11   12   13 14   15 16

Sax (More Relaxed)
A   **A**
Melody

Bbg   c F Bbg c F Bb EbEoBbgc FBbg c F Bbg c F Bb EbEoBb
1   2   3   4   5   6   7   8   9   10 11 12 13 14   15 16

B   **A**

D7   G7   C7   F7   Bbg c F Bbg c F   Bb EbEoBb
1 2   3   4   5   6   7 8 9   10   11   12   13 14   15 16

A
                Tentative   **Applause**

 Bb
 1 2 3 4 5 6 7 8

CHAPTER TWELVE

"Shaw Nuff"—Dizzy Gillespie All Star Quintette (SCCJ E-7)

The instrumentation is trumpet, alto sax, piano, bass, and drums. Recorded in 1945, the tempo is a sparkling 280, and the key is bb. I recommend counting this piece in two beats per measure, or 140 per minute. Obviously this is all solo, but you should be sure to listen carefully to the fast unison line which the sax and trumpet play together in the third eight bar phrase of the piece. The bebop line that follows is equally fascinating and awe-inspiring. The harmonic progression goes by so quickly that one is tempted to avoid even trying to listen to it. However, you have heard it before; this tune is also based on "I Got Rhythm" changes.

    Notice also that the composition breaks into thirty-two-measure units (A A B A) and that the total structure is introduction (24 measures), bebop line (32), alto (32), trumpet (32), piano (32), bebop line (32), introduction (24). In other words, the piece has a very tight structure. But it does go by quickly. It is incredible how they play so well together, as if they can anticipate what each other will do.

Intro
Primarily Drums
Bass/Piano Unison

1 2 3 4 5 6 7 8

Melody   **Sax/Trumpet Line Piano**
Sax/Trumpet in Thirds

bb   eb   bb   B7   N.C.
1 2   3 4   5 6   7 8   1 2 3 4   5 6 7 8

A   **A**
Bebop Line in Unison

Bbg c F7d G   c F7f BbEbEod g c F Bbg c F7d G   c Ff BbEbEoBb
1   2   3   4   5   6   7   8   1   2   3   4   5   6   7 8

B   **A**
Continued Bebop Line in Unison

D7   G7   C7   F7   Bbg c F7d G   c Ff   BbEbEoBb
1 2 3 4 5 6 7   8   1   2   3   4   5   6   7 8

A   **A**
Sax Solo

Bbg c F7d G   c F7f BbEbEod g c F Bbg c   F7d G   c Ff BbEbEoBb
1   2   3   4   5   6   7   8   1   2   3   4 5   6   7 8

B   **A**
Sax Solo Continued

D7   G7   C7   F7   Bbg c F7d G   c Ff   BbEbEoBb
1 2 3 4 5 6 7   8   1   2   3   4   5   6   7 8

A   **A**
Trumpet Solo

Bbg c F7d G   c F7f BbEbEod g c F Bbg c F7d G   c Ff BbEbEoBb
1   2   3   4   5   6   7   8   1   2 3   4   5   6   7 8

B   **A**
Trumpet Solo Continued

D7   G7   C7   F7   Bbg c F7d G   c Ff BbEbEoBb
1 2 3 4 5 6 6   8   1   2   3   4 5   6   7 8

A   **A**
Piano Solo

Bbg c F7d G   c F7f BbEbEod g c F Bbg c F7d G   c Ff   BbEbEoBb
1   2 3   4 5   6   7 8 1   2 3   4 5   6   7 8

B   **A**
Piano Solo Continued

D7   G7   C7   F7   Bbg c F7d G   c Ff   BbEbEoBb
1 2 3 4 5 6 7   8 1   2   3 4 5   6   7 8

Intro
Primarily Drums

1 2 3 4 5 6 7 8

Melody				**Sax/Trumpet**			
Sax/Trumpet in Thirds				**Line**		**Piano**	**Hold**
bb	eb	bb	B7	N.C.			
1 2	3 4	5 6	7 8	1 2 3 4		5 6	7 8

"KoKo"—Charlie Parker's Re-boppers (SCCJ E-8)

The instrumentation of this piece is alto sax (Parker), trumpet and piano (Gillespie), bass (Curly Russell), and drums (Max Roach); the recording was made in 1945. The meter signature is 4/4, but do not try to count it that way. In 4/4 it goes at 300 beats per minute, so count it in two, and you can slow down to 150. The tune is in Bb and is based on the chord changes to Charlie Barnett's "Cherokee."

     The basic form of this piece is A A B A, but it takes sixty-four measures to complete the cycle. You will notice that Gillespie's role in this piece is to play the beginning section with Parker and the conclusion. Gillespie plays piano during Parker's solo. Therefore, this piece is primarily a solo vehicle for Charlie Parker. This is a classic Bird solo, and many people play it in transcribed form. Notice the way that he uses the entire tonal and physical range of the alto sax; this is bebop at its finest.

Intro	**Trumpet Solo with Drums**
Trumpet/Sax	
N.C.	N.C.
1 2 3 4 5 6 7 8	1 2 3 4 5 6 7 8

Sax Solo	**Main Melody**
	Trumpet/Sax **Break**
N.C.	N.C.
1 2 3 4 5 6 7 8	1 2 3 4 5 6 7 8

A
Sax Solo

‖: Bb   f   Bb7   Eb   Ab7   Bb   C7   c   G7   c   F
   1   2   3   4   5   6   7   8   1 2   3 4   5   6   7   8

A
Sax Solo Continued

Bb   f   Bb7   Eb   Ab7   Bb   C7   c   F7   Bb
1   2   3   4   5   6   7   8   1   2   3 4   5   6   7   8

B
Sax Solo Continued

c#   F#7   B   b   E7   A   a   D7   G   g   C7   c   F7
1   2   3   4   5   6   7   8   1   2   3 4   5   6   7   8

A
Sax Solo Continued

Bb   f   Bb7   Eb   Ab7   Bb   C7   c   G7   c   F :‖
1 2   3   4   5 6   7 8   1 2   3 4   5   6   7   8

Drum Solo

N.C.
‖: 1 2 3 4 5 6 7 8   1 2 3 4 5 6 7 8 :‖

Intro **Trumpet/Sax**	**Trumpet Solo with Drums**
N.C. 1 2 3 4 5 6 7 8	N.C. 1 2 3 4 5 6 7 8
Sax Solo	**Main Melody** **Trumpet/Sax Bass**
N.C. 1 2 3 4 5 6 7 8	N.C. F 1 2 3 4 5 6 7 8

CHAPTER THIRTEEN
"Subconscious Lee"—Lennie Tristano Quintet (SCCJ F-9)

This piece uses alto sax (Lee Konitz), piano (Lennie Tristano), guitar (Billy Bauer), bass (Arnold Fishkin), and drums (Shelly Manne) and was recorded in 1949. In the key of C, the tempo is 240; if that is too fast, count it with two beats per measure at 120. The composition is based on the chord changes to the standard "What is this thing called love?" and you will notice that the chord changes are quite a bit easier to follow.

A thirty-two-measure song form with an A A B A structure, the piece is obviously arranged at the beginning. Listen carefully to the melodic improvisation, the relaxed sense about the playing, and the generally relaxed style, even at a fairly fast tempo.

A   **A**
Group

g	C7	f		d	G7	C		g	C	f		d		G7	C
1	2	3	4	5	6	7	8	9	10	11	12	13	14	15	16

B   **A**
Group

c	F	Bb		Ab		d	G	g	C	f		d		G7	C
1	2	3	4	5	6	7	8	9	10	11	12	13	14	15	16

A   **A**
Piano Solo

g	C7	f		d	G7	C		g	C	f		d		G7	C
1	2	3	4	5	6	7	8	9	10	11	12	13	14	15	16

B   **A**
Piano Solo Continues

c	F	Bb		Ab		d	G	g	C	f		d		G7	C
1	2	3	4	5	6	7	8	9	10	11	12	13	14	15	16

A   **A**
Guitar Solo

g	C7	f		d	G7	C		g	C	f		d		G7	C
1	2	3	4	5	6	7	8	9	10	11	12	13	14	15	16

B   **A**
Guitar Solo Continues

c	F	Bb		Ab		d	G	g	C	f		d		G7	C
1	2	3	4	5	6	7	8	9	10	11	12	13	14	15	16

A   **A**
Alto Solo

g	C7	f		d	G7	C		g	C	f		d		G7	C
1	2	3	4	5	6	7	8	9	10	11	12	13	14	15	16

B   **A**
Alto Solo Continues

c	F	Bb		Ab		d	G	g	C	f		d		G7	C
1	2	3	4	5	6	7	8	9	10	11	12	13	14	15	16

A
Piano Solo   **A**
                                        Guitar Solo

```
g   C7  f       d   G7  C    g   C   f       d   G7  C
1   2   3   4   5   6   7   8   9  10  11  12  13  14  15  16
```

B   **A**
Alto Solo   **Piano Solo**

```
c   F   Bb      Ab      d   G   g   C   f       d   G7  C
1   2   3   4   5   6   7   8   9  10  11  12  13  14  15  16
```

A
Group (Alto/Guitar/Piano Unison Line)   **Held**
                                                             C

```
1   2   3   4   5   6   7   8   ||
```

"Boplicity"—Miles Davis and His Orchestra (SCCJ F-8)

The instrumentation of this classic piece of cool jazz is trumpet, trombone, French horn, tuba, alto sax, baritone sax, piano, bass, and drums. The piece was recorded in 1949 and was an arrangement of a tune by Miles Davis called "Cleo Henry"; the arranger was Gil Evans. The tempo is 136, and the key is F. The soloists are Gerry Mulligan on baritone sax, Miles Davis on trumpet and John Lewis on piano.

The importance of this piece is both the solo technique used to express cool and also the way the arranger blends lines in the ensemble sections. Cool is expressed both through playing technique and through the unusual combination of musical instruments. The structure is based on a thirty-two-measure song form—A A B A—and the chord changes are fairly easy to follow. g is the 2 chord; C7 is the 5 chord; and F is the one chord.

For those who are following chord changes, the basic progression is not too difficult. However, if you were to examine some of the alterations you would find some very unusual textures. The genius of Gil Evans is certainly expressed in the way he orchestrated tonal colorings.

A   **A**
Ensemble Melody

```
g F      C7F  c F   Bb C7  F   g  F c   F   c F   Bb C7       F
1    2   3    4    5  6 7  8   9    10  11  12   13  14 15    16
```

B   **A**
Ensemble Melody

```
c  F  Bb      bbEb    AbabgC  g F    c  F   c F   Bb C7      F
1  2  3  4   5  6    7   8    9      10 11  12    13  14 15  16
```

Baritone Sax Solo

```
g F       C7F  c F  Bb C7  F   g F c   F   c F   Bb C7      F
1     2     3   4    5  6 7 8   9       10  11   12  13 14 15  16
```

B   **A**

Ensemble   Trumpet   **Ensemble**

```
c  F  Bb  bbEbgbAbDb  C7  g F   c  F   c F   Bb C7      F
1  2  3 4    5      6   7   8   9  10  11  12  13  14 15  16
```

A   **A**

Ensemble with Trumpet Solo Trumpet Solo

```
g F       C7F  c F  Bb C7  Gb F  g F c   F   c F  Bb  BF D g C  F
1     2     3   4    5  6    7   8 9   10  11  12  13   14   15  16
```

B   **A**   **Ext.**

Piano Solo   **Ensemble**

```
c  F  Bb  bbEbabDbg  C7  g     C F  c F   Bb C7  C7  gC7
1  2  3 4   5      6   7   8  9 10  11 12  13 14  15   16
```

Held Chord

F7

CHAPTER FOURTEEN

"Pent-Up House"—Sonny Rollins Plus Four (SCCJ H-2)

This abridged version of the 1956 recording of "Pent-Up House" (the piano solo is shortened) features tenor sax (Rollins), trumpet (Clifford Brown), piano, bass, and drums (Max Roach). The key is G and the tempo is 176. The entire composition is based on a sixteen-measure phrase you hear at the beginning. The chord changes to the first trumpet statement are slightly changed, but they are based on the original chord changes.

      I have simplified the chord changes somewhat at the beginning; the actual reading is Am7D7b9 at the beginning. I have also used a number of repeat signs because this is primarily a solo vehicle in structure. This was one of the last recordings Clifford Brown made, and, in fact, the group is actually the Clifford Brown-Max Roach Quartet recording with Sonny Rollins.

Tenor Pickup to Melody
1
A Melody

```
||: a D  a D  GAb  G  a D  a D  GAbGd G   dG   c   F7  a D   a D  GAbG :||
    1    2    3     4 5  6    7 8  9      10  11  12  13    14   15 16
```

Trumpet

a	D7	G	E7	a	D7	G		d	G	c	F7	a		D7	Ga	b	Bb
1	2	3	4	5	6	7	8	9	10	11	12	13	14	15			16

Trumpet (5 Choruses—Drum Crashes During Third Chorus)
Five Times

‖: a D7 G E7 a D7 G d G7 c F7 a D7 GabBb :‖

1 2 3 4 5 6 7 8 9 10 11 12 13 14 15 16

Trumpet   Sax

a	D7	G	E7	a	D7	G		d	G	c	F7	a		D7	Ga	b	Bb
1	2	3	4	5	6	7	8	9	10	11	12	13	14	15			16

Sax (Five Choruses—Piano Stronger During Fifth Chorus)

‖: a D7 G E7 a D7 G d G7 c F7 a D7 GabBb :‖

1 2 3 4 5 6 7 8 9 10 11 12 13 14 15 16

Sax   Piano

a	D7	G	E7	a	D7	G		d	G	c	F7	a		D7	Ga	b	Bb
1	2	3	4	5	6	7	8	9	10	11	12	13	14	15			16

Piano

a	D7	G	E7	a	D7	G		d	G	c	F7	a		D7	Ga	b	Bb
1	2	3	4	5	6	7	8	9	10	11	12	13	14	15			16

Sax   Drums Piano Drums Sax   Drums   Trp   Drums

‖: a D7 G E7 a D7 G d G7 c F7 a D7 GabBb :‖

1 2 3 4 5 6 7 8 9 10 11 12 13 14 15 16

Drum Solo

‖: N.C.   :‖

1 2 3 4 5 6 7 8 9 10 11 12 13 14 15 16

A Melody

‖: a D a D GAb G a D a D GAbG d G d G c F7 a D a D GAbG :‖

1 2 3 4 5 6 7 8 9 10 11 12 13 14 15 16

Two chords

G

"Moon Rays"—Horace Silver Quintet (SCCJ G-6)

This composition features Silver on piano, Art Farmer on trumpet, and Clifford Jordan on tenor sax, joined by Teddy Kotick on bass and Louis Hayes on drums. Recorded in 1958, the tempo is 130 and the key is Eb. Like many Silver tunes, it shifts back and forth between Latin and swing and is balladlike in quality. However, the piano solo definitely gets funky. The structure is very easy to hear, although the chord changes are a bit sticky to analyze; it is a thirty-two-measure unit in A A B A form. Generally speaking, there are sevenths and ninths all over the place, hidden in the voicings of Horace Silver. The following chord changes reveal the basic chords, but not all of the alterations.

A
Bb Pedal note .... **Latin Feel**   **Break**

f		BbEb	f#		f		a	ab	g	C7	f		Bb		EbAbEbAb	
1	2	3	4		5	6	7	8	9	10	11		12	13	14	15	16

A
Bb Pedal Note .... **Latin Feel**   **Break**

f		BbEb	f#		f		a	ab	g	C7	f		Bb	EbAbEbAb	
1	2	3 4		5	6	7 8	9	10	11	12	13	14	15	16

B

a	D7	G		Bb		a		c#	c	b	Eb	a	D g C f Bb
1	2	3	4	5	6	7 8	9	10	11	12	13	14	15	16

A
Bb Pedal Note .... **Latin Feel**   **Break**

f		BbEb	f#		f		a	ab	g	C7	f		Bb	EbAbEbAb	
1	2	3 4		5	6	7 8	9	10	11	12	13	14	15	16

A
Swing Tenor Solo

f	Bb	Ebf	g	C7f#	B7	f	Bb	f	a abg	f#B	f	Bb	EbAbEbAb
1	2	3	4	5	6	7	8	9	10 11	12	13 14	15	16

A

f	Bb	Ebf	g	C7f#	B7	f	Bb	f	a abg	f#B	f	Bb	EbAbEbAb
1	2	3	4	5	6	7	8	9	10 11	12	13 14	15	16

B

a	D7	G	abE7bb		Eb	a	D7	a	c#c	b	bbEba	D7	g C	f Bb
1	2	3	4	5	6	7	8	9 10		11	12	13	14 15	16

A

f	Bb	Ebf	g	C7f#	B7	f	Bb	f	a	abg	f#B	f	Bb	EbAbEbAb
1	2	3	4	5	6	7	8	9	10	11	12	13	14	15 16

A
Trumpet Solo

f	Bb	Ebf	g	C7f#	B7	f	Bb	f	a	abg	f#B	f	Bb	EbAbEbAb
1	2	3	4	5	6	7	8	9	10	11	12	13	14	15 16

A

f	Bb	Ebf	g	C7f#	B7	f	Bb	f	a	abg	f#B	f	Bb	EbAbEbAb
1	2	3	4	5	6	7	8	9	10	11	12	13	14	15 16

B

a	D7	G	abE7bb	Eb	a	D7	a	c#c	b	bbEba	D7	g C	f Bb
1	2	3	4	5	6	7	8	9	10	11	12	13 14	15 16

A

f	Bb	Ebf	g	C7f#	B7	f	Bb	f	a	abg	f#B	f	Bb	EbAbEbAb
1	2	3	4	5	6	7	8	9	10	11	12	13	14	15 16

A
Piano Solo

f	Bb	Ebf	g	C7f#	B7	f	Bb	f	a	abg	f#B	f	Bb	EbAbEbAb
1	2	3	4	5	6	7	8	9	10	11	12	13	14	15 16

A

f	Bb	Ebf	g	C7f#	B7	f	Bb	f	a	abg	f#B	f	Bb	EbAbEbAb
1	2	3	4	5	6	7	8	9	10	11	12	13	14	15 16

B

a	D7	G	abE7bb	Eb	a	D7	a	c#c	b	bbEba	D7	g	C	f Bb
1	2	3	4	5	6	7	8	9	10	11	12	13	14	15 16

A

f	Bb	Ebf	g	C7f#	B7	f	Bb	f	a	abg	f#B	f	Bb	EbAbEbAb
1	2	3	4	5	6	7	8	9	10	11	12	13	14	15 16

A
Funky Unison Line with Trumpet and Tenor

f	Bb	Ebf	g	C7f#	B7	f	Bb	f	a	abg	f#B	f	Bb	EbAbEbAb
1	2	3	4	5	6	7	8	9	10	11	12	13	14	15 16

A

f	Bb	Ebf	g	C7f#	B7	f	Bb	f	a	abg	f#B	f	Bb	EbAbEbAb
1	2	3	4	5	6	7	8	9	10	11	12	13 14	15	16

B

a	D7	G	abE7bb	Eb	a	D7	a	c#c	b	bbEba	D7	g C	f Bb
1	2	3	4	5	6	7	8	9	10	11	12 13	14	15 16

A

f	Bb	Ebf	g	C7f#	B7	f	Bb	f	a	abg	f#B	f	Bb	EbAbEbAb
1	2	3	4	5	6	7	8	9	10	11	12	13 14	15	16

A (Melody)
Bb Pedal Note .... **Latin Feel**   **Break**

f		BbEb		f#		f		a	ab	g	C7	f	Bb	EbAbEbAb
1	2	3 4		5	6	7	8	9	10	11	12	13	14	15 16

A
Bb Pedal Note .... **Latin Feel**   **Break**

f		BbEb		f#		f		a	ab	g	C7	f	Bb	EbAbEbAb
1	2	3 4		5	6	7	8	9	10	11	12	13	14	15 16

Ending (Latin Feel)   **Held Chord**

Eb		Ab		Eb	Ab		Eb	Ab		Eb	Ab		Eb		Ab
1		2		3			4			5			6		7

CHAPTER FIFTEEN

"Congeniality"—Ornette Coleman Quartet (SCCJ J-1)

This piece uses alto sax (Ornette Coleman), trumpet (Don Cherry), bass (Charlie Haden), and drums (Billy Higgins). It was recorded in 1959. The opening melody is in the key of Bb. The saxophone and trumpet solos are in the tempo of 230 beats per minute.

The problem with this type of piece is that the musicians have purposefully avoided standard chord progressions and phrase units. The whole idea of the music is to freely work off rhythmic and melodic motifs. However, there is a definite sense of structure. The piece begins and ends with contrasting melodies that are played in unison by sax and trumpet. The middle section of the piece is dominated by solos (sax, then trumpet), with the bass setting up a walking pattern without definitive chords, and the drummer keeping time.

I have analyzed the first and last sections as having two parts— A being fast and B being slow. I have indicated the number of measures in each solo and shown where there are some particularly memorable devices which you might hear.

Opening Melody Section in Bb.
A is fast   B is slow

A hold B   A hold B   A hold B   A hold A   B

Tempo is 230
Sax Solo   163 measures
Measures 120–130 Quote a Theme by
Rachmaninoff

Trumpet solo 8 measures lead-in, drum roll to 110 measures of trumpet solo. Measure 88 is "Surrey with the Fringe on Top."
Sax and trumpet back together at Ms. 111.
Opening section

A hold B A hold B A hold B A hold B A ‖

"Free Jazz"—Ornette Coleman Double Quartet (SCCJ J-2)

The instrumentation of this piece is alto sax (Coleman), trumpets (Don Cherry and Freddie Hubbard), bass clarinet (Eric Dolphy), basses (Scott LaFaro and Charlie Haden), and drums (Billy Higgins and Ed Blackwell). This piece poses even more problems for those who would analyze it, if for only because the Smithsonian version is an excerpt of the thirty-six-minute piece.

The whole purpose of this type of music is to deny traditional phrase structures although there are certainly recognizable links between musicians, and the rhythm section does set up patterns. However, it is impossible to develop chord changes for this piece. When there is a recognizable tempo, it is about 160 per minute.

To chart this piece, I used a stopwatch and wrote down the number of seconds into the piece and what was happening at that point. If you can think of a different way to chart this type of piece, go ahead and do it. However, this is the only way that has worked for me. If you discover that you do not hear it the way I did, do not let that bother you. In fact, you may find memorable types of activity which I did not. Free jazz is clearly up for interpretation.

Min./Sec.

0.00	Group improvisation
12.76	Melody
25.92	Alto solo
58	Motive A
1 15	Background riff
1 40	Collective improvisation
2 07	Bass clarinet honking
2 25	Bass pattern changes
2 32	Bass drops out

2	39	Bass back/Alto solo
2	50	Collective improvisation
3	00	Alto dominates
3	25	Motive B (Alto)
3	56	Bass clarinet motive
4	08	Collective improvisation becomes riff
4	25	Double time—free bass
4	35	Double-time rhythm
4	50	Trumpet enters—dominant
5	05	Alto/trumpet free cadenzas
5	19	Stronger rhythm section
		Total improvisation
5	40	"Mary Had a Little Lamb"
5	50	Motive C
6	42	Blues motive—tonal
7	00	Riff background—tonal but melodically free
7	39	Alto and trumpet trade motives
8	00	Group improvisation
8	14	Rhythm dies down
8	25	Cadenzalike
8	34	Alto asserts a melody
8	40	Others join
8	98	Blues motive
9	29	Alto solo
9	47	Trumpet
9	52	Bass clarinet and others
10	04	All free
10	13	Original melody
10	26	Fade-out

CHAPTER SIXTEEN

"25 or 6 to 4"—Chicago

Chicago uses a standard rock band plus two trumpets, a saxophone, and trombone. Recorded in 1970, this piece is in Bb minor and the tempo is 152. The chord changes are pretty simple. After the experience you have had listening to chords, this should be a breeze.

Notice especially the way the band plays in basically a rock-and-roll style in the rhythm section and also the guitar solo, but the horns play in a riff-oriented style. The trombone throws in a little jazz lick at the end. Although not everyone is a Chicago fan, this group is considered to be one of the most successful jazz/rock ensembles, especially from a financial point of view.

Intro Rhythm Section—Bass Dominant/Intro + Horns/Verse 1/Verse 2
Four Times

‖ : bb			Gb	F	bb			Gb F : ‖
1	2	3	4		5	6	7	8

Refrain in Harmony

Gb		Db		Ab		Gb	
1	2	3	4	5	6	7	8

Horns Plus Guitar Solo/Verse 3/Verse 4
Three times

‖ : bb			Gb	F	bb			Gb F : ‖
1	2	3	4		5	6	7	8

Refrain in Harmony

Gb		Db		Ab		Gb	
1	2	3	4	5	6	7	8

Guitar Solo for Six Choruses/Intro Rhythm/Intro Rhythm + Horns/Verse 5/Verse 6
Ten Times

‖ : bb			Gb	F	bb			Gb F : ‖
1	2	3	4		5	6	7	8

Refrain in Harmony

Gb		Db		Ab		Gb	
1	2	3	4	5	6	7	8

Guitar Solo

bb			Gb	F	bb			Gb F
1	2	3	4		5	6	7	8

Chordal Conclusion with Horn Section

		Ritard		Held Chord
eb	Gb	C	Ab	C
1	2	3	4	5

"Birdland"—Weather Report

"Birdland" was recorded on Weather Report's 1977 album, "Heavy Weather." Weather Report uses bass, drums, percussion, keyboards (Josef Zawinul), and saxophones (Wayne Shorter). This piece is in G major, and the tempo is 156. The structure of this piece is actually fairly hard to follow, although there are numerous repeats. Much of the piece is in one chord, but the melodies themselves are quite complex. The opening basslike solo is actually produced on an arp synthesizer. This is a good example of jazz/rock, and it was commercially very successful. However, underneath its crowd appeal it is complex music, although there is not much improvisation.

Introduction
Arp Synthesizer

A
Bass Melody in Harmonics
Note

G   +drums   g
1 2 3 4 5 6 7 8   1 2 3 4 5 6 7 8 9 10 11 12

B-Add Sax
Notes

   F F   Eb F d F   Eb   F e g Fe FF#Ge   g F
1   2   3 4   5   6 7   8

Rhythm Interlude

G
1   2   3   4

C-Rhodes Piano Melody

F   G   F   G   F   G   F   G
1 2 3 4   5   6 7 8   9   10 11 12   13   14 15   16

D-Sax   **Bass Piano**

  G C Ab G   G   Ab G b   G
1 2   3 4 5 6   7   8 9 10 11   12 13 14 15 16

E-Main Melody Sax/Harmonized Melody/Harmonized
Melody
Three Times

||: G b e   C b E7 a G a C   G b e C   e C   G a C a :||
    1   2   3   4   5   6 7 8

Interlude (Rhythm)   **C-Rhodes Melody**

G   F
1   2   3   4   5   6   7   8

Sax Solo

G G b F E E b D D b7 Repeat G7
1   2   3   4   5   6   7   8   9   10   11   12   13   14

Interlude (Rhythm)

G
1   2   3   4

A-Bass Melody

G   g
1 2 3 4 5 6 7 8 9 10 11 12 13 14 15 16

B-Ensemble Melody

F   F   Eb   Fd   F   Eb   F e   g   F   e FF#e   g F
1   2   3   4   5   6   7   8

C-Middle Section of Rhodes Melody

G   F   G   F   G
1   2   3   4   5   6   7   8

E-Main Melody Sax/Harmonized Melody/Harmonized Melody
Three Times

‖ G b e   C   b   E7   a G a C   G b e C   e C   G a C a :‖
   1   2   3   4   5   6   7   8

Vamp on Part of Main Melody to Fade Out

G e   b   E7   a G a C G
1   2   3   4

CHAPTER SEVENTEEN

"A Love Supreme"—Carlos Santana and John McLaughlin

This piece uses two guitars, organ, bass, congas, and four drummers and was recorded in 1973. A fairly slow piece, its tempo varies, as does the key centers. The opening is on F#m, and the main vamp or chord center of the main section is in C minor Dorian (C D Eb F G A Bb C). A most interesting piece, it defies traditional charting because it is basically a chant or "mantra." The bass pattern fits the words "A Love Supreme."

The composition was originally composed by John Coltrane, who had religious experiences towards the end of his life. The album which these two guitarists created is called "Love Devotion and Surrender," a creed of the Hindu sect to which they both converted. Therefore, this is a religious album which explains the nature of the music. What is hard to understand is how such apparently diverse musicians could get together—John McLaughlin of Miles Davis fame and

Carlos Santana, of Latin rock fame. The result is an intriguing blend of high-speed technical virtuosity (McLaughlin) and distorted rock guitar (Santana). But as a piece of non-Western influence, it fits the discussion beautifully.

Beginning

f# ....

Bass Vamp in c Dorian

|| : _____ : ||

"Spain"—Chick Corea

The ensemble Corea used to create the tune was actually called Return to Forever and consisted of bass, drums, piano (Corea), saxophone/ flute, percussion, guitar, and vocalist. Recorded in 1972, the tempo is about 225, and it is in the key of B minor, although it shifts to G major in the middle. Although you may have some difficulty following the chord changes, they basically consist of a downward scale. There are two clear melodies in this piece, and they are what you should listen for in counting the phrases.

Also note that some of the phrase lengths are unusual. One of the intriguing qualities of Corea's music, even when it was pop-oriented, as this tune is, is that it generally flows through uneven phrases. The technical ability of the musicians used here is quite high, and even though the music may not sound hard, it is. It is sort of like improvising in 5/4 time; it is difficult until you get used to it. Notice the combination of the flute and the vocalist.

Also notice the longer repeat signs with a first and second ending. The first time through, you use the material and chords in the first ending. The second time through, you skip the first ending, read the second ending, and go on.

Electric Piano and Bass Intro (Freely)

bA	b	e G	F#	b	G	f#	e A7	DoD	G F#	b
1	2	3	4	5	6	7	8	9	10	11

Unison (Flute and Piano)
Rhythmic Melody
Rhythm Section Enters

|| : b		E7		F#7	
1	2	3	4	5	6

Main Melody (Flute and Voice)

G		F#7	e	A7	D		C#7	F#7	B	
1	2	3	4	5	6	7 8	9	10	11	12

Unison Melody (Bass, Flute, and Piano)
N.C. | 1st Ending: || 2nd Ending

		E D b	: || E D7 G	
1 2 3 4 5 6 7 8 9 10	11	12 13	11	12

Continued Melody

G			F#7				e		A7		
1	2	3	4	5	6	7	8	9	10	11	12
D		G	C#7	F#7			b		B7		
1	2	3	4	5	6	7	8	9	10	11	12

Unison Melody

e	A7	D	C#7	F#7	B	N.C.		E	D	G
1	2	3	4	5	6	7	8 1 2 3 4 5 6 7 8 9	10	11	

Flute Solo (6th Time Plays Previous Melody)
Six Times

|| : G			F#7				e		A7			
	1	2	3	4	5	6	7	8	9	10	11	12
D		G	C#7		F#7		b		B7			: ||
1	2	3	4	5	6	7	8	9	10	11	12
e	A7	D	C#7	F#7	B	N.C.			E D	G
1	2	3	4 5	6	7	8 1 2 3 4 5 6 7 8 9 10		11	12

Electric Piano Solo (6th Time Plays Previous Melody)
Six Times

|| : G			F#7				e		A7			
	1	2	3	4	5	6	7	8	9	10	11	12
D		G	C#7		F#7		b		B7			: ||
1	2	3	4	5	6	7	8	9	10	11	12
e	A7	D	C#7	F#7	B	N.C.			E D	G
1	2	3	4 5	6	7	8 1 2 3 4 5 6 7 8 9 10		11	12

Bass Solo (4th Time Plays Previous Melody)
Four Times

|| : G			F#7				e		A7			
	1	2	3	4	5	6	7	8	9	10	11	12
D		G	C#7		F#7		b		B7			: ||
1	2	3	4	5	6	7	8	9	10	11	12
e	A7	D	C#7	F#7	B
1	2	3	4 5	6	7 8

Unison (Flute and Piano)
Rhythmic Melody

b		E7		F#7	
1	2	3	4	5	6

Main Melody (Flute and Voice)

G		F#7		e	A7	D		C#7	F#7	B
1	2	3	4	5	6	7	8	9	10	11	12

Unison Melody (Bass, Flute, and Piano)
N.C.   Chord Chord   Chord

|E		D		b		||				
1	2	3	4	5	6	7 8 9 10	11	12	13

CHAPTER EIGHTEEN

"Opus in Pastels"—Stan Kenton

This piece is orchestrated for a saxophone section (one alto, two tenors, and two baritones), bass, and drums. An old standard of the Kenton band, it has been recorded many times; it is available in photocopy form from Creative World. Played at a very slow tempo, it is in the key of Eb. It has an introduction, then a set of variations on basically the same chord progressions; the third variation is shortened by four measures. A brief conclusion ends the piece. Notice that the bass accompanies the saxophones only in the introduction and conclusion, and it is bowed rather than plucked.

The style of writing for the saxophones is slightly reminiscent of super-sax writing, only at a very slow tempo. However, the technique is Kenton style, producing a very thick texture, because of the two baritones and the single alto.

Pickup Saxes and Bowed String Bass

f		f	E		EB		f E	Eb	f	Bb7
1	2	3	4	5	6	7	8 9	10	11	12

Main Melody
Saxes + Drums + Plucked Bass

||: Eb		E7		Eb	D	Eb	f		E7	Eb		:||
1	2	3	4	5	6	7	8	9	10	11	12

Saxes + Drum Rolls + Bowed String Bass

Eb	D	DbD	Eb	Ab	Gb	E7	Eb
1	2	3	4	5	6	7	8

Stronger Sax Soli + Drums + Plucked Bass
2nd Time Bowed Bass

```
||: Eb      E7     Eb  D  Eb  f     E7   Eb         :||
    1   2   3   4   5   6  7   8  9  10   11   12
```

Relaxed Conclusion (Bowed Bass and No Drums)

```
f        E7       Eb   f  Bb  Eb
1   2    3    4   5    6       7  8
```

"Cherry Juice"—Thad Jones/Mel Lewis

A contemporary arrangement for big band, this piece is in G minor, and the tempo is 224. Primarily a solo piece in the Basie tradition, the arranging style takes advantage of super-sax ensemble writing and some unusual rhythm surprises. A thirty-two-measure A A B A structure the chord changes are fairly easy to hear. A begins on Gm and does a turnaround to D7 (or 1 to 5), and B starts on C7 (the 4 chord) and returns to D7 (the 5 chord). There are some slight variations on the basic progression in the transitions and interludes. The piece ends with held chords.

Introduction (Saxes with Chords) Piano Solo

```
E7EbD     EbD  Eb     DDbC7   E7a D   g
1   2     3    4      5       6      7 8      9  10  11  12  13  14  15  16
```

A   **A′**
Unison Sax Line

```
g        F  Bb  Eb   a  D7  g          F   BbEb7  D7  g   G7
1   2 3  4  5   6    7  8   9  10  11  12  13     14  15  16
```

B   **A**
Sax Line Continued

```
C7G#C7   C7G#C7   C7GC7  a  D7  g          F   BbEb D   g   D7
1   2    3    4   5   6  7 8 9  10  11  12  13   14  15  16
```

A   **A′**
Flügelhorn Solo with Rhythm Section

```
||: g       F  BbEb   a  D7  g          FBb  Eb  D7  g   G7
    1 2 3   4  5  6    7  8   9  10  11  12   13  14  15  16
```

B   **A′**
Unison Sax Line—2nd Time Brass Figures

```
C7          C      BbA7  D7  g          F   BbEb  D7  g   D7
1   2 3  4 5 6     7     8   9  10  11  12  13    14  15  16
```

Ensemble Interlude

A'
Tenor Solo with Rhythm

G AbG		GAbG	Bb Eb7	D7	g		F BbEb	D7	g	D7
1 2 3	4	5 6	7 8	9 10	11	12	13	14	15	16

B
Tenor Sax Solo Continued

A'

C7	C	BbA7	D7	g		F	BbEb	D7	g	D7
1 2 3	4 5 6	7	8	9 10	11	12	13	14	15	16

A
Tenor Sax Solo Continued/Trb. Brass Background

A'

g	F	BbEb7	a	D7	g		FBb	Eb	D7	g	D7
1	2 3	4	5	6	7 8	9 10	11	12	13	14 15	16

B'
Ensemble Interlude

A'
Tenor Sax with Rhythm

C7	C	BbA7	D7	g		F	BbEb	D7	g	D7
1 2 3	4 5 6	7	8	9 10	11	12	13	14	15	16

A
Ensemble Shout Chorus—Chord Changes Rhythmically Varied

A'

g	F	BbEb7	a	D7	g		FBb	Eb	D7	g	D7
1	2 3	4	5	6	7 8	9 10	11	12	13	14 15	16

B
Shout Chorus Continued

A

C7G#C7	C7G#C7	C7GC7	a	D7	g		F	BbEb7D7	g	D7
1 2	3 4	5 6	7 8	9 10	11	12	13	14	15	16

A
Super Sax

A'

g	F	Bb7Eb7	a	D7	g		F	BbEb7	D7	g	G7
1	2 3	4	5	6	7 8	9 10	11	12	13	14 15	16

B
Super Sax Continued

A

C7G#C7	C7G#C7	C7GC7	a	D7	g		F	BbEb7D7	g	D7
1 2	3 4	5 6	7 8	9 10 11		12	13 14		15	16

A''
Transition Interlude

A'''

gBbA	D7g f	BbEb	a	D7	g	BbA	D g f		BbEb D	g e	EbD G
1 2	3	4 5 6	7 8	9 10	11	12	13	14 15		16	

B   **A′**
Piano Solo

C7					Bb7	a	D7	g			F	BbEb7	D7	g	G7
1	2	3	4	5	6	7	8	9	10	11	12	13		14	15	16

A   **A**

g		F	BbEb7	D7	g	D7	g			F	BbEb7	D7	g	D7
1	2 3	4	5	6	7	8	9 10 11	12	13	14	15	16

Conclusion   **Five Holds**

g Db	G		C G	Gb7				F Bb	Eb Ab	g
1	2	3	4	5	6	7	8	9	10	11

CHAPTER NINETEEN

"Steppin'"—World Saxophone Quartet (SCCJ I-4)

This piece, recorded in 1981, features alto flute, two soprano saxophones, and bass clarinet. Like the Ornette Coleman pieces analyzed earlier, it is difficult to place a key on this piece, although much of it sounds as if it is in C#, which is highly unlikely. There also is no consistent tempo, although they do clearly at times set up tempos that are recognizable. There is thematic material to this piece, and there is free improvisation. In my analysis I have used the stopwatch technique that I used with "Free Jazz" and "Congeniality." If you feel that another form of analysis would be more appropriate, feel free to experiment. For the sake of the following analysis, RF = rhythmic figure and FI = free improvisation (no distinct rhythm).

Min.	*Sec.*	
0		RF
9.5		RF with chords
26		Chords only (theme)
42		RF
51.5		RF with chords
1	08	Chords only (theme)
1	26	RF with group improvisation
1	46	Blues figure
1	54	RF stops
2	10	Moving bass line
2	28	FI (blues and tonal)
2	43	FI (based on RF)
2	56	FI (from part of blues)
3	10	Call and response
3	22	FI
3	35	Call and response (blues)
3	45	FI

4	04	Individual solos
4	32	RF (suggested but not stated explicitly)
4	40	FI
4	55	Chords working towards cadence
5	08	Blues figures
5	19	FI (pointilistic—very thin or few sounds)
5	26	RF suggested
5	36	FI
6	05	"Summertime" suggested
6	17	Cadence
6	18	RF
6	28	RF with chords
6	45	Chords only (theme)
7	02	RF
7	08	RF with brief chords to
7	21	Chord held
7	29	Applause

"Who Can I Turn To"—Wynton Marsalis

This piece features Marsalis on trumpet, Herbie Hancock on piano, Ron Carter on bass, and Tony Williams on drums. Recorded in 1982, the piece is in Eb and the tempo is about 62 beats per minute, quite slow. The introductory section is improvised and vague in tempo, accompanied only by piano. When the regular tempo starts at the "A Tempo" marking, Marsalis plays through an interpretation of this jazz standard. Trumpet and piano trade four-measure units and then two-measure units in the double-time section. Then we have a return to the basic melody with trumpet improvisation at the end. A fairly standard piece in structure, it is made up of one sixteen-measure phrase that is repeated.

Improvised Introduction (Trumpet and Piano)
Hold

Eb EEb Gb G Gb Db D   Db   E F E Bb Bbo A D A D e D

Does not fit into measures because it is flexible time

Free Arpeggios on Chords Trumpet

ab   G   B7 bb   b G   c F Bb7 E

Unmeasured
A Tempo

Eb f	g c	B7 bb	Eb7 A	Ab		g	c B bb Eb
1	2	3	4	5	6	7	8

Main Section Continues

Ab	D7	g	C7f	B	Bb7	Db7	c	F	B	Bb7
9		10	11	12		13	14	15	16	

Variation One

Eb	F	g	c	Cb7bb		Eb	AbD7	G	c	a	ab
1	2	3	4			5	6	7		8	

Double-Time Feel   Double Time

Eb	G	bof	Bb	Db7	f	Bb7	Eb	D7	Db	C7	g	Bb7
9		10		11		12	13		14		15	16

Variation Two
Trumpet   Piano   Trumpet

Eb	f	g	B7	bb	Eb7	Ab		D7	g	c
1	2		3	4	5	6		7	8	

Variation Two (Continued)
Piano   Trumpet

Ab	a	D7g	C7	f	B7	Bb7	Db7	C7	B7	Bb7	Bb7
9		10	11		12		13	14	15		16

A Tempo (Original Melody)

Eb	f	g	c	B	bb	Eb7	Ab	D7	G7	c	a	ab
1	2		3		4	5	6		7	8		

Continued
Ritard Hold Hold

g	Gbo	f	Bb7	‖	Bb7		Free obligatto
9		10	11				12 13 14 15 16

Discography

All recordings listed are currently available as of the summer of 1987. Recordings analyzed in the book are preceded by an asterisk. Of course, these are not all of the good records available; this is simply representative. If your local record store does not have these records on the shelf, do not be surprised; you may have to special-order them. You might also check at college and public libraries. Collections are located at the end of the list.

ADDERLEY, JULIAN "CANNONBALL"
"Jazz Workshop Revisited."   Landmark, LLP-1303.

"Mercy, Mercy, Mercy."   Capitol, SN-16153.

"The Sextet."   Mile, 9106.

AIRTO MOREIRA
"Brazilian Heatwave."   Accord, SN-7184.

AKIYOSHI, TOSHIKO-LEW TABACKIN BIG BAND
"Farewell to Mingus."   JAM, 003.

ARMSTRONG, LOUIS
"Armstrong and Hines."   Smithsonian, 2002.

"Louis Armstrong and King Oliver."   Milestone, M47017.

"Louis Armstrong and Sidney Bechet." in NY   Smithsonian, 2026.

"The Louis Armstrong Story Vols. 1–4."   Columbia, CL 851-4.

"Plays W. C. Handy."   Columbia, Jazz.

"Masterpieces CJ-40242."

ART ENSEMBLE OF CHICAGO
"People in Sorrow."   Nessa, 3.

BARBIERI, GATO
"Callente."   A&M, SP-3247.

BARNET, CHARLIE
"Best of Charlie Barnet."   2-MCA, 4069E.

COUNT BASIE
"Best."   2-MCA, 4050.

COUNT BASIE AND JOE WILLIAMS
"Count Basie Swings, Joe Williams
   Sings."   Verve, 825770-1.

BECHET, SIDNEY
"Master Musician."   2-Blueb, AXM2-5516.

"Sessions."   Storyv, 4028E.

BEIDERBECKE, BIX
"Story, Vols. 1–2."   Col, Cl 844-5.

BENSON, GEORGE
"Cookbook."   Col, PC-9413.

"Silver Collection."   Verve, 823450-2(CD).

BERIGAN, BUNNY
"Big Band Sound of Bunny Berigan."   Folk,
   FJ-2819.

"Complete Bunny Berigan, Vol. 1."   2-
   Bluebird, AXM2-5584.

BLAKE, EUBIE
"Blues and Ragtime."   Bio, 1011Q.

BLAKE, EUBIE AND NOBLE SISSIE
"Early Rare Recordings."   Eubie Blake Music,
   EBM-4.

BLAKEY, ART
"Jazz Messengers."   Odys, PC-37021.

BLOOD SWEAT AND TEARS
"Blood Sweat and Tears."   Columbia, PC-
   9720.

"Child Is Father to the Man."   Columbia, PC-
   9619.

BRAXTON, ANTHONY
"3 Compositions."   Del, 415.

BRECKER, MICHAEL
*"Michael Brecker."   MCA, C-5980(C).

BROWN, CLIFFORD
"Clifford Brown All Stars."   Emarcy, EXPR-
   1007.

"Jam Session."   Emarcy, EXPR-1012.

BROWN, JAMES
"Best of James Brown."   Polydor, 6340.

BROWN, LES
"1946."   Circle, CLP-90.

"Les Brown and His Band of Reknown With
   Harry James."   Ranwood, RC-8225 (C).

BROWN, MILTON AND HIS BROWNIES
"Pioneer Western Swing Band."   MCA,
   1509E.

BRUBECK, DAVE
"Gone With the Wind/Time Out."   2-Col,
   CG-33666.

"Take Five."   CSP, JCS-9116.

"Trio" (Brubeck, Tjader, Crotty).   2-Fan,
   24726.

"Two Generations of Brubeck."   Atlantic, SD-
   1645.

*"Impressions of Japan."   Col, CS 9012.

BURRELL, KENNY AND JOHN COLTRANE   2-
   Prest, 24059.

BURTON, GARY
"Paris Encounter" (with S.
   Grappelli).   Atlantic, SD-1597.

"Gary Burton and Keith Jarrett."   Atlantic,
   SD-1577.

BYAS, DON
"Don Byas."   GNP, 9027.

BYRD, CHARLIE
"Brazilville."   Concord Picante, CJP-173.

CARTER, BENNY
"1938 & 1946."   Swing, SW-8403.

CARTER, RON
"Parade."   Mile, 9088.

CHARLES, RAY
"The Genius of Ray Charles."   Atlantic, SD-
   1312.

"Soul Brothers" (with Milt
   Jackson).   Atlantic, SD-1279.

CHICAGOANS   MCA, 1350.

CHICAGO
"Chicago Transit Authority."   2-Col, CG-8.

*"Chicago 2."   2-Col, PG-24.

CHRISTIAN, CHARLIE
"Charley Christian."   Arc. Folk, 219E.

CHRISTY, JUNE
"Big Band Specials."   Pausa, 9039.

CLARKE, STANLEY
"Children of Forever."   Pol, 827559.

"Stanley Clarke."   Col, PE-36973.

CLOONEY, ROSEMARY AND WOODY
      HERMAN
"My Buddy."   Concord Jazz, CJ-226.

COBHAM, BILLY
"Crosswinds." Atlantic, SD-7300.

COLE, NAT KING
"Early 1940s." 2-Mark, 56 739.

COLE, RICHIE
"Alto Madness." Muse, 5155.

"Side by Side" (with Phil Woods). Muse, 5237.

COLEMAN, ORNETTE
"Free Jazz." Atlantic, SD-1364.

COLTRANE, JOHN
"Ascension." MCA, 29020.

"Cosmic." MCA, 29025.

"Crescent." MCA, 29016.

"Giant Steps." Atlantic, SD-1311.

"A Love Supreme." MCA, 5660.

"My Favorite Things." Atlantic, SD 1361.

"Soultrane." Fan./OJC, OJC-246.

COLTRANE, JOHN WITH ARCHIE SHEPP
"Newport 1965." MCA, 29019.

COLTRANE, JOHN WITH MILES DAVIS
"Live in Stockholm." 2-AVI.

COREA, CHICK
"The Chick Corea Elektric Band." GRP, Records A-9535.

"Return to Forever." Col, PC-36359.

*"Light as a Feather." Pol, PD-5525.

COREA, CHICK AND LIONEL HAMPTON
"Live and Midem." Who's, 21016.

CROSBY, BING AND COUNT BASIE
"Bing and Basie." Em, 824705 (CD).

DAVIS, MILES
"Birth of the Cool." Cap, N-16168.

"Bitches Brew." 2-Col, J2C-40577.

"In a Silent Way." Col, CJ-40580.

"Kind of Blue." Col, PC 8163.

"Miles Ahead." Col, PC-8633E.

" 'Round about Midnight with Coltrane." Col, PC-8649E.

"Sketches of Spain." Col, PC 8271.

"At Newport" (with Theolonius Monk). Col, PC-8978.

"Dig" (with Sonny Rollins). Fan, OJC 005.

DIMEOLA, AL
"Splendido Hotel." 2-Col, C2X-36270.

DOBBINS, BILL
"Textures." Telarc, 5003.

DODDS, JOHNNY
"Paramount Recordings." Herwin, 115.

DOLPHY, ERIC
"Last Date." Fontana, 822226-2 (CD).

"Eric Dolphy and Cannonball Adderly." Arc. Folk, 227.

THE DORSEY BROTHERS
"The Fabulous Dorseys in Hi-Fi." 2-CSP, JC2-8.

DORSEY, JIMMY AND HIS ORCHESTRA
"1939–40." Hindsight, HSR-101.

"1948." Hindsight, HSR-203.

DORSEY, TOMMY AND HIS ORCHESTRA
"I'll See You in My Dreams" (with Sinatra). 2-Pair, PDL2-1008.

D'RIVERA, PAQUITO
"Paquito Blowin'." Col, FC-37374.

ECKSTINE, BILLY
"Everything I Have Is Yours." Verve, 819442-1.

ELDRIDGE, ROY
"The Nifty Cat." New World, NW-349.

ELLINGTON, DUKE
"Carnegie Hall Concert" (1946). Musicraft, 2002.

"Duke Ellington: The Blanton-Webster B." 4-Bluebird, 5659-1-RB29.

"The Duke Ellington Small Bands." Fantasy, F-9640.

"The Symphonic Ellington." Atlantic, SD-1688.

"First Time" (with Basie's band)." Col, CJ-40586.

ELLIS, DON
"New Ideas." Pausa, 7607.

EVANS, BILL
"Crosscurrents." Fan, 9568.

FARMER, ART
"You Make Me Smile." Soul. N, SN-1076.

FARMER, ART AND BILL EVANS
"Modern Art." Pausa, 9025.

FARRELL, JOE
"Skateboard Park." Xanadu, 174.

FERGUSON, MAYNARD
"Best of Maynard Ferguson."   Col, PC-36361.
"Chameleon."   Col, PC-33007.
"Conquistador."   Col, PC-34457.
FISCHER, CLARE
"Alone Together."   Discovery, DS-820.
"Machaca."   Discovery, DS-835.
FITZGERALD, ELLA
"And Her Orchestra 1940."   Sunb, 205.
"These Are the Blues."   Verve, 829536-2 (CD).
"Ella and Louis."   2-Verve, 2V6S-8811.
"Ella and Basie."   Verve, 2304049-1.
"Cote d'Azur" (with Ellington).   Verve, V6-4072.
GETZ, STAN
"The Girl from Ipanema."   5-Verve, 823611-1.
"Best of Stan Getz."   Col, JC-36403.
"Focus."   Verve, UMV-2071.
"Stan the Man."   2-Verve, 815239-1.
"Getz/Almeida."   Verve, 823149 (CD).
"Getz Meets Mulligan in Hi-Fi."   Verve, UMV-2657.
"The Brothers" (with Zoot Sims).   Fan, OJC 008.

GILLESPIE, DIZZY
"And His Big Band."   Philips, 830224-2 (CD).
"Dee Gee Days."   2-Savoy Jazz, SJL-2209.
"The King of Bop."   Arc. Folk, 346.
GOODMAN, BENNY
"Complete Benny Goodman, Vol. 1."   RCA, AXM2-5505.
"Carnegie Hall Jazz Concert."   Col, OSL 160.
GORDON, DEXTER
"Tower of Power."   Prest, 7623.
"Long Tall Dexter."   2-Savoy Jazz, SJL-22114.
"Who's Who Presents" (with L. Hampton).   Who's, 21011.
"A Day in Copenhagen" (with Slide Hampton).   Pausa, 7058.
GRAPPELLI, STEPHANE
"Stephane Grappelli."   Arc. Folk, 311.
"Giants" (with Jean-Luc Ponty).   Pausa, 7074.
GRAY, GLEN AND CASA LOMA ORCHESTRA
"1943–46."   Hindsight, HSR-120.

HAMPTON, LIONEL
"Best of Lionel Hampton."   2-MCA, 4075E.
"Steppin' Out."   MCA, 1315.
HANCOCK, HERBIE
*"Best of Herbie Hancock."   Col, JC-36309.
*"Headhunters."   Col, PC-32731.
"An Evening with Chick Corea."   2-Col, PC2-35663.
"Quartet."   2-Col, C2-38275.
HARRIS, EDDIE
"Steps Up."   Steepl, SCS-1151.
HARRISON, WENDELL
"Birth of a Fossil."   Rebirth, WHR-140.
HAWKINS, COLEMAN
"Body and Soul."   Bluebirds, 5717-2-RB (CD).
"Coleman Hawkins and Benny Carter."   Swing, 8403.
"Hawkins Encounters Webster."   Verve, 823120 (CD).
"Classic Tenors" (with Lester Young).   Doc, FW-38446.
HERMAN, WOODY
"Early Autumn."   Cap, M-11034.
*"Thundering Herd."   Fan, 9452.
"Woodchopper's Ball."   MCA, MCAC-20279.
HINES, EARL
"South Side Swing."   MCA, 1311.
HODGES, JOHNNY
"Hodge Podge."   CSP, JEE-22001.
HOLIDAY, BILLIE
"Greatest Hits."   Col, CL-2666.
HUBBARD, FREDDIE
"Ride Like the Wind."   Elek./Mus, E1-60029.

JACKSON, MILT AND JOHN COLTRANE
"Bags and Trane."   Atlantic, SD-1368.
JACKSON, MILT AND COLEMAN HAWKINS
"Bean Bags."   Atlantic, 90465-1.
JACQUET, ILLINOIS
"The Cool Rage."   2-Verve, VE2-2544.
JAMAL, AHMAD AND GARY BURTON
"In Concert."   Personal, 51004.
JAMES, BOB
"Touchdown."   Col, PC-35594.
JAMES, BOB AND DAVID SANBORN
"Double Vision."   War, 25393-1.

JAMES, HARRY AND HIS ORCHESTRA
"Greatest Hits with Frank Sinatra." Col, PC-9430E.

JARRETT, KEITH
"Spirits." 2-ECM, 829467-1.

JOBIM, ANTONIO CARLOS
"E Convidados." Polydor, 826665-1.

JOHNSON, JAMES P.
"1917–21, Rare Piano Rolls." Bio, 1003Q.

JONES, THAD-MEL LEWIS ORCHESTRA
*"Live in Munich." Hori, 724.

JOPLIN, SCOTT
"1916, Classic Solos." Bio, 1006Q.

JORDAN, LOUIS
"Greatest Hits, Vol. 2 (1941–1947)." MCA, 1337.

KAYE, SAMMY AND HIS ORCHESTRA
"1944–46." Hindsight, HSR-207.

KENTON, STAN AND ORCHESTRA
"Artistry in Rhythm." Sunb, 213.

*"Greatest Hits." Cap, N-16182.

"Kenton/Wagner." Cre, W 1024.

"West Side Story." Cre, W. 1007.

KIRK, RAHSAAN ROLAND
"Pre-Rahsaan." 2-Prest, 24080.

KONITZ, LEE
"Subconscious-Lee." Fan./OJC, OJC-186.

KRUPA, GENE
"Gene Krupa with Anita O'Day." CSP, JCL-753.

"Original Drum Battle" (with Buddy Rich). Verve, V68484.

LATEEF, YUSEF
"Yusef Lateef." 2-Prest, 24007.

LAWS, HUBERT
"Afro-Classic." CTI, 8019.

LEADBELLY
"Good Morning Blues. Biograph, 12013.

LIEBMAN, DAVE
"Picture Show." PM, PMR-023 (C).

LUNCEFORD, JIMMIE
"And Band 1939–42." Sunb, 221.

MCINTOSH, LADD
"Energy Featuring Joe Farrell." Sea Breeze, SB-2007.

MCPARTLAND, JIMMY
"On Stage." Jazzo, 16.

MAHAVISHNU (MCLAUGHLIN, JOHN)
"Mahavishnu." War, 25190-1.

MANGIONE, CHUCK
"Feels So Good." A&M SP-3219.

MANNE, SHELLY
"Plays Richard Rogers." Discovery, 783.

MARSALIS, WYNTON
*"Wynton Marsalis." Col, FC-37574.

MASAKELA, HUGH
"Techno Bush." Jive, JL8-8210.

MENDES, SERGIO
"Brasil '66." A&M, SP-4116.

MENZA, DON
"Horn of Plenty." Pausa, PR-7170.

METHENY, PAT
"Rejoicing." ECM, 817795-2 (CD).

"Song X" (with Ornette Coleman). Geffen, GHS-24096.

MINGUS, CHARLES
"Better Git Hit in Your Soul." 2-Col, CG-30628.

"Mingus Ah Um." Col, CJ-40648.

"Pithecanthropus Erectus." Atlantic, SD-8809.

"Portrait with Dolphy, Byard." 2-Prest, 24092.

"Reincarnation" (Mingus Dynasty). Soul N, SN-1042.

MODERN JAZZ QUARTET
"European Concert." Atlantic, SD2-603.

"Modern Jazz Quartet." Prestige, 24005.

"With Sonny Rollins." Atlantic, SD-1299.

MONK, THELONIUS
"Blue Monk, Vol. 2." Prest, 7848E.

"Monk's Blues." Col, PC-9806.

"Pure Monk." 2-Mile, 47004.

"Monk with Coltrane." Fan./OJC, 039.

MORTON, FERDINAND "JELLY ROLL"
"Jelly Roll Morton." Arc. Folk, 267E.

MULLIGAN, GERRY
"Little Big Horn." GRP Records, A-9503.

"Meets the Saxophonists." Verve, 827436-2 (CD).

NAVARRO, FATS
"Fat Girl." 2-Savoy Jazz, SJL-2216.

NEW ORLEANS RAGTIME ORCHESTRA
"Creole." Arhoo, 1058.

NEW ORLEANS RHYTHM KINGS
"New Orleans Rhythm Kings." 2-Mile, 47020.

NEW YORK SAXOPHONE QUARTET
"An American Experience." Stash, 220.

NICHOLS, RED AND HIS 5 PENNIES
"1929–31 with Goodman." Sunb, 137.

NOONE, JIMMIE AND EARL HINES
"At the Apex Club." MCA, 1313.

O'DAY, ANITA
"Big Band Sessions." 2-Verve, VE2-2534.

"Time for Two" (with Cal Tjader). Verve, UMJ-3287.

ORIGINAL DIXIELAND JAZZ BAND
"1943." GHB, 100.

ORY, KID
"Creole Jazz Band 1944–45." Good T, 12022.

PARKER, CHARLIE
"Bird: The Savoy Recordings." 2-Savoy Jazz, SJL-2201.

PEPPER, ART
"Art Pepper Quartet." Gal, 5151.

PETERSON, OSCAR
"The Trio." Verve, 2304194.

PONTY, JEAN-LUC
"Cosmic Messenger." Atlantic, SD-19189.

POWELL, BUD
"Genius of Bud Powell." 2-Verve, VE2-2506.

PURIM, FLORA
"500 Miles High." Mile, 9070.

"Humble People." George W, GW-3007.

RARE SILK
"New Weave." Polydor, 810028-2 (CD).

REDMAN, DON AND HIS ORCHESTRA
"For Europeans Only." Steep, SCC-6020/21.

REID, RUFUS
"Perpetual Stroll." Theresa, 111.

REINHARDT, DJANGO
"Quintet of Hot Club of France." GNP, 9001.

RICH, BUDDY
"This One's for Basie." Verve, 817788-2 (CD).

"Rich Versus Roach." Mercury, EXPR-1016.

RIDLEY, LARRY
"Sum of the Parts." Strata-East, 19759.

ROACH, MAX
"Jazz in 3/4 Time." Em, 826456-1.

"Standard Time." 2-Em, 814190-1.

"Birth and Rebirth" (with Anthony Braxton). Black Saint BSR-0024.

"Best" (with Clifford Brown). GNP, 18E.

ROLLINS, SONNY
"Moving Out." Fan./OJC, 058.

"Plus Four." Fantasy/OJC, OJC-243.

"Sonny Rollins, Vol. 2." Blue, BST-81558.

SANDERS, PHAROAH
"Shukuru." Theresa, TR-121.

SANTAMARIA, MONGO
"Afro Roots." 2-Prest, 24018.

SCHULLER, GUNTHER
"Happy Feet: Tribute to Paul Whiteman." GC, 31043.

"The Road from Rags to Jazz." 2-GC, 31042.

SHANK, BUD
"This Bud's for You." Muse, 5309.

SHANKAR, RAVI
"Who's to Know?" ECM, 827269-2 (CD).

SHAW, WOODY
"In the Beginning." Muse, 5298.

SHEARING, GEORGE
"So Rare." Savoy Jazz, SJL-1117.

"The Reunion" (with S. Grappelli). Pausa, 7049.

"An Elegant Evening" (with Mel Torme). Concord Jazz, CJ-294.

"The Swinging's Mutual" (with Nancy Wilson). Pausa, 9021.

SHEPP, ARCHIE
"On Green Dolphin Street." Denon, CD-7262 (CD).

SHEW, BOBBY
"Breakfast Wine." Pausa, PR-7171.

SHORTER, WAYNE
"Adam's Apple." Blue, BST-84232.

SILVER, HORACE
"And The Jazz Messengers." Blue, BST-81518.

"Song for My Father." Blue, BST-84185.

SIMS, ZOOT
"Zoot Sims Quartets." Fantasy/OJC, OJC-242.

SINGERS UNLIMITED
"With Rob McConnell Boss Brass." Verve/MPS, 817486-1.

SMITH, BESSIE
"The Bessie Smith Story, Vols. 1–3." 3-Col, CL 855-7.

SMITH, WILLIE "THE LION"
"Willie 'The Lion' Smith." GNP, 9011.

SOPRANO SUMMIT
"Big Horn Jazzfest." Jazzo, 56.

SPYRO GYRA
"Spyro Gyra." MCA, 37149.

STITT, SONNY
"Sonny's Back." Muse, 5204.

"Stitt Plays Bird." Atlantic, SD-1418.

"Sonny Stitt/Sonny Rollings and Dizzy." Verve, 825674-2 (CD).

SUBRAMANIAN, DR. L
"Mani and Co." Mile, M-9138.

"Conversations" (with S. Grappelli). Mile, 9130.

SUN RA
"Sun Song with Arkestra." Del, 411E.

SUPERSAX
"Chasin' the Bird." Verve, MPS821867-2 (CD).

"Plays Bird, Vol. 2—Salt Peanuts." Pausa, PR-9028.

SWINGLE SINGERS
"Anyone for Mozart." Philips, 826948-2 (CD).

"Jazz Sebastian Bach." Phi, 824544-1.

TATUM, ART
"The Legend." Pausa, 9017.

"King and Queen" (with Mary Lou Williams). Hall, 607E.

TEAGARDEN, JACK
"Big Big Sound of Jack Teagarden." Folk, FJ-2819.

TENOR CONCLAVE FAN./OJC, 127.

TERRY, CLARK
"Serenade to a Bus Seat." Fan./OJC, 066.

"In Orbit" (with Thelonius Monk). Riv, 6167.

TJADER, CAL
"Live at the Funky Quarters." Fan, 9409.

THE TONIGHT SHOW BAND
"The Tonight Show Band." Amherst, AMH-3311.

TORME, MEL
"Duke Ellington & Count Basie Songbooks" Verve, 823248-1.

"Sings His California Suite." Discovery, 910.

TRISTANO, LENNIE
"Lennie Tristano Quartet." 2-Atlantic, SD2-7006.

TURRENTINE, STANLEY
"Cherry" (with Milt Jackson). CTI, 8010.

"Jubilee Shout." Blue Note, BST-84122.

TYNER, MCCOY
"Fly with the Wind." Mile, 9067.

VAUGHAN, SARAH
"The Divine Sarah, with Bud Powell." Musicraft, 504.

"No Count Sarah" (with Thad Jones). mEmarcy, 824057-2 (CD).

"Irving Berlin Songbook" (with Eckstine). Verve, 822526-1.

VENUTI, JOE
"Violin Jazz." Yazoo, 1062.

"Stringing the Blues." 2-CSP, JC2-24.

VSOP
"Quintet." Col, C2-34976.

WALLER, THOMAS "FATS"
"Ain't Misbehavin'." RCA, LPM-1246.

WASHINGTON, DINAH
"The Bessie Smith Songbook." Emarcy, 826663-1.

WATANABE, SADAO
"Dedicated To Charlie Parker." Denon, CD-7689(CD).

"Iberian Waltz" (with Charlie Mariano). Denon CD-7690(CD).

WATERS, ETHEL
"1921–24."   Bio, 12022.

WATTS, ERNIE
"Sanctuary."   Qwest/War, 25513-1.

WEATHER REPORT
*"Heavy Weather."   Col, PC-34418.

"Mr. Gone."   Col, PC-35358.

WEBSTER, BEN
"The Horn."   Circle, 41.

"Ben Webster Meets Don Byas."   Verve/
   MPS827920-2 (CD).

"Soulmates" (with Josef Zawinul).   Fan./
   OJC, 109.

WILSON, PHIL
"Getting It All Together."   Outra, 1.

WILSON, TEDDY
"And His All Stars. Vol. 1."   Musicraft, 502.

WINDING, KAI
"Incredible Trombones."   MCA, 29062.

"Israel" (with JJ Johnson).   A&M, SP9-3008.

"Early Modern" (with Sonny Stitt).   Hall,
   612E.

WOODS, PHIL
"At the Vanguard."   Ant, AN-1013.

"Birds of A Feather."   Ant, AN-1006.

"Phil Woods and Lew Tabackin."
   Omnisound, 1033.

WORLD SAXOPHONE QUARTET
"Live at Brooklyn Academy of Music."
   Black Saint, BSR-0096.

"Steppin' with the W.S.Q."   Black Saint, BSR-
   0027.

YOUNG, LESTER
"The Complete Savoy Recordings."   2-Savoy
   Jazz, SJL-2202.

Anthologies and Collections

AC-DC BLUES   Stash 106

ALTO SUMMIT   Pausa 7026

ATLANTIC JAZZ, VOLS. 1–12   15-Atlantic 81712-1

ATLANTIC RHYTHM AND BLUES, VOLS. 1–7   Atlantic 7-81293-9

THE BASS   3-Impulse 9284

BEBOP BOYS   2-Savoy Jazz SJL-2225

BEBOP REVISITED   Xanadu 120,24,72,97,205,208

BIG BAND ERA   2-RCA VPM-6043

*BIG BAND JAZZ   Smithsonian RC030

BLACK SWING TRADITION   2-Savoy Jazz SJL-2246

THE BLUES SUMMIT MEETING   2-Mobile Fidelity 518

BOOGIE WOOGIE RARITIES   Mile 2009

BOOGIE WOOGIE TRIO   Story v. 4006

BROTHERS AND OTHER MOTHERS   2-Savoy Jazz SJL-2210

CHICAGO JAZZ   Bio. 12005

CHICAGO JAZZ   Bio. 12043

CHOCOLATE DANDIES   Swing SW-8448

THE COMPLETE KEYNOTE COLLECTION   21-Keynote 830121-1

CONCORD JAZZ GUITAR COLLECTION   2-Concord Jazz CJ-160

Bibliography

Allen, Walter C., and Brian Rust. *King Joe Oliver.* London and New York: Sidgwick and Jackson, 1958.

Armstrong, Louis. *My Life in New Orleans.* New York: Prentice-Hall, 1954.

Basie, Count. *Good Morning Blues: The Autobiography of Count Basie, As Told to Albert Murray.* New York: Random House, 1986.

Bechet, Sidney. *Treat It Gentle: An Autobiography.* New York: Hill and Wang, 1960.

Berendt, Joachim. *The Jazz Book.* New York: Lawrence Hill, 1975.

Berger, Morroe, Edward Patrick, and James Patrick. *Benny Carter: A Life in American Music.* Metuchen, New Jersey: Scarecrow Press, 1982.

Berton, Ralph. *Remembering Bix: A Memoir of the Jazz Age.* New York: Harper and Row, 1974.

Blesh, Rudi, and Harriet Janis. *They All Played Ragtime.* New York: Oak Publications, 1971.

———. *Shining Trumpets—A History of Jazz.* New York: Alfred A. Knopf, 1946.

Brooks, Tilford. *America's Black Musical Heritage.* Englewood Cliffs, N.J.: Prentice-Hall, Inc., 1984.

Brask, Ole, and Dan Morgenstern. *Jazz People.* New York: Abrams, 1976.

Broonzy, William, and Yannick Bruynoghe. *Big Bill Blues.* London: Cassell, 1955.

Brown, Charles T. *The Art of Rock and Roll,* 2d ed. Englewood Cliffs, N.J.: Prentice-Hall, Inc., 1987.

———. *Music U.S.A.: America's Country & Western Tradition.* Englewood Cliffs, N.J.: Prentice-Hall, Inc., 1986.

———, editor. *Proceedings of the National Association of Jazz Educators, Volumes 1–8.* Manhattan, Kansas: Jazz Educator's Press, 1981–8.

Brunn, H. O. *The Story of the Original Dixieland Jazz Band.* Baton Rouge: Louisiana State University Press, 1960.

Bruyninckx, Walter. *50 Years of Recorded Jazz, 1917–1967.* Mechelen, Belgium: Published privately, n.d.

Budds, Michael J. *Jazz in the Sixties.* Iowa City: University of Iowa Press, 1978.

Calloway, Cab, and Bryant Rollins. *Of Minnie the Moocher and Me.* New York: Crowell, 1976.

Carr, Ian. *Miles Davis.* New York: William Morrow and Company, 1982.

Charles, Ray, and David Ritz. *Brother Ray.* New York: Dial Press, 1978.

Charters, Samuel B, and Leonard Kunstadt. *Jazz: A History of the New York Scene.* New York: Doubleday, 1962.

———. *The Country Blues,* Rev. ed. New York: Da Capo, 1975.

Chilton, John. *Who's Who of Jazz, 4th ed.* New York: Da Capo Press, 1985.

Cole, Bill. *John Coltrane.* New York: Schirmer Books, 1976.

Courlander, Harold. *Negro Folk Music.* New York: Columbia University Press, 1963.

———. *Miles Davis: A Musical Biography.* New York: WIlliam Morrow, 1974.

Dale, Rodney. *The World of Jazz.* Cambridge: Basinghall Books Limited, 1980.

Dance, Stanley. *The World of Count Basie.* New York: Scribner's Sons, 1980.

———. *The World of Duke Ellington.* New York: Scribner's Sons, 1970.

———. *The World of Earl Hines.* New York: Scribner's Sons, 1977.

———. *The World of Swing.* New York: Scribner's Sons, 1974.

Dapogny, James. *Ferdinand "Jelly Roll" Morton. The Collected Piano Music.* New York: G. Schirmer, 1982.

Davies, John R. T., and Laurie Wright. *Morton's Music.* Essex, England: Storyville Publications, 1968.

Davis, Nathan T. *Writings in Jazz,* 3d ed. Scottsdale, Arizona: Gorsuch Scarisbrick Publishers, 1985.

Delaunay, Charles. *Hot Discography.* Translated by Ian Munro Smyth. Paris: Hot Jazz, 1936.

Driggs, Frank and Harris Lewine. *Black Beauty/White Heat: A Pictorial History of Classic Jazz.* New York: Morrow, 1982.

Ellington, Duke. *Music Is My Mistress.* Garden City, New York: Doubleday, 1973.

Ellington, Mercer, and Stanley Dance. *Duke Ellington in Person.* New York: Da Capo Press, 1979.

Ellison, Ralph. *Shadow and Act.* New York: Random House, 1964.

Ewen, David. *The Life and Death of Tin Pan Alley.* New York: Funk & Wagnalls, 1964.

Feather, Leonard. *The Book of Jazz: A Guide from Then till Now.* New York: Horizon Press, 1965.

———. *The Encyclopedia of Jazz.* New York: Da Capo Press, 1984.

———. *The Pleasures of Jazz.* New York: Horizon Press, 1976.

Frith, Simon. *Sound Effects—Youth, Leisure, and the Politics of Rock 'n' Roll.* New York: Pantheon Books, 1981.

Gammond, Peter, ed. *Duke Ellington: His Life and Music.* New York: Da Capo Press, 1977.

Giddins, Gary. *Riding on a Blue Note.* New York: Oxford University Press, 1981.

———. *Rhythm-a-Ning.* New York: Oxford University Press, 1985.

Gillespie, Dizzy, and Al Frazer. *To Be or Not to Bop.* Garden City, New York: Doubleday, 1979.

Gillet, Charlie. *The Sound of the City: The Rise of Rock and Roll.* New York: Sunrise Books, 1970.

Gitler, Ira. *Jazz Masters of the Forties.* New York: Macmillan Company, 1966.

———. *Swing to Bop.* New York: Oxford University Press, 1986.

Goddard, Chris. *Jazz Away from Home*. London: Paddington Press, 1979.

Goldberg, Joe. *Jazz Masters of the Fifties*. New York: Macmillan Company, 1965.

Goodman, Benny, and Irving Kolodin. *The Kingdom of Swing*. New York: Stackpole Sons, 1939.

Gridley, Mark. *Jazz Styles*, 2d ed. Englewood Cliffs, N.J.: Prentice-Hall, Inc., 1985.

Hadlock, Richard. *Jazz Masters of the Twenties*. New York: Macmillan, 1965.

Hamm, Charles. *Yesterdays, Popular Song in America*. New York: Norton, 1979.

Hammond, John, and Irving Townsend. *John Hammon on Record—An Autobiography*. New York: Penguin Books, 1981.

Handy, W. C., ed. *Blues: An Anthology*. New York: Da Capo Press, 1926.

———. *W. C. Handy: Father of the Blues*. New York: Collier Books, 1970 (first published in 1941).

Harris, William J. *The Poetry and Poetics of Amiri Baraka—The Jazz Aesthetic*. Columbia, Missouri: University of Missouri Press, 1985.

Haskins, Jim. *The Cotton Club*. New York: Random House, 1977.

———. *Black Music in America*. New York: Thomas Y. Crowell, 1987.

Hentoff, Nat. *The Jazz Life*. New York: Da Capo Press, 1975.

Hentoff, Nat, and Nat Shapiro. *Hear Me Talkin' to Ya: An Oral History of Jazz*. New York: Dover Publications, 1966.

Hentoff, Nat, and Albert McCarthy, eds. *Jazz: New Perspectives on the History of Jazz*. New York: Da Capo Press, 1974.

Hodier, Andre. *Jazz: Its Evolution and Essence*. New York: Da Capo Press, 1986.

———. *Toward Jazz*. New York: Da Capo Press, 1976.

———. *The Worlds of Jazz*. New York, Grove, 1972.

Holiday, Billie, and William Dufty. *Lady Sings the Blues*. New York: Doubleday, 1956.

Jepsen, Jorgen Grunnet. *Jazz Records: A Discography*. Holte, Denmark: K. E. Knudsen, 1963.

Jewell, Derek. *Duke—A Portrait of Duke Ellington*. New York: Norton, 1977.

Jones, LeRoi. *Blues People*. New York: William Morrow & Co., 1963.

Jones, Max, and John Chilton. *Louis: The Louis Armstrong Story*. New York: Little, Brown, 1972.

Jost, Ekkehard. *Free Jazz*. Graz, Austria: Universal Edition, 1974.

Keepnews, Orrin and Bill Grauer. *A Pictorial History of Jazz*. New York: Crown Publishers, 1966.

Keil, Charles. *Urban Blues*. Chicago: University of Chicago Press, 1966.

Kinkle, Roger D. *The Complete Encyclopedia of Popular Music and Jazz 1900–1950*. New Rochelle, NY: Arlington House, 1974.

Kirkeby, Ed. *Ain't Misbehavin': The Story of Fats Waller*. New York: Da Capo Press, 1975.

Krehbiel, Henry Edward. *Afro-American Folksongs—A Study in Racial and National Music*. New York: Frederick Ungar Publishing Co., 1962 (first published in 1913).

Leonard, Neil. *Jazz and the White Americans*. Chicago: University of Chicago Press, 1962.

de Lerma, Dominique-Rene. *Reflections on Afro-American Music*. Kent, Ohio: Kent State University Press, 1973.

Litweiler, John. *The Freedom Principle*. New York: Morrow, 1984.

Lomax, Alan. *Mister Jelly Roll*. Berkeley and Los Angeles: The University of California Press, 1973 (first edition 1950).

Lyons, Len. *The 101 Best Jazz Albums, A History of Jazz on Records*. New York: William Morris and Company, Inc., 1980.

Malone, Bill. *Country Music U.S.A.,* 2d ed. Austin, Texas: University of Texas Press, 1985.

Martin, Henry. *Enjoying Jazz*. New York: Schirmer, 1986.

McCalla, James. *Jazz: A Listener's Guide*. Englewood Cliffs, N.J.: Prentice-Hall, 1982.

Mecklenburg, Carl Gregor Herzog Zu, and Waldemar Scheck. *Die Theorie des Blues Im Modernen Jazz*. Baden-Baden: Verlag Valentin Koerner, 1971.

———. *International Jazz Bibliography*. Graz, Austria: Universal Edition, 1969 (supplements in 1970–1975).

Meeker, David. *Jazz in the Movies*. New York: Da Capo Press, 1982.

Megill, Donald D., and Richard S. Demory. *Introduction to Jazz History*. Englewood Cliffs, N.J.: Prentice-Hall, Inc., 1984.

Meller, Wilfrid. *Music in a New Found Land*. New York: Alfred A. Knopf, 1965.

Merrian, Alan P., and Robert J. Benford. *A Bibliography of Jazz*. New York: Da Capo Press, 1970.

Mingus, Charles. *Beneath the Underdog*. New York: Alfred A. Knopf, 1971.

Moon, Peter. *A Bibliography of Jazz Discographies*. 2d ed. Middlesex, England: British Institute of Jazz Studies, 1972.

Murray, Albert. *Stompin' the Blues*. New York: McGraw-Hill, 1976.

Nanry, Charles. *The Jazz Text*. New York: D. Van Nostrand Company, 1976.

Nathan, Hans. *Dan Emmett and the Rise of Early Negro Minstrelsy*. Norman, Oklahoma: University of Oklahoma Press, 1977.

Nketia, J. H. Kwabena. *The Music of Africa*. New York: Norton, 1974.

Oliver, Paul. *Savannah Syncopators, African Retentions in the Blues*. New York: Stein and Day, 1970.

Ostransky, Leroy. *Understanding Jazz*. Englewood Cliffs, N.J.: Prentice-Hall, Spectrum Books, 1977.

Owens, Thomas. *Charlie Parker: Techniques of Improvisation*. Ph.D. dissertation, Los Angeles: University of California, 1974.

Panassie, Hugues. *The Real Jazz*. London: Smith and Durrell, 1942.

Pareles, Jon, and Patricia Romanow, eds. *The Rolling Stone Encyclopedia of Rock and Roll*. New York: Summit Books, 1983.

Pierson, Nathan. *Goin' to Kansas City*. Chicago: University of Illinois Press, 1987.

Placksin, Sally. *American Women in Jazz*. Wideview Books, 1982.

Priestley, Brian. *Mingus: A Critical Biography*. New York: Da Capo Press, 1984.

Ramsey, Frederic, Jr. and Charles Edward Smith. *Jazzmen*. New York: Harcourt, Brace, Harvest Book, 1939.

Reisner, Robert. *Bird: The Legend of Charlie Parker*. New York: Da Capo Press, 1975.

————. *The Literature of Jazz. A Preliminary Bibliography*. New York: New York Public Library, 1954.

Roach, Hildred. *Black American Music*. Boston: Crescendo Publishing Co., 1973.

Russell, Ross. *Jazz in Kansas City and the Southwest*. Berkeley: University of California Press, 1971.

Rust, Brian. *Jazz Records, 1897–1942*. New Rochelle, New York: Arlington House, 1978.

————. *The American Dance Band Discography, 1917–1942*. New Rochelle, N.Y.: Arlington House, 1975.

Sargeant, Winthrop. *Jazz, Hot and Hybrid*. 3d ed. New York: Da Capo Press, 1975 (first edition 1938).

Schafer, William J., and Johannes Riedel. *The Art of Ragtime*. Baton Rouge: Louisiana State University Press, 1973.

Schenkel, Steven M. *The Tools of Jazz*. Englewood Cliffs, N.J.: Prentice-Hall, Inc., 1983.

Schuller, Gunther. *Early Jazz: Its Roots and Musical Development*. New York: Oxford University Press, 1968.

————. *Musings*. New York: Da Capo Press, 1986.

————, *Schwann Record and Tape Guide*. New York: Schwann, Summer 1987.

Shaw, Arnold. *Honkers and Shouters—The Golden Years of Rhythm and Blues*. New York: Macmillan, Collier Books, 1987 reprint.

Simkins, C. O. *Coltrane: A Biography*. New York: Herndon House, 1975.

Simon, George T. *The Big Bands*. Rev. ed. New York: Collier, 1974.

Simosko, Vladimir, and Barry Tepperman. *Eric Dolphy: A Musical Biography and Discography*. New York: Da Capo Press, 1979.

Southern, Eileen. *The Music of Black Americans*. New York: Norton, 1971.

————, ed. *Readings in Black American Music*. New York: Norton, 1971.

Spellman, A. B. *Black Music: Four Lives in the Bebop Business.* New York: Schocken Books, 1970.

Stambler, Irwin, and Grelun Landon. *The Encyclopedia of Folk, Country & Western Music,* 2d ed. New York: St. Martin's Press, 1983.

Starr, S. Frederick. *Red and Hot, the Fate of Jazz in the Soviet Union.* New York and Oxford: Oxford University Press, 1983.

Stearns, Marshall Winslow. *Jazz Dance: The Story of American Vernacular Dance.* New York: Macmillan, 1968.

———. *The Story of Jazz.* New York: Oxford University Press, 1970 (first published in 1956).

Stewart, Rex. *Jazz Masters of the Thirties.* New York: Da Capo Press, 1980.

Sudhalter, Richard M. *Bix: Man and Legend.* New Rochelle, New York: Arlington House, 1974.

Tanner, Paul, and Maurice Gerow. *A Study of Jazz,* 5th ed. Dubuque, Iowa: William C. Brown, 1983.

Taylor, Arthur. *Notes and Tones.* New York: Perigee Books, 1977.

Taylor, Billy. *Jazz Piano: History and Development.* Dubuque, Iowa: W. C. Brown Co., 1982.

Tirro, Frank. *Jazz, A History.* New York: Norton, 1977.

Ulanov, Barry. *Duke Ellington.* New York: Da Capo Press, 1975.

Ward, Ed, Geoffrey Stokes, and Ken Tucker. *Rock of Ages.* Englewood Cliffs, N.J.: Prentice-Hall, Inc., 1986.

Waters, Ethel, and Charles Samuels. *His Eye Is on the Sparrow.* New York: Doubleday, 1950.

Werner, Otto. *The Origin and Development of Jazz.* Dubuque, Iowa: Kendall/Hunt Publishing Co., 1984.

Whitcomb, Ian. *After the Ball: Pop Music from Rag to Rock.* New York: Simon and Schuster, 1973.

Wilder, Alec. *American Popular Song. The Great Innovators 1900–1950.* New York: Oxford University Press, 1972.

Williams, Martin. *Jazz Masters in Transition 1957–1969.* New York: Macmillan, 1970.

———. *Jazz Masters of New Orleans.* New York: Macmillan, 1979.

———, ed. *Jazz Panorama.* New York: Collier Books, 1964 (first published 1958).

———. *The Jazz Tradition, New and Revised Edition.* New York: Oxford University Press, 1983.

———. *Where's the Melody?* New York: Pantheon Books, 1969.

———. *Jazz Heritage.* New York: Oxford University Press, 1985.

Wilson, John S. Jazz: *The Transition Years, 1940–1960.* New York: Appleton-Century-Crofts, 1966.

Index

"Crazy Blues": blues recordings, 58
Creoles: black culture in New Orleans, 34, 35; Latin influence, 155
Crosby, Bing: big bands, 88, 90
Cry: African vocal tradition, 16
Culture: black power and bebop, 105; blues as rural form, 21–22; free jazz, 132; jazz as reflection, 3, 177; New Orleans, 33–34, 35; urbanization and blues, 24–25, 26–27
"Cutting" contests: boogie-woogie, 53
Cyrille, Andrew: free jazz, 134

D

Dance: big bands, 69, 70; expression of black attitudes, 19
Davis, Anthony: jazz in 1980s, 171
Davis, Kay: big bands, 90
Davis, Miles: biographical note, 123; "Boplicity," 218–19; cool jazz, 115, 117–18; electronics, 146, 150; Herbie Hancock, 152; hard bop, 124; jazz in 1980s, 170; rock devices, 145–46
Davis, Sammy, Jr.: big bands, 90
"Dead Man Blues": analysis, 190–92
Debussy, Claude: influence on jazz, 155
DeJohnette, Jack: free jazz, 134
Depression: cultural setting of big bands, 68–69
Desmond, Paul: "Koto Song," 158; West Coast jazz, 118
Detroit: hard bop musicians, 125; musical entertainment, 25
Detroit/Montreux Festival: jazz in 1980s, 172
DiMeola, Al: jazz/rock, 148; Return to Forever, 159
"Dinah": analysis, 193–94
"Dippermouth Blues": analysis, 27–29
Dixieland: big bands, 74, 97; blues as early form, 26; combo jazz, 98–99; improvisation, 8, 74; jazz singing, 60; Jelly Roll Morton, 57; New Orleans piano style, 54; rhythmn, 75; styles compared, 46
Dolphy, Eric: free jazz, 133, 134
Domnerus, Arne: European jazz, 155
Dorsey, Tommy: big band revival, 161; big band vocalists, 90
Drums: bebop style, 109, 110; free jazz, 134; hard bop, 126; jazz/rock, 146; Max Roach, 130; West Coast jazz, 119

E

Earth, Wind and Fire: jazz/rock, 145
Eastman School of Music: jazz in 1980s, 173
Eldridge, Roy: "I Can't Believe That You're in Love With Me," 102; "Rockin' Chair," 201, 202
Electric Flag: jazz/rock, 145
Electronics: Miles Davis, 146, 150; hard bop, 128; jazz/rock, 150; Josef Zawinul, 148
Ellington, Duke: big bands, 76, 90, 161; biographical note, 86; classical music, 116, 154; "Cottontail," 206–8; European tours, 154; "KoKo," 84–85; riff style, 81, 83; urban blues, 27

Ellis, Don: electronics, 150
El-Zabar, Kahil: jazz in 1980s, 171
Embellishment: spirituals and improvisation, 18
Entertainment: Chicago in 1920s, 43; classic blues, 26; Depression and big bands, 68; Detroit, 25; New Orleans, 24–25, 34
Erskine, Peter: jazz in 1980s, 171
Europe: early jazz tours, 154; jazz festivals and musicians, 155
Evans, Gil: "Boplicity," 218; Miles Davis, 123

F

Ferguson, Maynard: big band revival, 165–66
Feza, Mongezi: jazz in Africa, 156
Field hollers: African vocal tradition, 16
Fitzgerald, Ella: big band singing, 90, 91; biographical note, 93; influence on vocal improvisation, 175; vocal jazz in 1980s, 174; "You'd Be So Nice to Come Home To," 209–10
Form: defined, 7
Forrest, Helen: big bands, 90
"4 or 5 Times": analysis, 200–201
Free-form jazz: Ornette Coleman, 176; European influence, 155
"Free jazz": analysis, 224–25; style elements, 136
Freeman, Bud: Austin High group, 45
Free Spirits: jazz/rock, 148
Frissell, Bill: jazz in 1980s, 171
Fuller, Curtis: hard bop, 126
Funerals: street bands in New Orleans, 35
Funk: jazz/rock, 144
Funky style: gospel piano playing, 126; hard bop, 125–26; Horace Silver, 130; use of term, 124
Fusion: Ornette Coleman, 176; Chick Corea, 160; defined, 143

G

Gaye, Marvin: vocal style, 175
Getz, Stan: "Body and Soul," 120; Horace Silver, 130; West Coast jazz, 119
Gillespie, Dizzy: bebop, 105; biographical note, 113; development of jazz, 108; European tours, 154; "KoKo," 215; Latin influence, 155; "Night in Tunisia," 111; Charlie Parker, 113; rock elements, 149; "Shaw Nuff," 213–15
Giuffre, Jimmy: West Coast jazz, 119
Goodman, Benny: big band vocalists, 90; biographical note, 78–79; combo jazz, 98, 99, 101; Dixieland, 45; Lionel Hampton, 103; riff style, 83
Gordon, Dexter: hard bop, 124; jazz in 1980s, 170
Great Awakening: hymns and spirituals, 18
Guaraldi, Vince: West Coast jazz, 119
Guillin, Lars: European jazz, 155
Guitar: bebop, 110; Charlie Christian, 101; hard bop, 126; jazz/rock, 146; T-Bone Walker, 29, 30; West Coast jazz, 119
Gulda, Friedrich: European jazz, 155

P

Pace, Harry: blues recordings, 59
Paramount: blues recordings, 59
Paris: black jazz musicians, 154
Parker, Charlie: bebop, 105, 107–8; biographical note, 113; Ornette Coleman, 136; hard bop, 124; "KoKo," 215–16
Parliament/Funkadelic: jazz/rock, 145
Pederson, Oerstad: European jazz, 155
Peer, Ralph: country blues, 59–60
Pell, Dave: West Coast jazz, 119
"Pent-Up House": analysis, 219–20
Pepper, Art: West Coast jazz, 119
Philadelphia: hard bop musicians, 125
Piano: Count Basie, 86; bebop, 110; boogie-woogie, 26; combo jazz musicians, 101; free jazz, 134; funky style and gospel, 126; hard bop, 126; jazz/rock, 146; "Night in Tunisia," 111; Bud Powell, 109, 111; Cecil Taylor, 134; Lennie Tristano, 123; West Coast jazz, 119
Poland: independent development of jazz, 157
Ponty, Jean-Luc: jazz/rock, 148
Powell, Bud: bebop style, 109; "Night in Tunisia," 111–12
Previn, Andre: West Coast jazz, 119
Puckwana, Dudu: jazz in Africa, 156
Punk/jazz: Ornette Coleman, 140
Purim, Flora: Return to Forever, 159

R

Radio: popularity of big bands, 70
Ragtime: early jazz styles, 42; Jelly Roll Morton, 57
Railroad: boogie-woogie, 26
Rainey, Ma: blues recordings, 59; early blues, 21; Bessie Smith, 63
Records: popularity of blues, 58
Redman, Don: big band arrangements, 76; biographical note, 78; "Stampede," 76–77
Red Onion Jazz Babies: "Cake Walking Babies from Home," 189–90; Dixieland, 37
Religion: African cultural tradition, 14–15; camp meetings, 18–19; Catholicism and slavery, 14, 15; Great Awakening, 18; Protestantism and slavery, 14–15; Protestant religious music, 17–18
Rent parties: boogie-woogie, 26; classic blues, 26
Return to Forever: Chick Corea, 159–60; jazz/rock, 148; "Spain," 229–31
Rhythmn: African tribal music, 15–16; beat, 6; big bands, 71; combo jazz styles, 99–100; defined, 6; Dixieland, 36; hard bop, 125; jazz and rock, 150; riff bands, 81; swing style, 74–75
Riedel, Georg: European jazz, 155
Riff bands: jazz/rock, 144; solo passages, 74
Roach, Max: bebop style, 109; biographical note, 130; hard bop, 125, 126
Rock-and-roll: boogie-woogie, 54; Miles Davis, 145–46; jazz, 149, 175–76; jazz/rock, 143; jump blues, 27; rhythmn, 75
"Rockin' Chair": analysis, 201–2

Rodby, Steve: jazz in 1980s, 201–2
Rogers, Shorty: West Coast jazz, 119
Rollins, Sonny: hard bop, 126; jazz in 1980s, 170; "Pent-Up House," 219–20
Round Midnight: black musicians in Paris, 154; Herbie Hancock, 152; jazz in 1980s, 170
Rugolo, Pete: Stan Kenton, 168
Russell, Curly: bebop style, 109

S

"St. Louis Blues": analysis, 198–99
Sanders, Pharoah: free jazz, 133
Santana: jazz/rock, 145; Latin influence, 155; "A Love Supreme," 228–29
Saxophone: bebop, 110; Sidney Bechet, 41; big bands, 71, 73; John Coltrane, 127–28; cool jazz, 117; Dixieland, 38; free jazz, 133; hard bop, 124, 126; Coleman Hawkins, 101; Woody Herman, 162; identification, 10–11; Charlie Parker and bebop, 107–8; Wayne Shorter, 153; West Coast jazz, 119
Scale: John Coltrane, 128; Miles Davis, 146; defined, 23; free jazz, 135; modal improvisation in bebop, 107; oriental influence, 155
Scat song: defined, 60–61
Schlippenbach, Alexander von: European jazz, 155
Schoenberg, Arnold: influence on jazz, 155
Shank, Bud: West Coast jazz, 119
"Shaw Nuff": analysis, 213–15
Shepp, Archie: free jazz, 133; University of Massachusetts, 173
Shorter, Wayne: biographical note, 153; hard bop, 126; jazz/rock, 148
Shout chorus: big bands, 73
Shouts: camp meetings, 18–19
Silver, Horace: biographical note, 130; hard bop, 126; Latin influence, 155; "Moon Rays," 221–23
Sims, Zoot: West Coast jazz, 119
Sinatra, Frank: big bands, 90
"Singing the Blues": analysis, 192–93
Slavery: cultural history, 13–15, 16, 17
Smith, Bessie: biographical note, 63; "Lost Your Heart Blues," 187–88; "St. Louis Blues," 198–99; vocal quality, 59, 60
Smith, Carson: West Coast jazz, 119
Smith, Clara: vocal quality, 59
Smith, Mamie: blues recordings, 58, 59
Smith, Marvin: jazz in 1980s, 171
Smith, Willie "The Lion": boogie-woogie, 54
Solo: bebop, 106; big bands and improvisation, 74; Coleman Hawkins, 103; combo style jazz, 98, 100; riff bands, 80
Soul: jazz/rock, 144
"Spain": analysis, 229–31
Spirituals: improvisation, embellishment, and syncopation, 18
Spyro Gyra: jazz/rock, 148
"Stampede": analysis, 76–78
"Steppin'": analysis, 234–35
Stewart, Slam: "I Got Rhythmn," 211–13
Stitt, Sonny: hard bop, 124
Stockhausen, Karlheinz: influence on jazz, 155

Stomp: defined, 50
Strayhorn, Billy: big band arrangements, 76; Duke Ellington, 83, 86
"Struttin' with Some Barbecue": analysis, 39–40
"Subconscious Lee": analysis, 216–18
Sun Ra: African influence, 156; free jazz, 134
"Sweethearts on Parade": analysis, 61–62; Armstrong as vocalist, 60
Syncopation: defined, 7; spirituals, 18

T

Tabackin, Lew: Toshiko Akiyoshi, 160; big band revival, 166; Japanese influence, 119
Tatum, Art: harmonic variation, 107
"Taxi War Dance": analysis, 204–6
Taylor, Cecil: free jazz, 134, 135
Tempo: defined, 6
Ten Wheel Drive: jazz/rock, 145
Terry, Clark: Miles Davis, 123; on riffs, 81
Teschemacher, Frank: Austin High group, 45; Dixieland, 45
Texture: bebop and cool jazz, 116; riff bands, 81
"These Foolish Things": analysis, 208–9; vocal improvisation, 91
Tonight Show Band: big band revival, 166
Torme, Mel: big bands, 88; jazz in 1980s, 174
Tristano, Lennie: biographical note, 122–23; cool jazz, 117; "Subconscious Lee," 216–18
Trombone: bebop, 110; big bands, 72; Dixieland, 37; hard bop, 124–25, 126; West Coast jazz, 119
Trumbauer, Frankie: "Singing the Blues," 192–93
Trumpet: bebop, 110; big bands, 71–72; Dixieland, 37; free jazz, 133–34; Dizzy Gillespie, 113; hard bop, 124, 126; identification, 10–11; West Coast jazz, 119
Turrentine, Stanley: hard bop, 126
"25 or 6 to 4": analysis, 225–26

U

Ulmer, James Blood: jazz in 1980s, 172
University of Miami: jazz in 1980s, 173
Urbanization: big bands, 68; classic blues, 24–25, 26–27

V

Vallee, Rudy: big bands, 90
Vaudeville: black minstrelsy, 18; early jazz, 51
Vaughn, Sarah: "All Alone," 91–92; big bands, 88
Venuti, Joe: European tours, 154
Vibraphone: bebop, 110; Lionel Hampton, 99

W

Walker, T-Bone: biographical note, 29–30
Waller, Fats: Count Basie, 85; boogie-woogie, 54; European tours, 154; "I Ain't Got Nobody," 197–98
Ward, Helen: big bands, 90
Watanabe, Sadao: Toshiko Akiyoshi, 160; jazz in Japan, 156
"Watermelon Man": African influence, 156; analysis, 129–30, 150–52
Waters, Ethel: biographical note, 62; blues recordings, 59; vocal style, 60
"Weather Bird": analysis, 46–47
Weather Report: "Birdland," 226–28; jazz/rock, 148; Wayne Shorter, 153
Webb, Chick: Ella Fitzgerald, 93
Webster, Ben: "Cottontail," 206
Weiss, Pamela: jazz in 1980s, 172
Wertico, Paul: jazz in 1980s, 171
West Coast jazz: "Body and Soul," 120; Brubeck quartet, 158; cool jazz, 115–16
White, Maurice: Earth, Wind and Fire, 145
"Who Can I Turn To": analysis, 235–36
Williams, Clarence: boogie-woogie, 54; Bessie Smith, 63
Williams, Cootie: "Cottontail," 206
Williams, Martin: jazz information, 6
Williams, Tony: jazz/rock, 146
Wills, Bob and His Texas Playboys: combo jazz, 98; Bing Crosby, 88, 90
Wilson, Cassandra: jazz in 1980s, 175
Winding, Kai: European jazz, 155
"Woodchopper's Ball": solo passages, 74
Woods, Phil: European performances, 154; hard bop, 126
Woodwinds: Eric Dolphy, 134; free jazz, 133
World Saxophone Quartet: free jazz, 137; "Steppin'," 234–35
World War II: big bands, 69, 97
Wright, Eugene: West Coast jazz, 119
Wroblonski, Jan: independent development of jazz in Europe, 157

Y

"You'd Be So Nice to Come Home To": analysis, 209–10
Young, Lester: "Taxi War Dance," 204

Z

Zawinul, Josef: jazz/rock, 146, 148